SUZUKI
GT550

A COMPILATION OF 3 FACTORY MANUALS

SERVICE  MANUAL

DISC BRAKE SERVICE MANUAL   VM28SC CARBURETOR MANUAL

1972  **1977**

A Floyd Clymer Publication - 2025 VelocePress.com

PREFACE

TRADEMARKS & COPYRIGHT

SUZUKI® is the registered trademark of the SUZUKI MOTOR CO., LTD. and this publication is not sponsored by or endorsed by the trademark owner. We recognize that some words, model names and designations, for example, mentioned herein are the property of the trademark holder. We use them for identification purposes only. This is not an official publication however; it may include non-copyright works of the trademark holder.

INTRODUCTION

Welcome to the world of digital publishing ~ the book you now hold in your hand was printed using the latest state of the art digital technology. The advent of print-on-demand has forever changed the publishing process, never has information been so accessible and it is our hope that this book serves your informational needs for years to come. If this is your first exposure to digital publishing, we hope that you are pleased with the results. Many more titles of interest to the classic automobile and motorcycle enthusiast, collector and restorer are available via our website at www.VelocePress.com. We hope that you find this title as interesting as we do.

NOTE FROM THE PUBLISHER

The information presented is true and complete to the best of our knowledge. All recommendations are made without any guarantees on the part of the author or the publisher, who also disclaim all liability incurred with the use of this information.

INFORMATION ON THE USE OF THIS PUBLICATION

This manual is an invaluable resource for those interested in performing their own maintenance. However, in today's information age we are constantly subject to changes in common practice, new technology, availability of improved materials and increased awareness of chemical toxicity. As such, it is advised that the user consult with an experienced professional prior to undertaking any procedure described herein. While every care has been taken to ensure correctness of information, it is obviously not possible to guarantee complete freedom from errors or omissions or to accept liability arising from such errors or omissions. Therefore, any individual that uses the information contained within, or elects to perform or participate in do-it-yourself repairs or modifications acknowledges that there is a risk factor involved and that the publisher or its associates cannot be held responsible for personal injury or property damage resulting from the use of the information or the outcome of such procedures.

WARNING!

One final word of advice, this publication is intended to be used as a reference guide, and when in doubt the reader should consult with a qualified technician.

www.VelocePress.com

IMPORTANT INFORMATION REGARDING PAGE NUMBERS

Each of the three manuals included in this publication have their own index. The page numbers that correspond to each individual index are printed to the bottom of each page.

The page numbers printed to the top of each page are the page numbers within the book to enable quick access to each of the three individual manuals. They are referenced below:

Book page number 1	SERVICE (WORKSHOP) MANUAL
Book page number 87	DISC BRAKE MANUAL
Book Page number 115	VM28SC CARBURETOR MANUAL

SUZUKI
SERVICE MANUAL

MODEL

SERVICE GUIDE

INTRODUCTION

This manual has been prepared to provide service operators with necessary information for the maintenance and the repairs of the motorcycle. The contents are made plain so that less-experienced mechanics may carry out the proper jobs according to the items of assembly and disassembly instructions. For fully qualified mechanics, the necessary service data for the inspections and repairs is provided in this manual. Since it is above all important on servicing a motorcycle to know throughly its construction and the necessary data, it is highly recommended for those who are engaged in servicing GT550 to study beforehand this manual notwithstanding their technical ability.

We trust the publication of this manual would be of assistance in the service activity as well as in the study of GT550.

SUZUKI MOTOR CO., LTD.
Export Service Section

2nd edition

LEFT AND RIGHT SIDE VIEWS

CONTENTS

		Page
1.	SPECIFICATIONS	4
2.	PERFORMANCE CURVES	6
3.	GENERAL INSTRUCTION	7
4.	SPECIAL TOOLS	8
5.	NECESSARY MATERIALS	10
6.	TROUBLE SHOOTING	12
7.	ENGINE	
	7–1. REMOVAL	15
	7–2. DISASSEMBLY AND ASSEMBLY	22
	7–3. NECESSARY POINTS ON ASSEMBLY	28
	7–4. SUZUKI RECYCLE INJECTION SYSTEM	36
	7–5. ENGINE LUBRICATION SYSTEM	37
	7–6. CARBURETOR	40
	7–7. STARTER SYSTEM	44
	7–8. CLUTCH	46
	7–9. TRANSMISSION	47
	7–10. AIR CLEANER	48
	7–11. ENGINE ELECTRICAL	49
8.	BODY	
	8–1. FRONT FORK	58
	8–2. REAR SHOCK ABSORBER	60
	8–3. BRAKES	61
	8–4. WHEELS	63
	8–5. DRIVE CHAIN	68
	8–6. BODY ELECTRICAL	70
9.	SPECIFICATIONS FOR INSPECTION AND REPAIR	73
10.	TIGHTENING TORQUE	76
11.	IMPORTANT FUNCTIONAL PARTS	77

* PERIODICAL INSPECTION LIST
* WIRING DIAGRAMS
   - **For standard specification**
   - **For USA & CANADA specification**
* EXPLODED VIEW OF ENGINE

1. SPECIFICATIONS

DIMENSIONS & WEIGHT

Overall length	2,160 mm (85.0 in)
Overall width	850 mm (33.5 in)
Overall height	1,100 mm (43.3 in)
Wheel base	1,405 mm (55.3 in)
Road clearance	150 mm (5.9 in)
Tires, front	3.25–19 4PR
rear	4.00–18 4PR
Dry weight	187 kg (412 lb)

PERFORMANCE

Maximum speed	176 – 184 kph (110 – 115 mph)
Acceleration	13.5 sec (SS 1/4 mile)
Climbing ability	26° (tan θ = 0.48)

ENGINE

Type	2 stroke, air cooled, gasoline
Piston displacement	543 cc (33.2 cu-in)
Bore X Stroke	61 X 62 mm (2.40 X 2.44 in)
Cylinders	Three in line, aluminium
Corrected compression ratio	6.8 : 1
Maximum horsepower	50 hp/6,500 rpm
Maximum torque	6.1 kg-m (44.1 ft-lb)/5,000 rpm
Starter	Electric & kick

FUEL SYSTEM

Carburetors	Three, Mikuni VM28SC
Air cleaner	Wet polyurethane filter
Fuel tank capacity	15 ltr(4.0/3.3 gal, US/Imp) including reserve 4.6 ltr(1.2/1.0 gal, US/Imp)

LUBRICATION SYSTEM

Engine	Suzuki CCI
Gear box	1,500 cc (3.17/2.64 pt, US/Imp)
Engine oil tank capacity	1.5 ltr (3.2/2.6 pt, US/Imp)

IGNITION SYSTEM

Type	Battery ignition
Ignition timing	24° (3.37 in piston stroke) BTDC
Spark plug	NGK B-7ES or Nippon Denso W-22ES

POWER TRANSMISSION

Clutch	Wet, multi-disc
Gear box	5-speed, constant mesh
Gear shifting	Left foot operated
Primary reduction ratio	2.242 (74/33)
Final reduction ratio	2.500 (40/16)

Gear ratios (Overall reduction ratios)

1st	2.864 : 1 = 37/13 (16.07)
2nd	1.736 : 1 = 33/19 (9.74)
3rd	1.363 : 1 = 30/22 (7.65)
4th	1.125 : 1 = 27/24 (6.31)
5th	0.923 : 1 = 24/26 (5.18)

SUSPENSION

Front suspension	Telescopic forks with hydraulic damper
Rear suspension	Swinging arm with hydraulic damper

STEERING

Steering angle	42° (right & left)
Castor	61°
Trail	118 mm (4.6 in)
Turning radius	2.5 m (8.2 ft)

BRAKES

Front brake	Right hand, two leading shoes, dual panel
Rear brake	Right foot, leading trailing shoes

ELECTRICAL EQUIPMENT

Generator	Alternator 12V 210W
Starter motor	12V 500W
Battery	12V 11AH
Fuse	20A
Head lamp	12V 50/40W
Tail/Brake lamp	12V 8/23W (3/32 cp)
Neutral indicator lamp	12V 3.4W
Speedometer lamp	12V 3.4W
Tachometer lamp	12V 3.4W
High beam indicator lamp	12V 3.4W
Turn signal indicator lamp	12V 1.7W
Turn signal lamp	12V 23W (32 cp)

* The specifications subject to change without notice.

2. PERFORMANCE CURVES

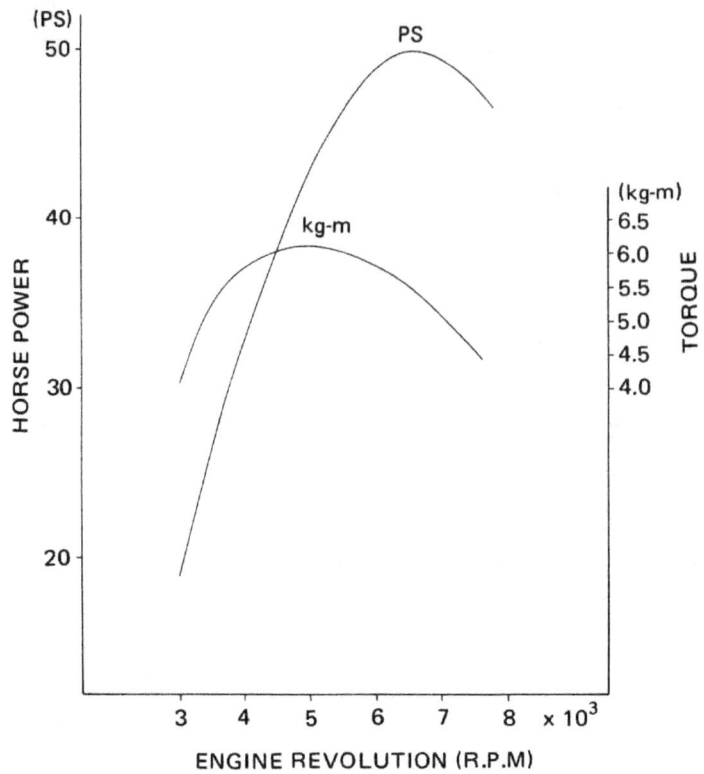

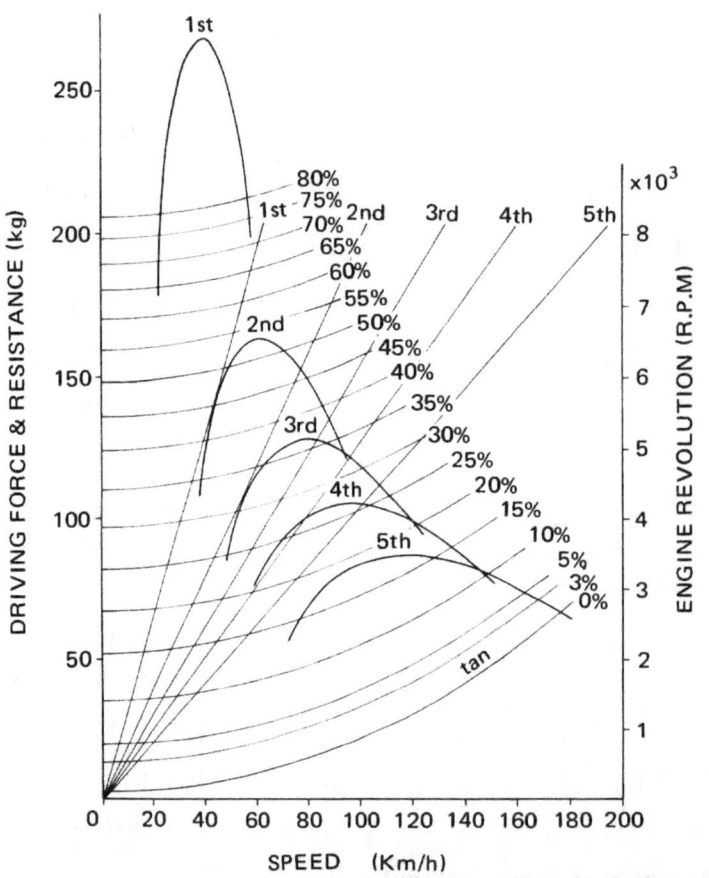

3. GENERAL INSTRUCTION

To keep the motorcycle in peak condition, advise your customers to follow these instructions and this will give top performance at all times.

3-1. BREAKING-IN

The life of the motorcycle depends on the breaking-in of the engine and the way in which the motorcycle is treated. Therefore, breaking-in with the best care is much important to prevent excessive wear of the parts and noise and to prolong the engine life. During the breaking-in period, do not operate the motorcycle at high speed nor allow the engine to run wide open. Keep to specified breaking-in engine speed limit. Gradually raise the speed as covered mileage increases.

> First 500 miles (800 km) .... below 4,000 rpm
> Up to 1,000 miles (1,600 km) .... below 5,000 rpm

3-2. FUEL AND OIL

The engine's moving parts such as crankshaft, crankshaft brearings, con-rod, piston and cylinder wall are lubricated by fresh oil pressure-delivered by Suzuki CCI system separately from the fuel supply. Put gasoline only in the fuel tank and engine oil in the oil tank.

> FUEL .... GASOLINE OF 85 – 95 OCTANE IN RESEARCH METHOD
> ENGINE OIL .... SUZUKI CCI OIL

* If Suzuki CCI oil is not available, non-diluent (non-self mixing type) two stroke oil with around SAE No.30 may be used instead.

> TRANSMISSION OIL .... MOTOR OIL OF SAE 20W/40, 1,500 cc (3.17/2.64 pt, US/IMP) CHANGE FIRST 1,000 KM (750 MILES) AND 3,000 KM (2,000 MILES) THEREAFTER.

* At the time of the first supply of oil after the transmission is overhauled, fill with 1,600 cc of oil.

3-3. GENUINE PARTS

When replacing parts, always use Suzuki genuine parts, which are precision-made under severe quality control. If imitation parts (not genuine parts) are used, good performance cannot be expected from the motorcycle and in the worst case, they may cause a breakdown.

3-4. PERIODICAL INSPECTION

To prolong the life of the motorcycle and avoid unforeseen occurrence of serious troubles, the periodical inspection is indispensable. Be sure to check the motorcycle periodically according to the list given at the end of this manual.

4. SPECIAL TOOLS

Special tools listed below are used to disassemble, assemble and to perform maintenance and service. These special tools make works easy which can not be done simply with ordinary tools and prevent the parts from damage. It is recommended to provide these special tools as shop equipment.

Ref. No.	Tool No.	Use for
1	09910-20113	Locking crankshaft
2	09930-10111	Removing or installing spark plug
3	09914-25810	Tightening or loosening crankcase bolt
4	09913-70122	Installing bearing and oil seal
5	09913-80111	Installing bearing and oil seal
6	09913-50110	Removing oil seal
7	09920-70111	Removing snap ring
8	09900-06103	Disassembling and assembling front fork
9	09940-10122	Tightening or loosening steering stem nut
10	09940-60112	Adjusting spoke tension
11	09930-20111	Adjusting contact point gap
12	09930-33310	Removing alternator rotor of KOKUSAN make
13	09930-50951	Removing alternator rotor of DENSO make
14	09920-51510	Locking clutch sleeve hub
15	09920-60310	Locking clutch sleeve hub
16	09900-09002	Tightening or loosening cross-head screw
17	09900-21802	Connecting or disconnecting drive chain
18	09900-25001	Checking electrical equipment
19	09900-27002	Checking or adjusting ignition timing
20	09900-28103	Checking electrical equipment
21	09931-00112	Checking or adjusting ignition timing
22	09900-28401	Checking battery capacity
23	09940-53110	Installing front fork oil seal

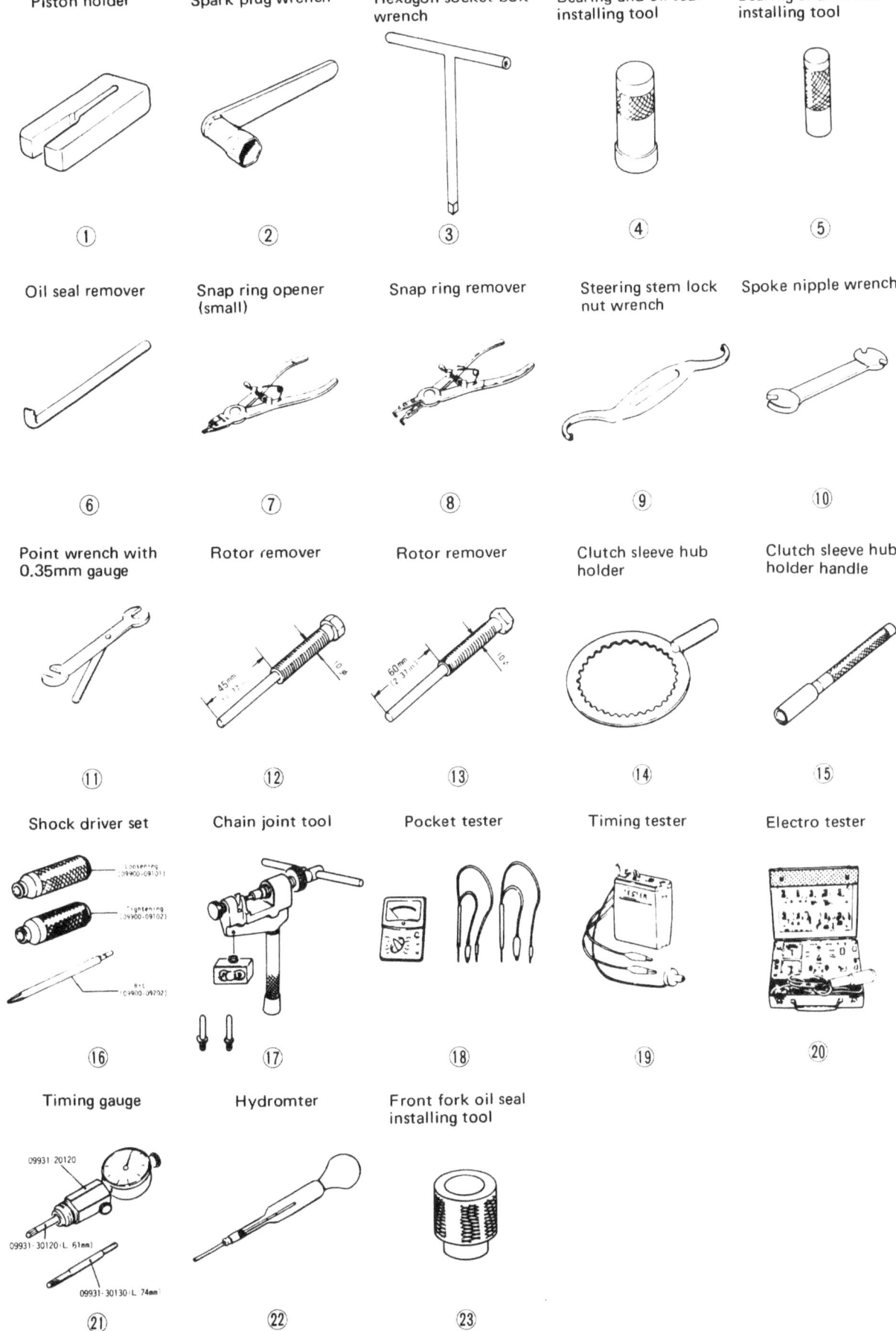

5. NECESSARY MATERIALS

GT550 necessitates the following materials in addition to the general service equipment, tools and other materials like lubricant, cleaning solvent, emery cloth and so forth. For further details, refer to the pertinent items in this manual.

5-1. THREAD CEMENT

Fig. 5-1-1   Optional part No.99000-32040

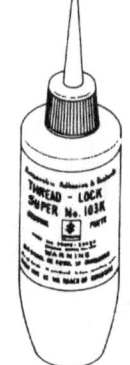

Fig. 5-1-2   Optional part No.99000-32030

This cement is applied to the thread of screws to be secured, such as the fitting screws for the starter clutch hub, gear shifting cam guide, kick starter guide and gear shifting arm stopper.

This cement is only used for securing the 2nd drive gear press-fitted over the counter-shaft end. Apply the cement to the inside surface of the gear when pressing it in.

5-2. LIQUID GASKET

This liquid is applied to the meeting surface of the crankcase being split into two halves and is to seal the crank chamber and the transmission box.

Fig. 5-1-3   Optional part No.99000-31010

5-3. EXHAUST COUPLER SEAL

This material is packed at the joint of exhaust coupler tube in order to prevent it from exhaust gas leakage.

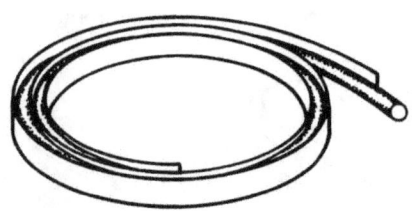

Fig. 5-1-4   Optional part No.99000-31020

5-4. GREASE
Suzuki Super Grease "A" or "C"

One of these two types should be used for lubrication of the crank and other oil seals. These greases are applied to the inside of oil seal where it meets with a shaft.

A type   Optional part No.99000-25010   C type   Optional part No.99000-25030

Fig. 5-1-5

6. TROUBLE SHOOTING

When a trouble occurs with a motorcycle, it is important to find the source of the trouble as rapidly as possible tracing it in the systematic procedure without bothering with parts which are functioning properly. This section dispences with the explanations about troubles, the cause of which may easily be found and explains only about the troubles necessitating systematic job to trace the causes.

6–1. STARTER MOTOR WILL NOT SPIN

6-2. ENGINE WILL NOT START

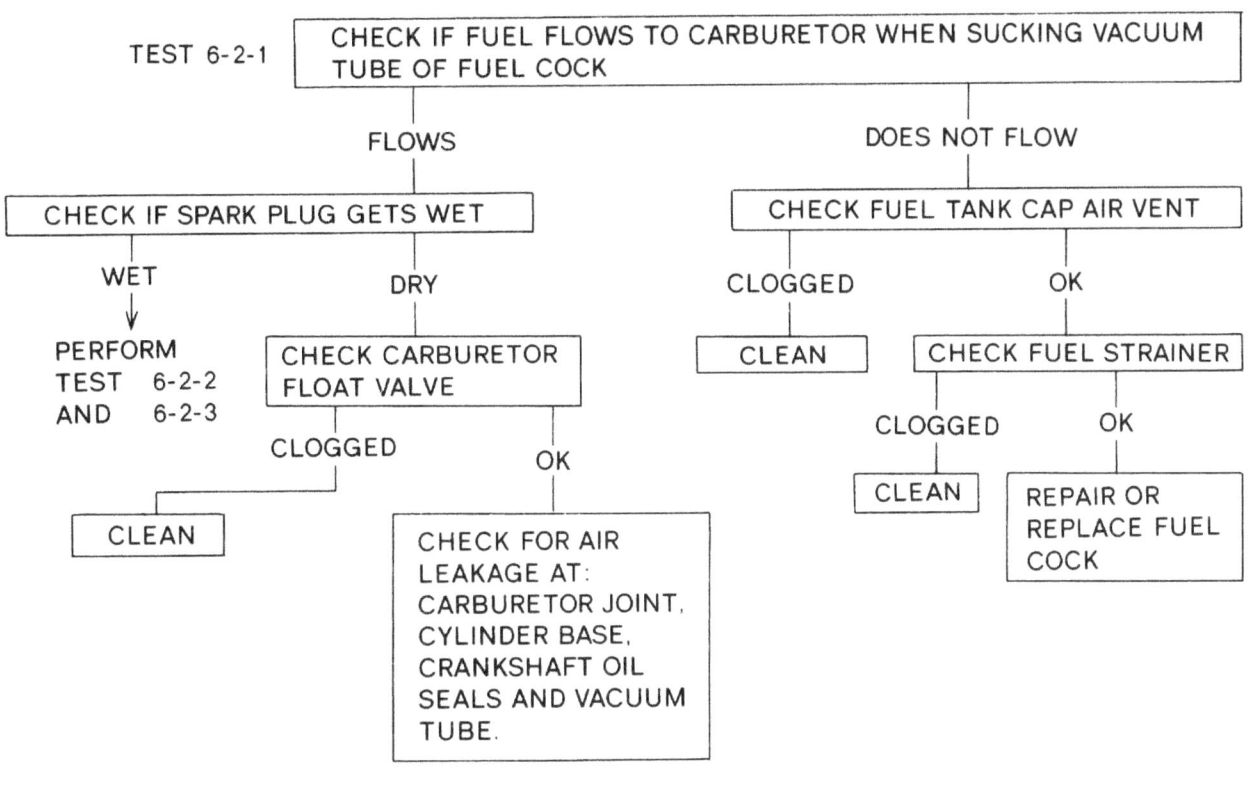

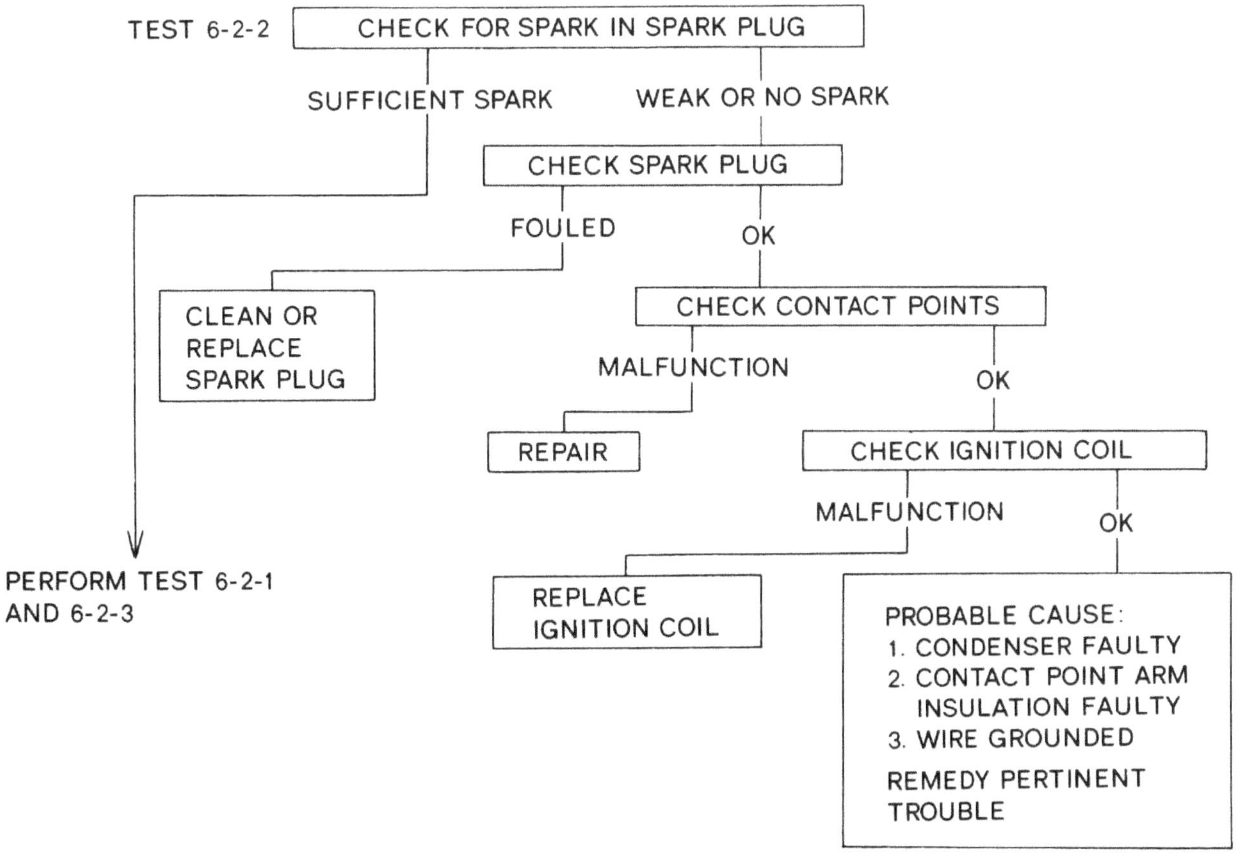

TEST 6-2-3 → CHECK FOR ENGINE COMPRESSION

- **SUFFICIENT COMPRESSION** → CHECK FOR VACUUM AT CARBURETOR INLET BY FEELING IT WITH HAND
  - **VACUUM** → PERFORM TEST 6-2-1 AND 6-2-2
  - **NO VACUUM** → PROBABLE CAUSE:
    1. CRANKSHAFT OIL SEAL DAMAGE
    2. CARBURETOR JOINT DAMAGED
    3. CYLINDER BASE GASKET DAMAGED

    REPLACE PERTINENT PART

- **NO COMPRESSION** → CHECK FOR COMPRESSION LEAKAGE AT CYLINDER HEAD GASKET
  - **LEAKAGE** → REPLACE GASKET
  - **OK** → PROVABLE CAUSE:
    1. CYLINDER WORN
    2. PISTON DAMAGED
    3. PISTON RING STUCK

    REPLACE OR RECTIFY PERTINENT PART

6-3. BATTERY TENDS TO DISCHARGE

CHECK CHARGING VOLTAGE (FIG. 6-3-1)

- **MORE THAN 14.5V** → CHECK FOR ELECTRICAL LEAK
  - **LEAK** → REPAIR
  - **NO LEAK** → REPLACE BATTERY
- **LESS THAN 13.5V** → CHECK ALTERNATOR VOLTAGE (FIG. 6-3-2)
  - **TOO LOW** → CHECK WIRING
    - **FAULTY** → REPAIR
    - **OK** → REPLACE ALTERNATOR
  - **OK** → CHECK RECTIFIER
    - **FAULTY** → REPLACE
    - **OK** → REPLACE OR ADJUST REGULATOR

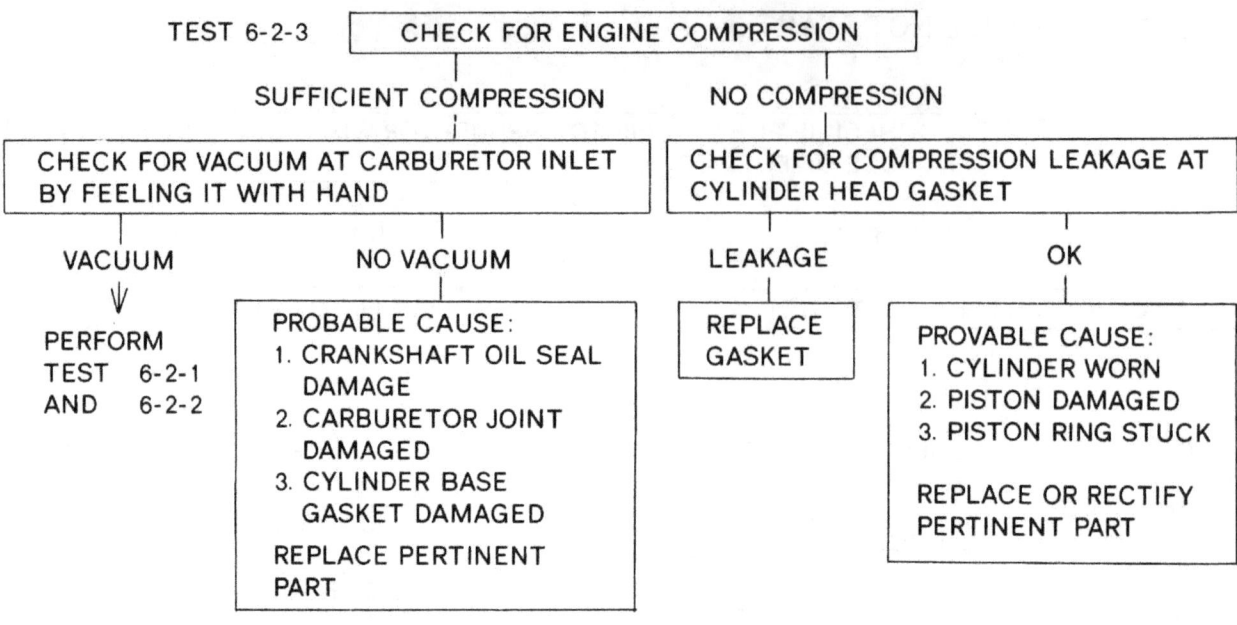

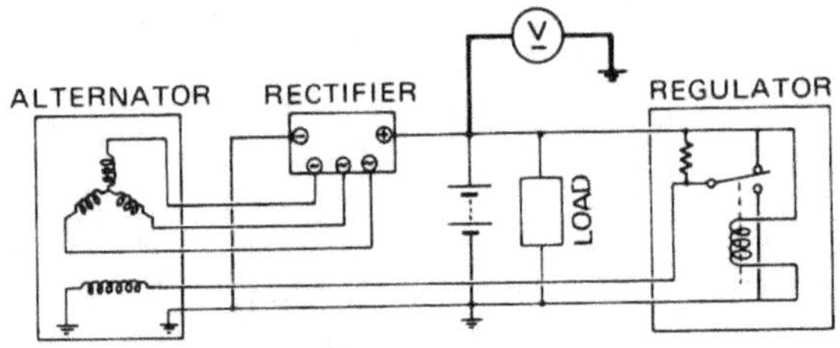

Fig. 6-3-1

Fig. 6-3-2

VOLTAGE TO BE 13.5 – 14.5V

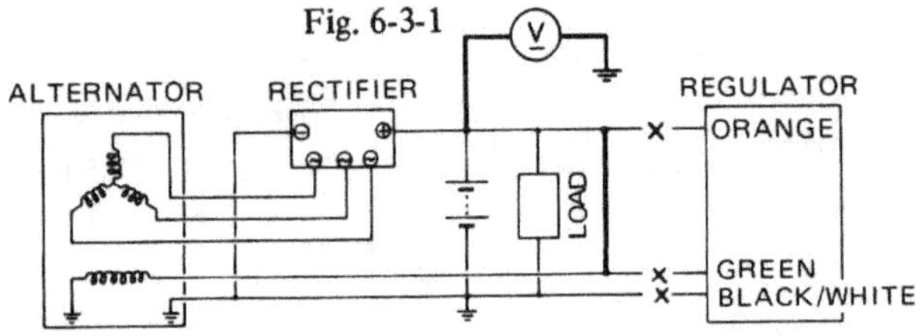

VOLTAGE TO BE:

	DENSO	KOKUSAN
1,500 RPM	18V	22V
2,500 RPM	31V	40V

NOTE: Figures are applicable under the condition that alternator is not heated.

7. ENGINE

7-1. REMOVAL

Prior to the removal operation, throughly clean the engine with a steam cleaner or cleaning solvent to remove road dirt. The removal procedure is as follow.

Fig. 7-1-1 Disconnecting fuel pipe

Required tool:

🖉 small size screw driver

Fig. 7-1-2 Removing fuel tank

Required tool: non

Remove the rubber band supporting the fuel tank at its rear end and lift up the rear part of the tank.

Fig. 7-1-3 Disconnecting battery ground cord

Required tool:

🔧 10mm or 🖉

Tightening torque:
40 – 70 kg·cm (2.9 – 5.1 lb-ft)

Fig. 7-1-4 Removing spark plug cap

Fig. 7-1-5 Disconnecting contact breaker lead wire

Disconnect the contact breaker lead wires at the coupler located behind the air cleaner box.

Fig. 7-1-6 Removing brake lamp switch

Required tool:

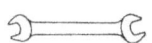 17 mm

Fig. 7-1-7 Disconnecting tachometer cable

Required tool:

Be sure not to lose the oil seal installed at the joint when removing the cable

Fig. 7-1-8 Disconnecting starter motor lead wire

Required tool:

 10 mm

Tightening torque:
40 – 60 kg-cm (2.9 – 4.4 lb-ft)

Disconnect the starter motor lead wire at the starter relay "M" terminal.

Fig. 7-1-9 Disconnecting alternator lead wire

Disconnect the alternator lead wire at the coupler shown in Fig.7-1-9. Since there are two similar couplers to each other, refer to each symbol drawn by the couplers so as to avoid misconnection.

 denotes rectifier coupler.

 denotes alternator coupler.

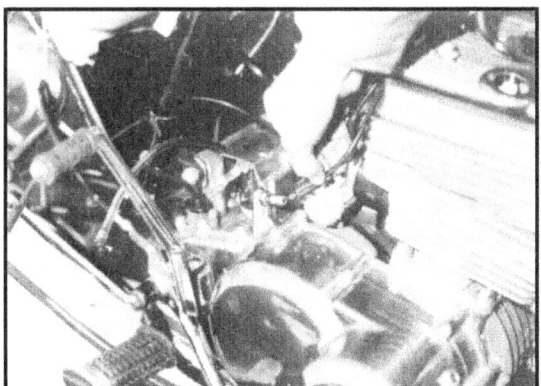

Fig. 7-1-10 Disconnecting oil pump control cable

Disconnect the oil pump control cable at the oil pump by removing the cable end piece as shown in the illustration.

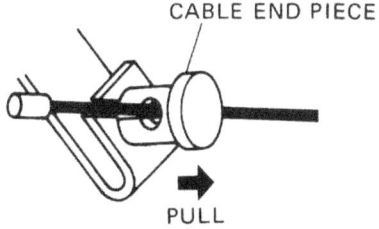

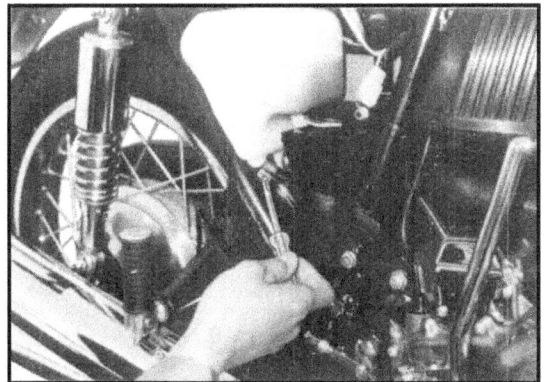

Fig. 7-1-11 Disconnecting oil inlet pipe

Required tool:

small size

Disconnect the oil pump inlet pipe at the oil tank outlet and block the outlet hole by the rubber cap of wheel inner tube inflator valve.

Fig. 7-1-12 Removing brake pedal

Required tool:

⊃━━⊂ or ○━━○ 19 mm

Tightening torque:
300 – 450 kg-cm (22 – 33 lb-ft)

Remove the brake pedal after removing the right footrest bar and loosening the rear brake cable.

Fig. 7-1-13 Removing air cleaner

Required tool:

⊤━━▭ 10 mm and ━━▭ small size

Tightening torque:
60 – 100 kg-cm (4.4 – 7.3 lb-ft)

Fig. 7-1-14 Removing carburetors

Required tool:

━━▭ small size

Fig. 7-1-15 Removing gear shifting lever

Required tool:

⊃━━⊂ 12 mm

Tightening torque:
130 – 230 kg-cm (9.5 – 17 lb-ft)

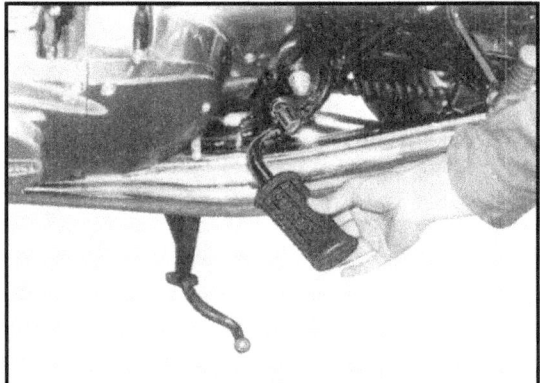

Fig. 7-1-16 Removing left footrest

Required tool:

 19 mm

Tightening torque:
300 – 450 kg-cm (22 – 33 lb-ft)

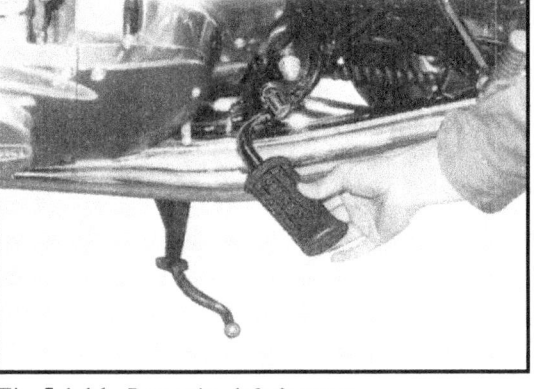

Fig. 7-1-17 Removing clutch release cover

Required tool:

big size

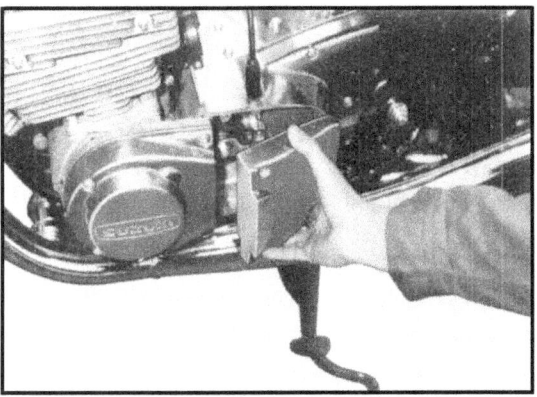

Fig. 7-1-18 Removing engine sprocket cover

Required tool:

big size

Fig. 7-1-19 Removing sprocket fitting plate

Required tool:

 10 mm

Tightening torque:
40 – 70 kg-cm (2.9 – 5.1 lb-ft)

After removing the fitting bolts, turn the fitting plate half pitch of the spline and take it off.

Pull out the drive sprocket from the drive shaft.

Fig. 7-1-20 Removing drive sprocket

Required tool:

 10 mm and  big size

Remove the left and right cylinder head covers in order that these do not hinder when dismounting engine.

Fig. 7-1-21 Removing cylinder head covers

Required tool:

 14 mm

Tightening torque:
180 – 280 kg-cm (13 – 20 lb-ft)

Remove both the right and left footrests.

Fig. 7-1-22 Removing rear footrest

Required tool:

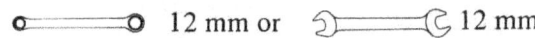 12 mm or 12 mm

Tightening torque:
90 – 140 kg-cm (6.6 – 10 lb-ft)

Remove both the right and left side mufflers.

Fig. 7-1-23 Removing muffler

20

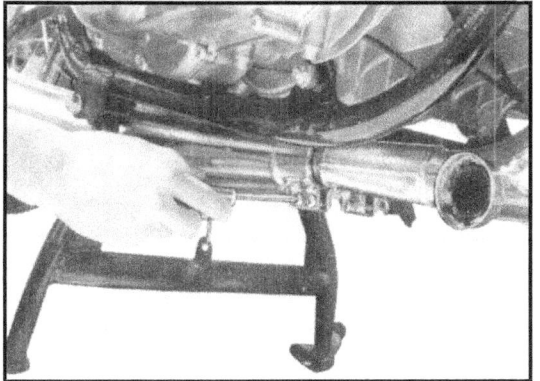

Fig. 7-1-24 Disconnecting muffler joint

Required tool:

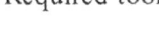 big size

After loosening two joints, pull out backward the inside two mufflers.

Fig. 7-1-25 Removing center exhaust pipe

Required tool:

 or  12 mm

Tightening torque:
90 – 140 kg-cm (6.6 – 10 lb-ft)

Fig. 7-1-26 Removing engine mounting bolts

Required tool:

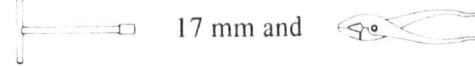 17 mm and

Tightening torque:
250 – 400 kg-cm (18 – 29 lb-ft)

Fig. 7-1-27 Removing engine mounting plate

Required tool:

 12 mm

Tightening torque:
130 – 230 kg-cm (9.5 – 17 lb-ft)

Fig. 7-1-28 Dismounting engine

Lift up the engine and move it to the right side.

CAUTION:
Do not pull up or move the engine by holding the gear shifting shaft otherwise the shaft may bend making it difficult to pull the shaft out.

7−2. DISASSEMBLY AND ASSEMBLY

This section gives an explanation of all the jobs necessary for separating the crankcase. When disassembling the engine, take the following steps. For reassembling the engine after necessary inspections or repairs, follow the reverse order of the disassembly.

Fig. 7-2-1 Removing cylinder head

1. Remove the cylinder head after unscrewing the fitting nuts.

    Required tool:

    ⊢──────▭ 14 mm

    Tightening torque:
    250 − 400 kg-cm (18 − 29 lb-ft)

Fig. 7-2-2 Removing cylinder

2. Pull out the SRIS rubber hoses connected to cylinder inlet side and remove the cylinders after unscrewing their fitting nuts.

    Required tool:

    o────o or ⊃────⊂ 14 mm

    Tightening torque:
    250 − 400 kg-cm (18 − 29 lb-ft)

3. After removing the cylinders, cover the crank chamber with clean rag to prevent a piston pin circlip or a foreign substance from dropping into it. Remove one piston pin circlip from the piston with a small screw driver or nose pliers. Now, the piston pin can be easily removed by pushing the other end of the pin with a rod. Fig. 7-2-3 & 7-2-4.

NOTE:
Each piston and its related parts should be installed in the original place when the assembly. Therefore, keep them separately so that the original position of each part may be identified.

Fig. 7-2-3 Removing piston pin circlip

Fig. 7-2-4 Removing piston pin

Fig. 7-2-5 Removing alternator stator

4. After disconnecting the neutral indicator lead wire at the switch, remove 3 pcs of alternator stator fitting screw and take off the stator.

Required tool:

large and small size

Fig. 7-2-6 Removing alternator rotor

5. Place the piston holder between the connecting rod and the crankcase in order to lock the crankshaft and after removing the rotor fitting bolt, screw-in the rotor remover and torque it firmly.

Required tool:

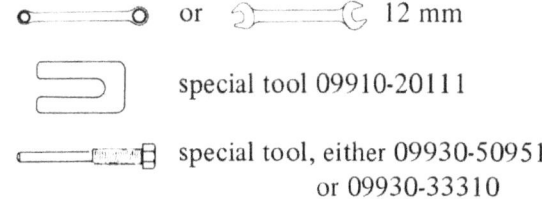

or 12 mm

special tool 09910-20111

special tool, either 09930-50951 or 09930-33310

Tightening torque:
90 – 140 kg-cm (6.6 – 10 lb-ft)

Fig. 7-2-7 Removing oil pump cover

6. Remove the oil pump cover.

   Required tool:

   ⌒ 8 mm

   ▬▭ small size

   Tightening torque:
   20 – 40 kg-cm (1.5 – 2.9 lb-ft)

Fig. 7-2-8 Removing oil pump

7. Unscrew the fitting bolts and remove the oil pump.

   Required tool:

   ▬▭ small size

   Tightening torque:
   20 – 40 kg-cm (1.5 – 2.9 lb-ft)

Fig. 7-2-9 Removing kick starter lever

8. Remove the kick starter lever from the kick shaft.

   Required tool:

   o━━o 14 mm

   Tightening torque:
   250 – 400 kg-cm (18 – 29 lb-ft)

Fig. 7-2-10 Removing engine right cover

9. After loosening the fitting screws, remove the engine right cover.

   Required tool:

   ▬▭ large size or impact driver

   The contact breaker is installed in the cover and the job in this item can be done without removing it.

Fig. 7-2-11 Removing clutch pressure plate

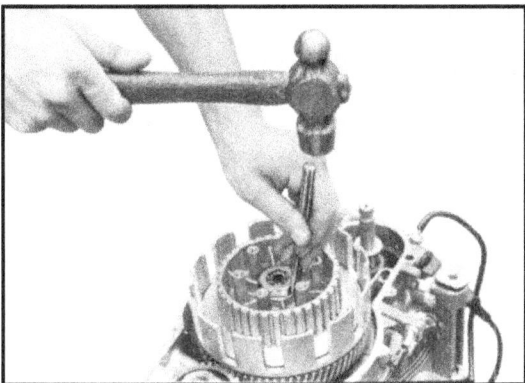

Fig. 7-2-12 Flattening lock washer

Fig. 7-2-13 Loosening clutch sleeve hub nut

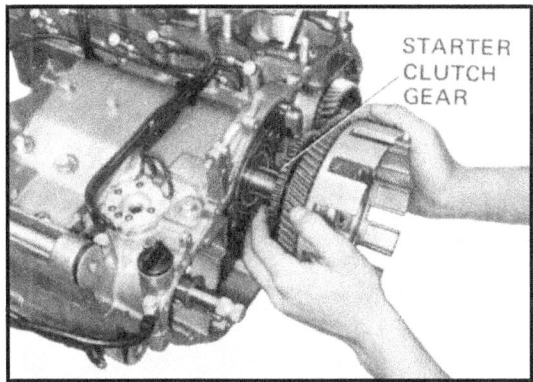

Fig. 7-2-14 Removing clutch housing and starter one-way clutch

10. Unscrew 6 pcs of the screws and remove the clutch pressure plate.

   Required tool:

    10 mm

   Tightening torque:
   40 – 70 kg-cm (2.9 – 5.1 lb-ft)

11. After removing the clutch plates and the push piece fitted on the end of the shaft by hand, flatten the clutch sleeve hub washer with a chisel and a hammer.

    Required tool:

    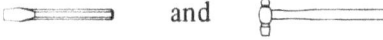

12. Loosen the clutch sleeve hub nut by holding the hub with the special tools.

    Required tool:

    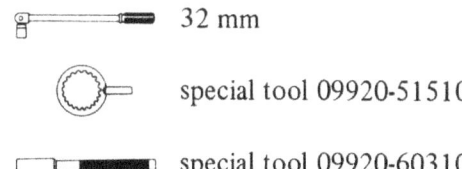

    32 mm

    special tool 09920-51510

    special tool 09920-60310

    Tightening torque:
    500 – 600 kg-cm (36 – 43 lb-ft)

13. Remove the clutch housing together with the starter clutch gear.

    NOTE:
    The starter one-way clutch is equipped behind the clutch housing. If the clutch housing is removed leaving the starter clutch gear on the shaft, the component parts of the starter clutch may come off the housing, which may give an inconvenience of repositioning them.

Fig. 7-2-15 Removing gear shifting shaft

14. Pull out the gear shifting shaft.

Fig. 7-2-16 Removing oil guide plate

15. Remove the oil guide plate.

    Required tool:

    impact driver

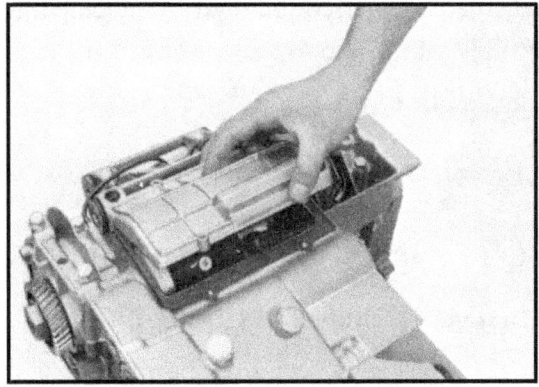

Fig. 7-2-17 Removing starter motor cover

16. After removing the fitting screws, take off the starter motor cover installed underneath the engine.

    Required tool:

    8 mm

    Tightening torque:
    20 – 40 kg-cm (1.5 – 2.9 lb-ft)

Fig. 7-2-18 Removing starter motor

17. Unscrew 2 pcs of the fitting screw and remove the starter motor.

    Required tool:

    10 mm

    Tightening torque:
    40 – 70 kg-cm (2.9 – 5.1 lb-ft)

Fig. 7-2-19 Loosening crankcase bolts

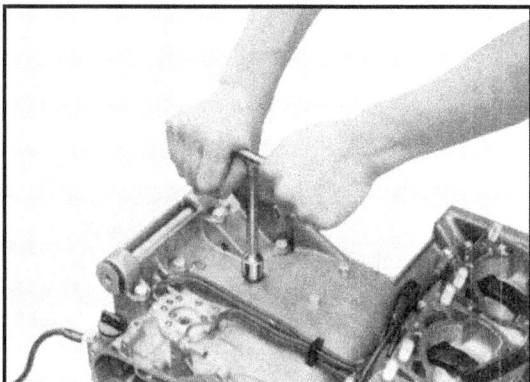

Fig. 7-2-20 Loosening crankcase bolts

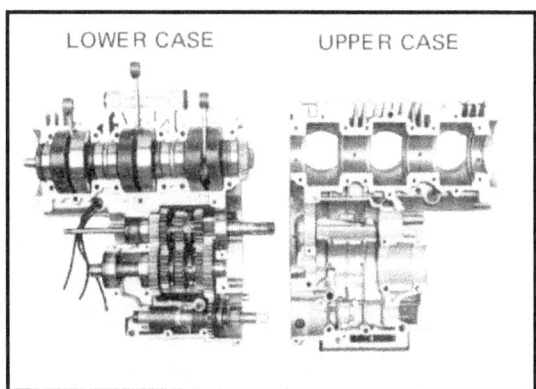

Fig. 7-2-21 Separated crankcase

18. Loosen all the crankcase joining bolts on the lower crankcase half.

    Required tool:

    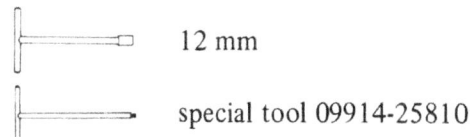

    12 mm

    special tool 09914-25810

    Tightening torque:
    130 − 230 kg-cm (9.5 − 17 lb-ft)

19. Loosen all the crankcase joining bolts on the upper crankcase half.

    Required tool:

    12 mm and 10 mm

    Tightening torque:
    6 mm bolt... 60 − 100 kg-cm (4.4 − 7.3 lb-ft)
    8 mm bolt... 130 − 230 kg-cm (9.5 − 17 lb-ft)

20. Hit the crankcase with a mallet or a soft hammer and separate it into upper and lower halves leaving inside parts on lower half of the case.

    Required tool:

    Mallet or soft hammer

7-3. NECESSARY POINTS ON ASSEMBLY

7-3-1. CYLINDER HEAD

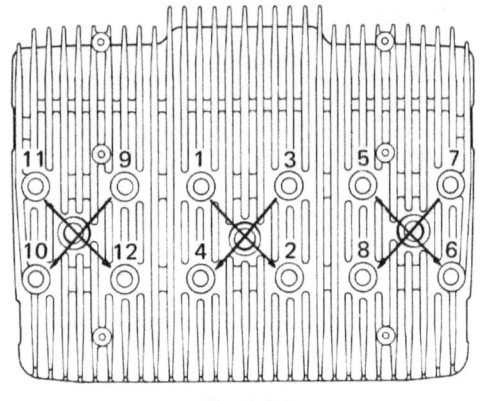

Fig. 7-3-1

When installing the cylinder head, tighten 4 bolts of each combustion chamber evenly in a crisscross fashion as illustrated in Fig. 7-3-1 so that each meeting surface of the combustion chamber may properly fit the same of respective cylinder.

Tightening torque:
250 – 400 kg-cm (18 – 29 lb-ft)

7-3-2. PISTON

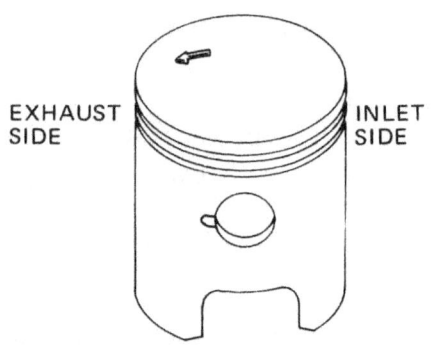

Fig. 7-3-2

The piston pin hole is off-center and the piston skirt is cut according to the shape of scavenging passage on the crankcase, therefore, the piston should be installed in proper direction. The arrow mark on the piston head indicates the exhaust side.

7-3-3. PISTON RING

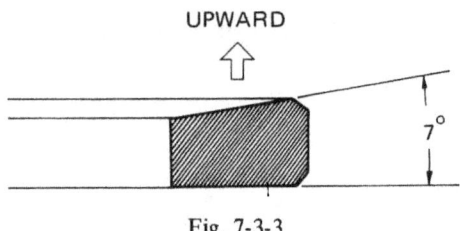

Fig. 7-3-3

Both the 1st and 2nd rings are of wedge type in their sectional views as illustrated in Fig. 7-3-3 and the ring grooves on piston are machined according to the shape of the rings. Therefore, the ring should be placed in proper direction otherwise the piston will not fit in the cylinder. For identifying upside, a stamped letter is put on the inclined surface.

7-3-4. CRANKSHAFT

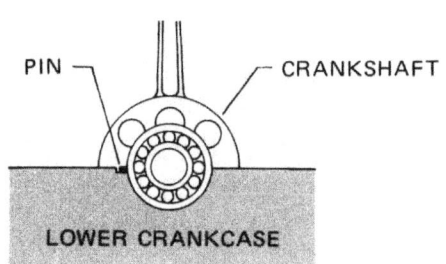

Fig. 7-3-4

When installing the crankshaft, pay attention to following point.

1) The pins on the crankshaft bearings should be placed in the grooves on the lower crankcase. Fig. 7-3-4.

2) All the movable oil seals on the crankshaft should be put to bearing side. Fig. 7-3-5.

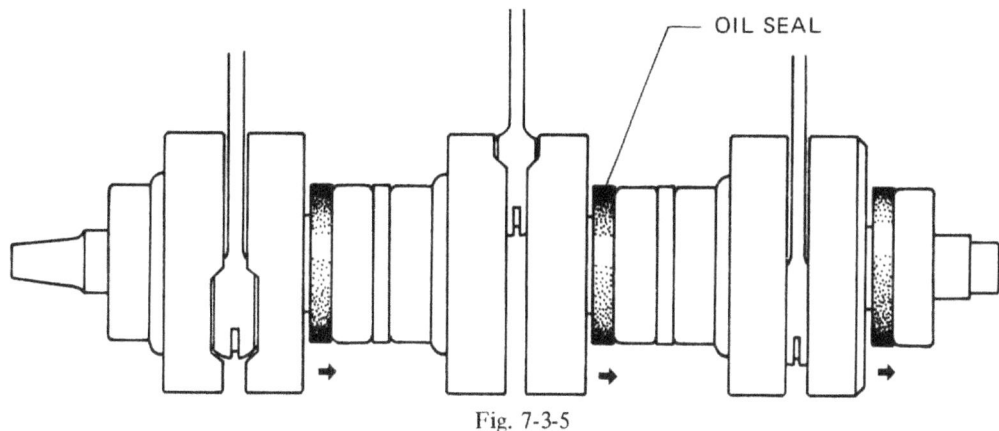

Fig. 7-3-5

3) In case that an impact or heavy stress is given to the connecting rod by any chance, it is necessary to check it for a bend. For this check, install the piston on the connecting rod without the piston ring in the state that the crankshaft is assembled on the crankcase and install the cylinder. In this condition, push the piston head at TDC to left and right. The piston should return to the neutral position or stay free position within the clearance when the pressure is released. If the piston tends to press the cylinder wall always to one side, that is, the piston is not positioned in center of the cylinder bore, the connecting rod is judged to be bent.

NOTE:

In case disassembly or assembly of the crankshaft is required, use the special jigs designed by the factory to get the proper alignment.

7-3-5. CYLINDER

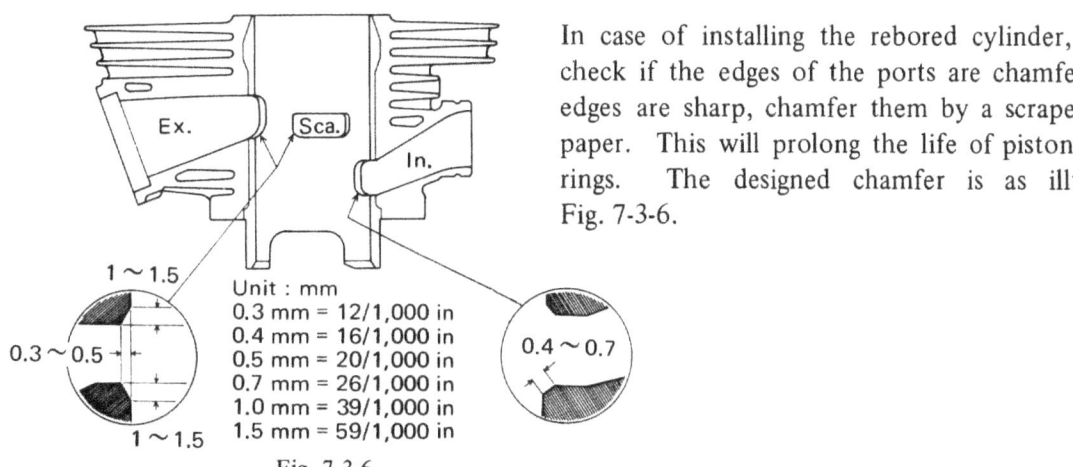

Fig. 7-3-6

In case of installing the rebored cylinder, be sure to check if the edges of the ports are chamfered. If the edges are sharp, chamfer them by a scraper or emery paper. This will prolong the life of piston and piston rings. The designed chamfer is as illustrated in Fig. 7-3-6.

7-3-6. INTAKE PIPE

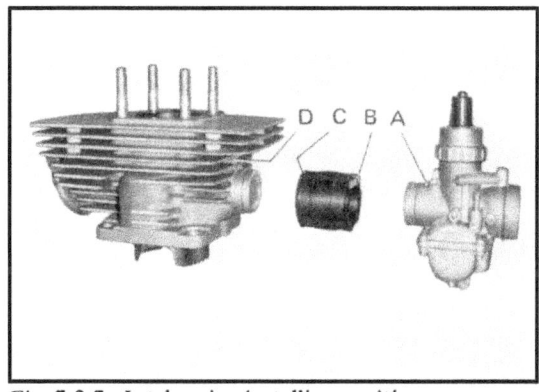

Fig. 7-3-7 Intake pipe installing position

When installing the intake pipe on the cylinder, align the notch "C" on the intake pipe with the rib on the cylinder "D" as illustrated in Fig. 7-3-7 so that the carburetor may be placed in proper position with engagement of "A" and "B".

7-3-7. SRIS HOSES

Two grommets are provided on the upper and lower crankcases respectively in order to hold the SRIS hoses and guide them to proper piping. Therefore, if only the hoses are set according to the indications on the grommets in the condition of proper grommet installation, the hoses will be set in the designed proper places. However, in case that the grommets are improperly installed on the crankcase, the proper piping will not be obtained resulting in malfunctioning of the system.

The installation of the grommets and the piping of SRIS hoses should be done as shown in Fig. 7-3-8.

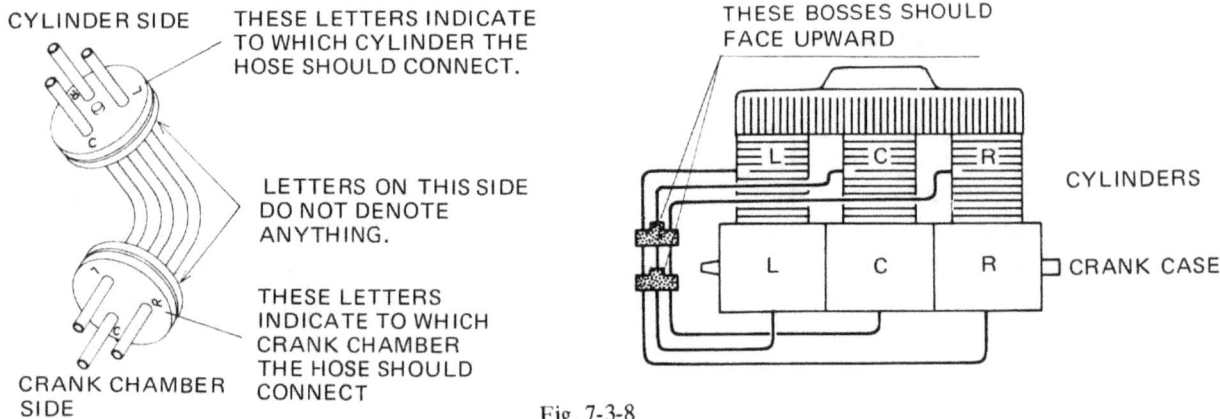

Fig. 7-3-8

7-3-8. ENGINE OIL PIPE

Fig. 7-3-9 Initial oil supply

At the time when the engine assembly is completed, the oil passages has not yet been filled with oil. If the engine is started and kept on running in this condition, the engine may suffer lack of lubrication causing a bearing noise or piston seizure. Therefore, be sure to supply CCI oil from the end of the oil pipes with a oil filler as shown in Fig. 7-3-9.

7-3-9. CLUTCH

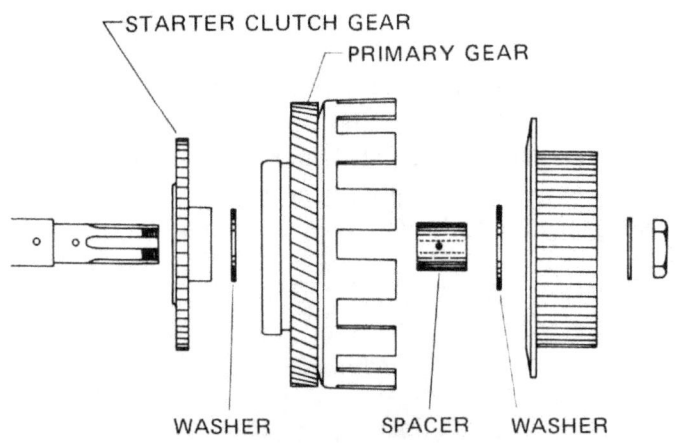

Fig. 7-3-10

1) On assembling the clutch, place the washer and the spacer in right position as shown in Fig.7-3-10.

2) When installing the primary gear on the shaft, the starter clutch gear should be installed to the primary gear beforehand otherwise the primary gear will not fit in proper place.

7-3-10. CLUTCH RELEASE

Fig. 7-3-11 Clutch release lever

1) The clutch release lever should be installed so that its end aligns with the embossed line provided on the engine left cover when the lever is fully returned. If the lever is found to be in improper position when assembling this mechanism, correct its position by changing the position of the plate "A" after removing the release lever and screws on the plate shown in Fig. 7-3-11.

Before tightening the nut "B", the screw "C" should be adjusted by the following procedure.
1. Turn the screw "C" clockwise until it becomes stiff.
2. Unscrew it by 1/2 turn from this position.
3. Keeping the screw in this state, tighten the nut "B".

2.) Two pieces of the clutch release rods are placed in the center hole of the countershaft. Each of the rod should be positioned with its round shape end facing clutch side.

7-3-11. GEAR SHIFTING FORKS

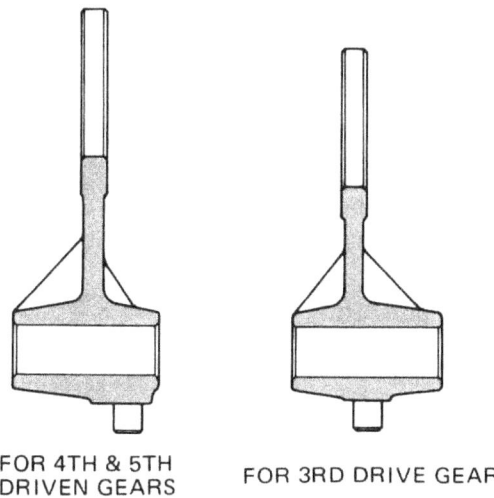

FOR 4TH & 5TH DRIVEN GEARS   FOR 3RD DRIVE GEAR

Fig. 7-3-12

There are 3 pcs of the gear shifting forks in the transmission. 2 forks out of 3 are identical and used for the 4th and 5th driven gears on the drive shaft. The rest has a different shape and is used for the 3rd drive gear on the countershaft. These shapes are drawn in Fig. 7-3-12.

7-3-12. TRANSMISSION

For the installation of gears, washers, circlips and bearings, refer to the illustration Fig. 7-3-13.

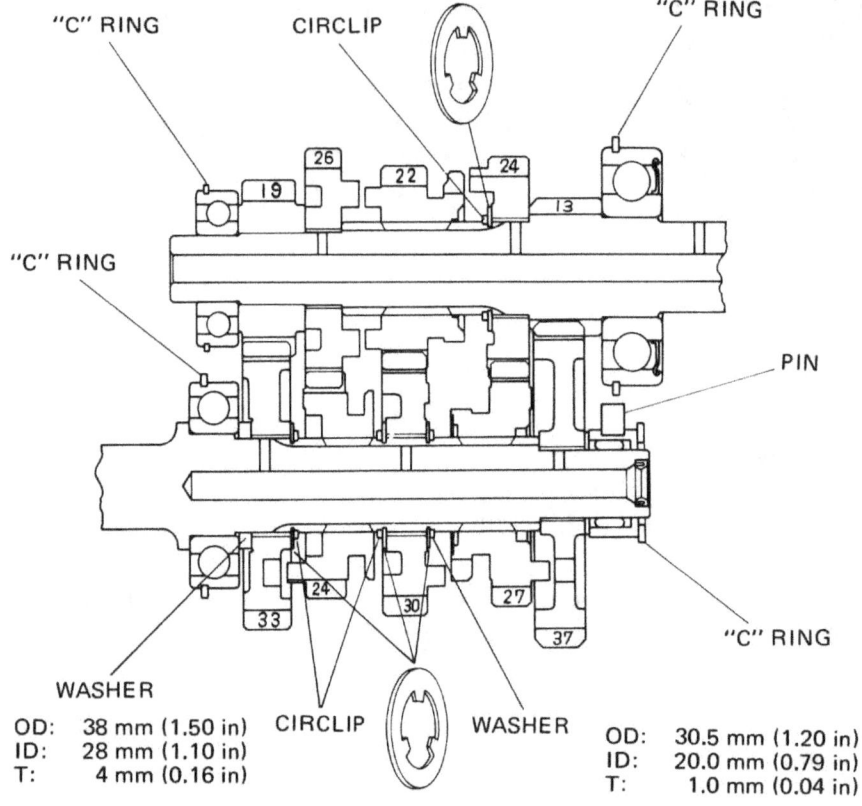

Fig. 7-3-13

OD: Outside Diameter
ID: Inside Diameter
T : Thickness

The figure on the gears in this illustration denotes the number of the teeth.

WASHER
OD: 38 mm (1.50 in)
ID: 28 mm (1.10 in)
T: 4 mm (0.16 in)

WASHER
OD: 30.5 mm (1.20 in)
ID: 20.0 mm (0.79 in)
T: 1.0 mm (0.04 in)

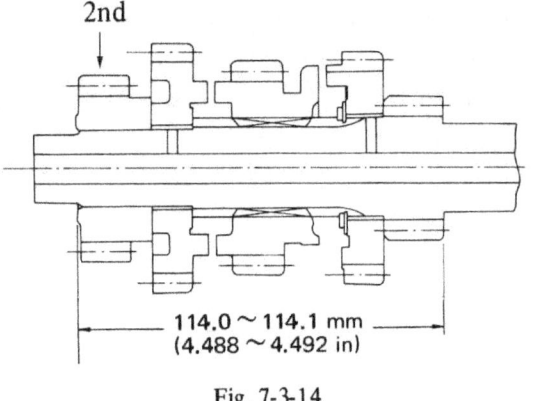

Fig. 7-3-14

The job of replacing the gears on the countershaft may scarcely be required. However, in case that this job is necessarily done, the 2nd gear installed by press-fit should be removed.

When installing the 2nd gear on the countershaft, the following points should be observed.

IMPORTANT: The measurement shown in Fig. 7-3-14 should be checked prior to disassembly as Suzuki repair shops have reported dimensions as low as:
111.0 ~ 111.1 mm (4.370 ~ 4.374 in)

1) Since the 2nd gear must transmit large torque of the countershaft, enough capacity in frictional force is required at the joint surface of the 2nd gear and countershaft. Suzuki Lock Super 103K (available as the genuine part) is cement applied to a joint of two materials to increase the frictional force to a great extent. When installing the second gear by press-fit, apply this cement to inside surface of the 2nd gear.

2) The press-fit should be made so as to have 114.0 – 114.1 mm (4.488 – 4.492 in) from the low gear end to the end of 2nd gear as shown in Fig. 7-3-14.

3) Removal of the 2nd gear from the countershaft is allowable only twice. At the third removal, replace with a new countershaft.

Fig. 7-3-15 Countershaft oil reservoir

When installing the countershaft oil reservoir, fit the boss in the groove on the case. This will locate the oil passage in a right position.

7-3-13. KICK STARTER

The component parts of the kick starter mechanism should be assembled as illustrated in Fig. 7-3-16.

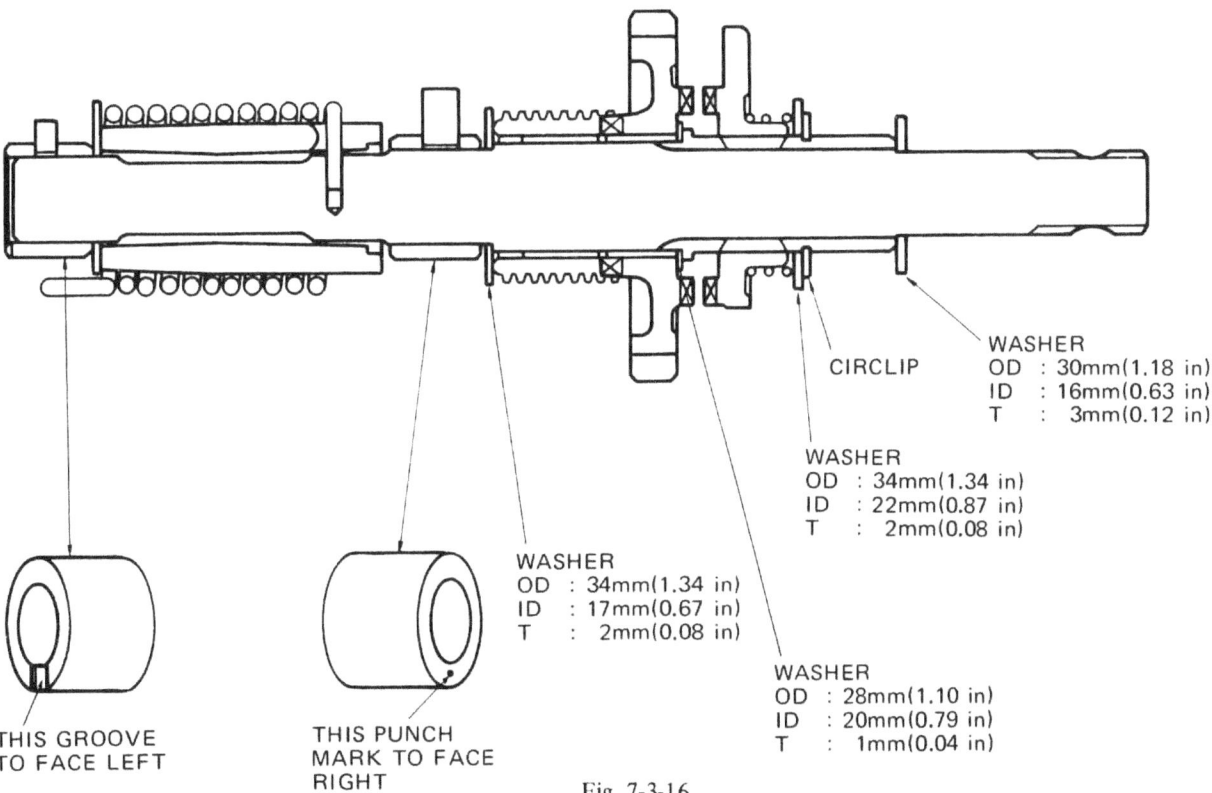

Fig. 7-3-16

Fig. 7-3-17 Assembling kick starter shaft

When the upper and lower crankcase are joined, be sure to check if the end of the kick starter spring is in the hole of the case as indicated by arrow mark in Fig. 7-3-17.

To give spring tension to the kick starter shaft, carry out the following procedure.

1) Install the ratchet wheel over the kick starter shaft so that the two punch marks align as shown in Fig. 7-3-18.

2) Twist the kick starter shaft approximately 3/4 turn anticlockwise and set the ratchet wheel so that its boss is caught in the stopper plate.

Fig. 7-3-18   Positioning ratchet wheel

7–3–14. CRANKCASE

1) Before joining the upper and lower crankcases, clean their meeting surfaces and coat the upper case surface with Suzuki liquid gasket 99000-31010 evenly and after drying it for approximately 5 minutes, take the assembly procedure of the engine.

2) The crankcase tightening bolts and clamps fixed together with them should be used in the positions shown in Fig. 7-3-19.

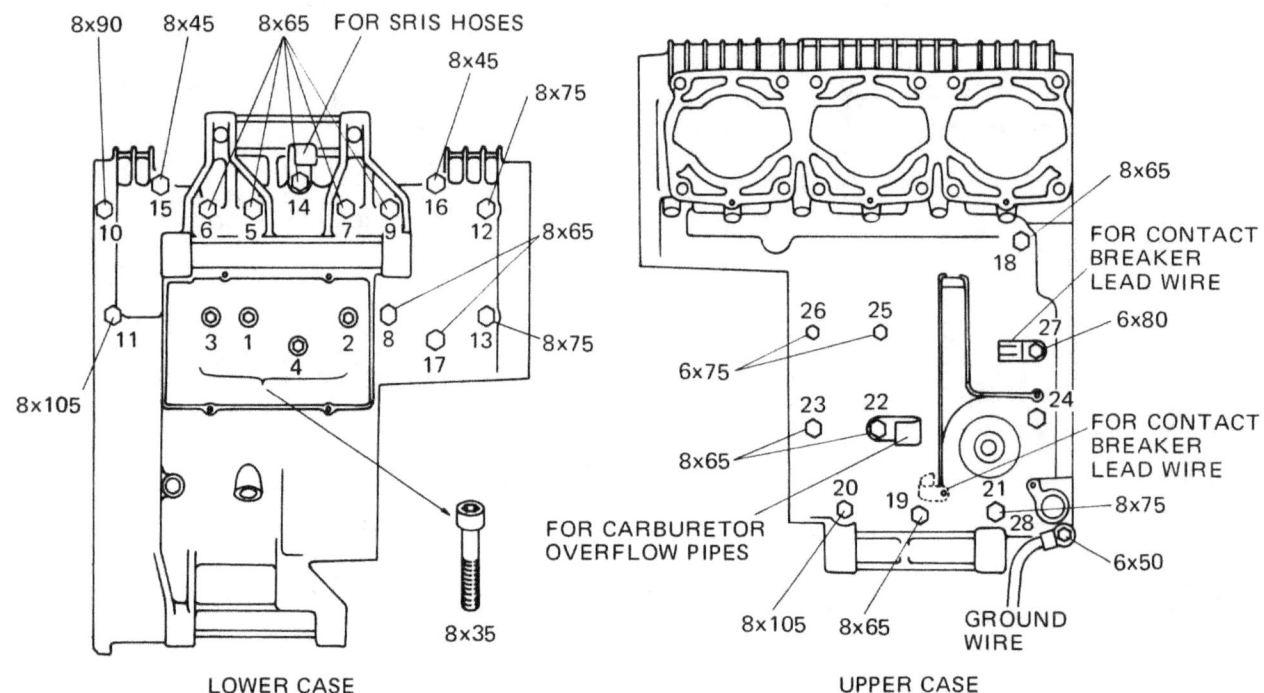

Fig. 7-3-19

* The figures on the case indicate the tightening order.
* The figures written like 8 × 45 denote the size of the bolt:

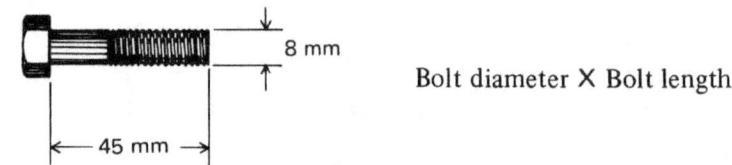

Bolt diameter × Bolt length

* Tightening torque: 6 mm bolt = 60 – 100 kg-cm (4.4 – 7.3 lb-ft)
                       8 mm bolt = 130 – 230 kg-cm (9.5 – 17 lb-ft)

7-3-15. EXHAUST PIPE AND MUFFLER

Fig. 7-3-20 Exhaust pipe position

Before tightening the exhaust pipe clamp bolts, check to see if there is enough clearance between the cylinder and the exhaust pipe clamp. The designed clearance is 1 – 2 mm (0.04 – 0.08 in).
This clearance can be adjusted by turning the clamp since it is screw-coupled with the exhaust pipe.

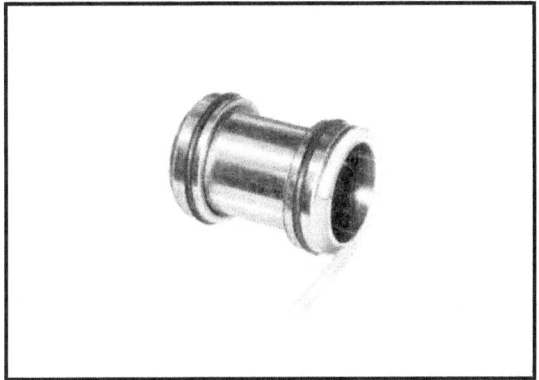

Fig. 7-3-21 Exhaust coupler seal

In order to seal thoroughly the joint of the exhaust coupler tube, put exhaust coupler seal (Suzuki genuine part 99000-31020) around both ends of the coupler tube.

NOTE:
Original thickness of the coupler seal is a little too large for the groove on the muffler in which the coupler seal and the end of the coupler tube are placed together. Therefore, it is necessary to lengthen beforehand the coupler seal by approximately 10% to make it thinner.

7-4. SUZUKI RECYCLE INJECTION SYSTEM (SRIS)

After the moving parts are lubricated with engine oil fed through CCI system, this used oil tends to accumulate in the bottom of crank chamber though it does little by little. Oil thus stored-up is discharged to the combustion chamber through the transfer port (scavenging port) when the engine is quickly accelerated causing as a result excessive smoke emission from the exhaust silencer.

SRIS has been designed in order to eradicate this undesirable phenomenon by transferring the residual oil into the cylinder without accumulating in the crank chamber and exhausting it little by little with invisible smoke.

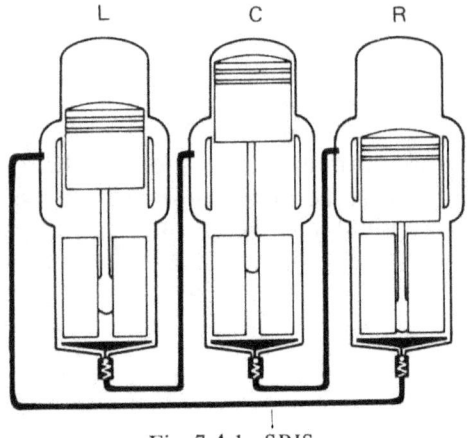

Fig. 7-4-1 SRIS

Oil from the crank chambers is delivered to the cylinders through the tubes connecting the crank chamber and the transfer port in the way shown in Fig. 7-4-1.

One-way valves are installed at the oil outlet of the crank chambers in order to check the reverse flow of oil. Pressure at each end of the tube always changes to positive and negative reciprocally while the engine is running and oil is sent to the cylinder whenever the crank chamber pressure is higher than that of the transfer port in excess of the one-way valve working pressure.

This action takes place in each crank chamber notwithstanding engine speed and load, which burns oil continuously and thoroughly resulting in no accumulation of oil in the crank chambers.

7-4-1. INSPECTION

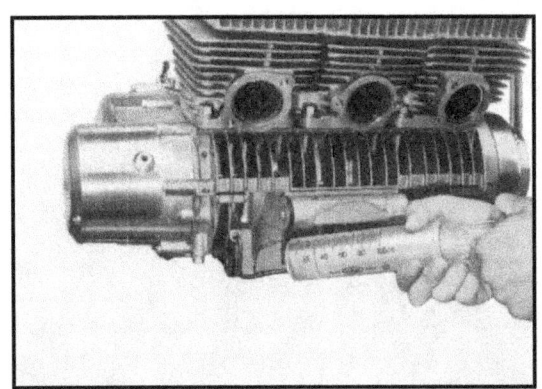

Fig. 7-4-2 Checking one-way valve

For checking the one-way valve on the crankcase, use a syringe to apply pressure or vacuum to it. In case the valve functions properly, air can be drawn by syringe but not be sent.

7-5. ENGINE LUBRICATION SYSTEM

7-5-1. CONSTRUCTION

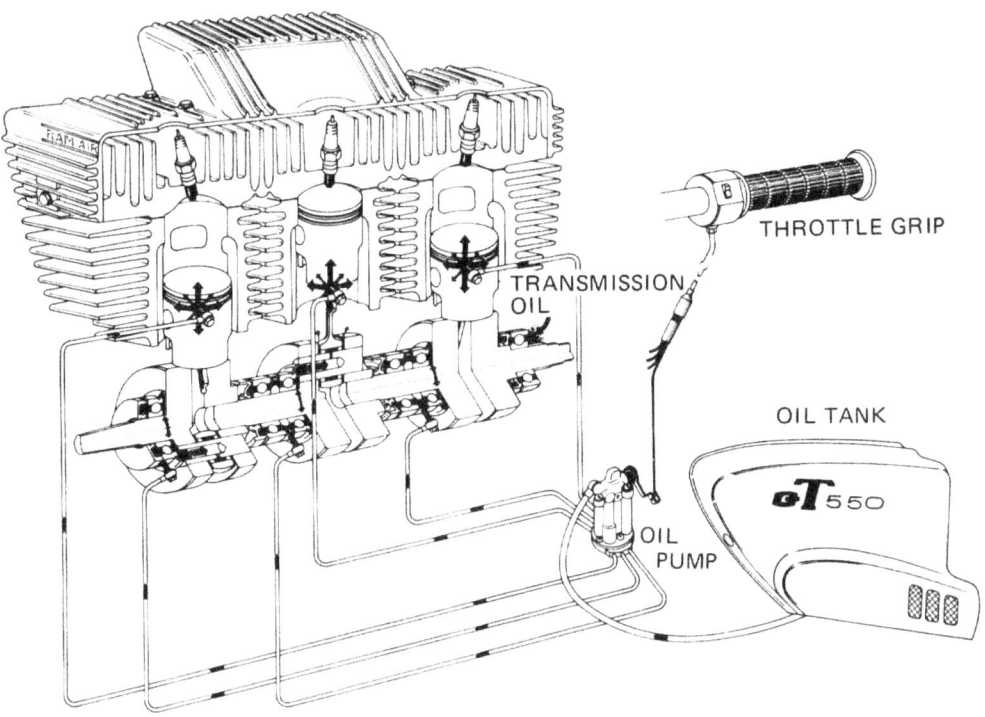

Fig. 7-5-1 Suzuki CCI lubrication system

The engine lubrication is of Suzuki CCI system same as other Suzuki models. The oil pump has 6 outlets connecting with respective oil feeding pipes and lubricate all the moving parts of the engine except the crankshaft right end bearing which is lubricated by transmission oil. The oil pump is driven by a warm gear engaging with the same on kick starter shaft and the driving power is transmitted from the engine through the clutch, the low gears and the kick starter gear.

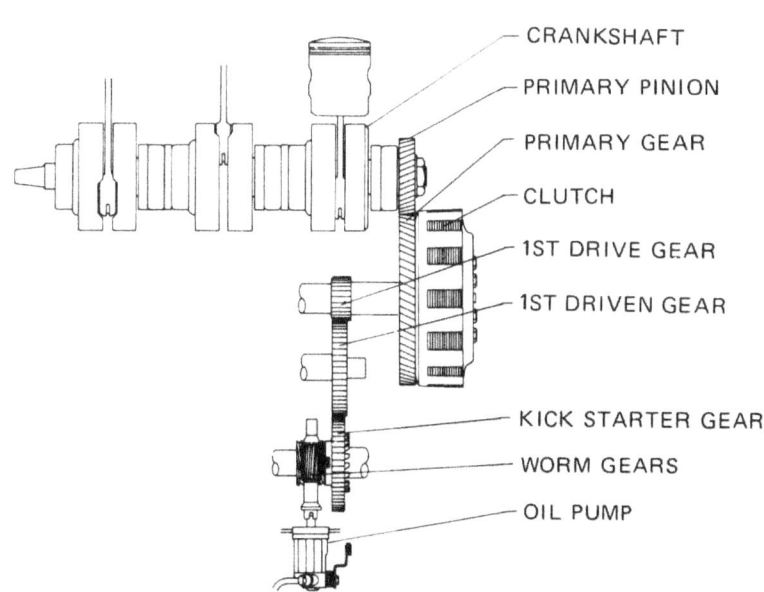

Fig. 7-5-2 Oil pump driving system

Fig. 7-5-2 and 7-5-3 show the oil pump driving system and the construction of the oil pump respectively.

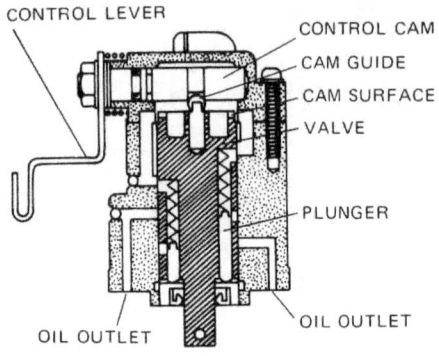

Fig. 7-5-3

In Fig. 7-5-3, the valve is always pressed upwards by the springs and its movement to upside is restricted by the control cam or the cam guide stationarily fitted on the pump body. The valve moves up and down according to the cam shape machined on its upper end as the valve rotates.

The discharge and suction of oil in the pump take place by the variation of inside volume of the valve resulting from the change of relative position of the plunger to the valve.

The control cam fitted on the control body is connected with the oil pump control lever and is to change the travel of the valve by limiting its maximum upward movement.

The discharging amount of oil is regulated by the prescribed valve travel and engine speed. Therefore, more oil is fed to the engine as the throttle grip is more opened and the engine speed increases.

The oil pump performance is shown in Fig. 7-5-4.

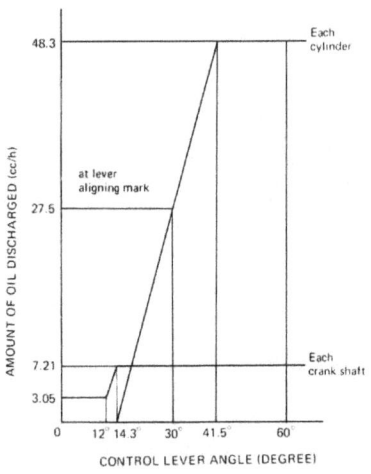

Fig. 7-5-4

* The discharging amount is measured when the valve speed is kept at 30 rpm which corresponds to the engine speed of 2,300 rpm.

7–5–1. ADJUSTMENT

Since the oil discharging amount of the oil pump is regulated in relation to the throttle opening by connecting the throttle wire to the control lever on the oil pump, the throttle wire adjustment must be considered to be very important factor for affecting engine lubricating condition.

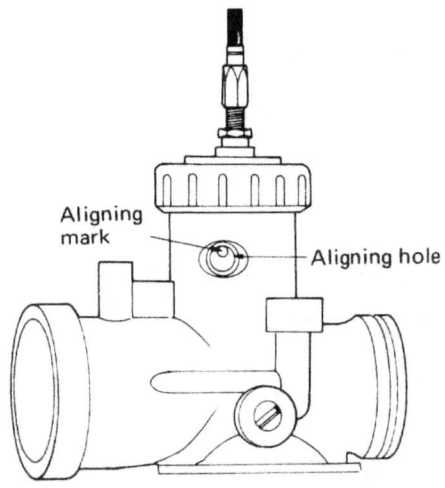

Fig. 7-5-5 Carburetor aligning marks

To adjust the oil pump by the throttle cable, perform the following procedure.

1) Remove the aligning hole plug on the right carburetor.

2) Wind up the throttle grip gradually and stop moving the grip just when an aligning mark on the side of throttle valve comes on upper end of the hole. Fig. 7-5-5.

Fig. 7-5-6 Adjusting oil pump

3) Holding the grip in the position mentioned in the previous item, adjust the cable adjuster so that a score on the oil pump lever align with the marking on the body Fig. 7-5-6.

NOTE:
The adjustment in this section should be done after the throttle wire adjustment for the carburetor has been made. The reverse procedure may cause the mal-adjustment of oil pump.

7-5-2. BLEEDING OF OIL LINES

Fig. 7-5-7 Bleeding oil lines

In case air is found in the oil inlet pipe, bleed the line by loosening the bleeder screw. If air is in the outlet pipes, carry out either the method 1) or 2) written below depending on amount of air.

1) Much air:
   Remove the oil pump and send oil with a oil filler to expel air as already explained in the section 7-3-8.

2) A little air:
   Start the engine with the oil control lever fully turned and keep the engine running at about 2,000 rpm till all air is expelled.

7-6. CARBURETOR

7-6-1. SPECIFICATION

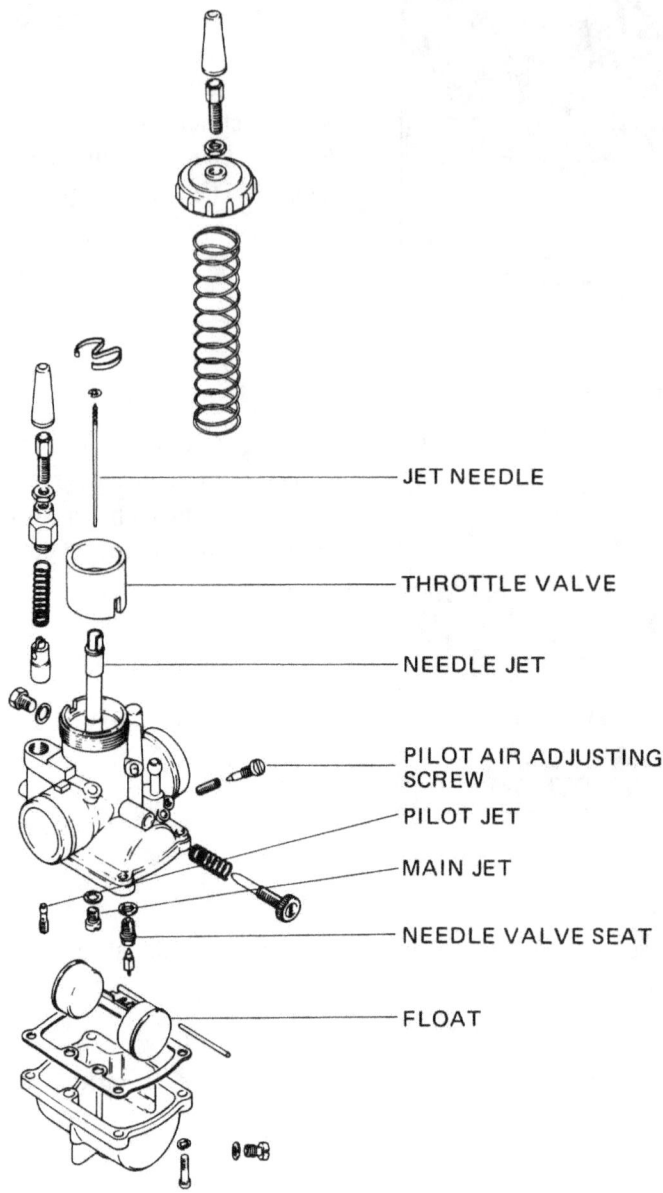

Fig. 7-6-1

Type	VM 28 SC
Main Jet (right & left carburetors)	No.95
(center carburetor)	No.92.5
Jet Needle	5DH21-3
Needle Jet	O-5
Throttle Valve Cut-away	2.5
Pilot Jet	27.5
By-pass	1.4
Pilot Outlet	0.5
Pilot Air Adjusting Screw	1-1/4 turns back
Needle Valve Seat	2.0
Starter Jet	60
Float Level	24.25 mm

7-6-2. ADJUSTMENT

I. CARBURETION

The adequate carburetion is determined according to the result of various tests mainly in consideration of engine power, fuel consumption and fuel cooling effect to the engine and jets settings are done so as to satisfy and balance all these conditions. Therefore, it is not recommended to replace the jet with the other size than original or to change the setting position of adjustable parts except when compensating the mixture ratio due to the different altitude or climate conditions. When the adjustment is necessarily required, carry out the job referring to the following points.

1) Fuel-air mixture ratio can be changed by following manners.

THROTTLE OPENING	METHOD TO CHANGE THE RATIO	STANDARD SETTING
SLIGHT	PILOT AIR ADJUSTING SCREW TO LEANER / TO RICHER	1-1/4
MEDIUM	JET NEEDLE TO LEANER / TO RICHER	3RD POSITION FROM TOP GROOVE
HIGH	MAIN JET Larger number : Richer mixture Smaller number: Leaner mixture	NUMBER: R & L CARB. 95 C CARB. 92.5

2) The fuel level inside the float chamber should also be set in proper position. To adjust the fuel level, measure the height of the float from the mixing chamber body in the way explained as follows.

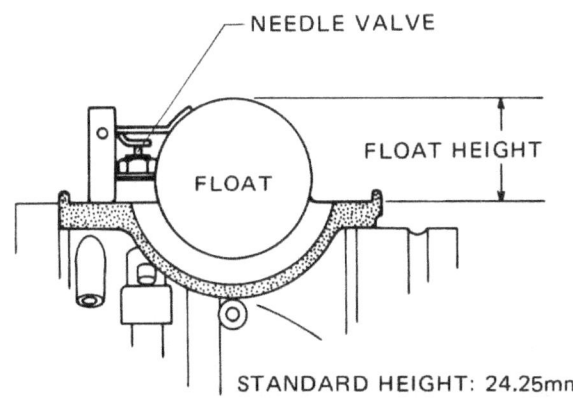

* Remove the float chamber.
* Hold the carburetor upside down with the float fitted to the mixing chamber body.
* Lower the float gradually and stop it just when the float tongue touches the upper end of the needle valve.
* Measure the distance between the float chamber fitted surface and bottom of the float as shown in Fig. 7-6-2.

STANDARD HEIGHT: 24.25mm (0.95 in.)

Fig. 7-6-2

II. IDLING ADJUSTMENT

This section explains the procedure to balance the working conditions of the carburetors in engine idling speed. Two methods for balancing the carburetors are described hereunder, each of which gives the same result. On taking either method, following jobs should be practiced beforehand.

* Warm up the engine for about 5 minutes.
* Replace the spark plug with of hotter type in order to avoid the plug fouling trouble which may take place when killing ignition during the adjusting procedure.
* The ignition timing should be properly adjusted since improper ignition timing may bring the unsuccessful result even though the procedure is carried out properly.
* Have enough throttle wire play on each carburetor so that the wire may not limit the throttle valve movement when adjusting.
* Set each pilot air screw to the specified turns (1¼).

1) METHOD 1

* Screw in the 3 throttle stop screws fully and unscrew them by about same turns so as to have the engine speed of approximate 1,500 rpm. In this state, the turning-back will roughly be 3-1/2.
* While the engine runs, kill ignition on one cylinder out of 3 either by grounding the corresponding contact point or by removing the spark plug cap of the same and adjust engine speed in this condition by the throttle stop screws as shown in Fig. 7-6-2.

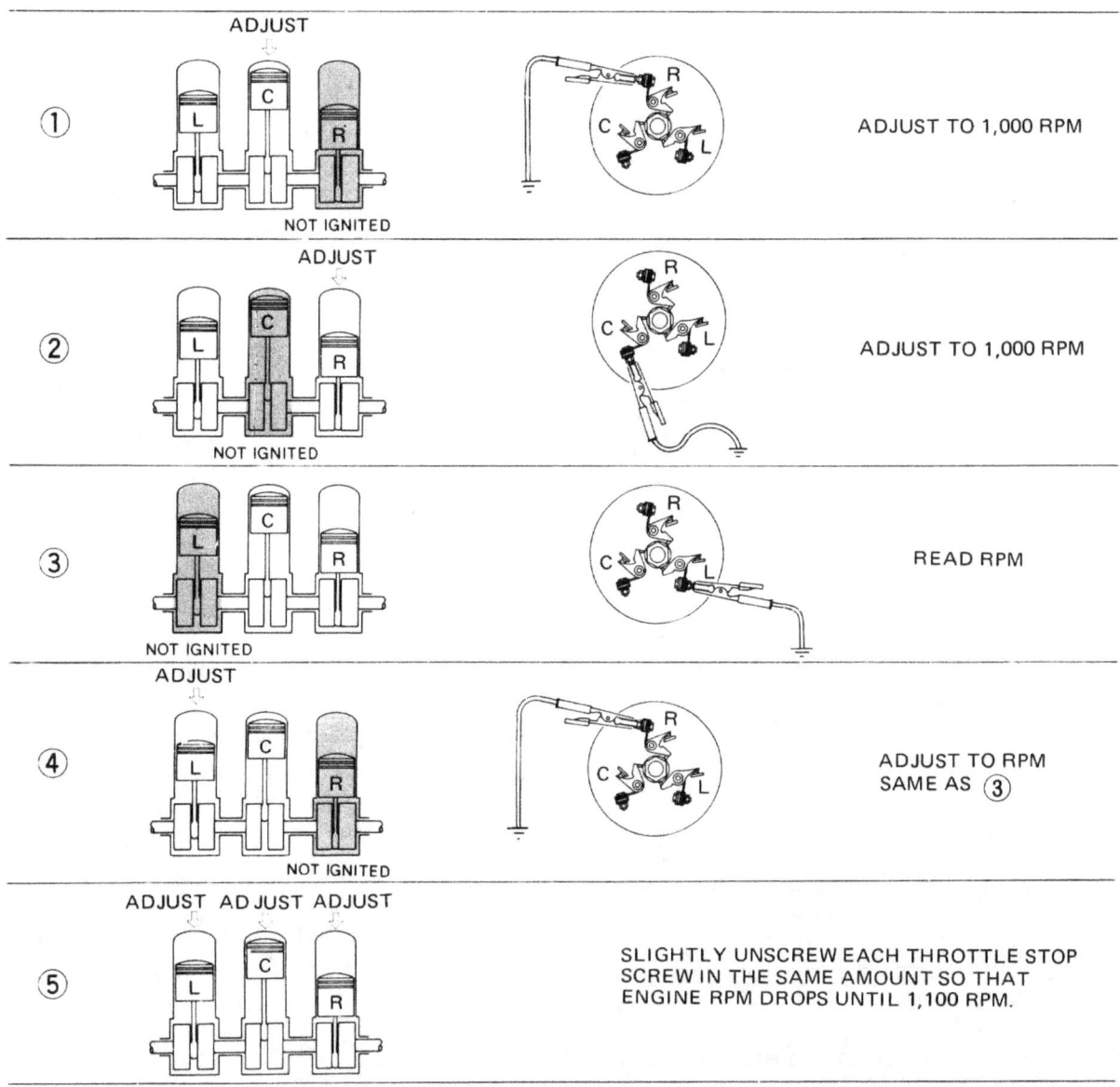

Fig. 7-6-3

2) METHOD 2

In the method 2, the adjustment is made on the carburetor fitted on a cylinder which is not ignited unlike the method 1.

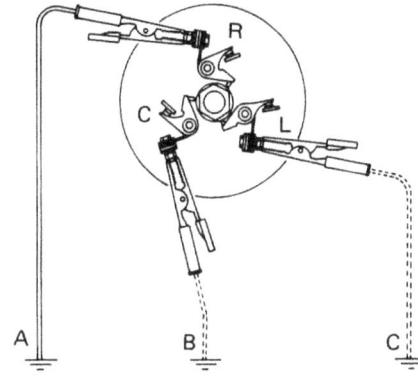

Fig. 7-6-4

① Perform the ground connection "A", "B" and "C" individually as shown in Fig. 7-6-4 and read the drop in engine rpm from that in the state without grounding.

* If the carburetors are balanced, the drop in rpm should be the same in each case.

* In the case that each drop of rpm varies among those in above three groundings:

If having a certain cylinder not ignited causes remarkable rpm drop as compared with the case done same for other cylinders respectively, unscrew the related throttle stop screw to the cylinder being not ignited, and if causes no or less rpm drop, screw-in the related throttle stop screw to the cylinder being not ignited.

② If the idling rpm with all the cylinders ignited is too high after the balance is properly made, unscrew 3 throttle screws by same turn respectively so as to have specified idling speed of 1,100 rpm.

③ After compensating the idling speed as described above, check the balance again by the procedure ① since this compensation may unbalance the carburetors to a certain extent.

NOTE:
If the relative position of the throttle stop screws or throttle wires is entirely changed, adopt the method 1 and in case of periodic inspection, simple idling speed adjustment, etc., carry out the method 2 for quicker job.

III. BALANCE OF THROTTLE VALVES AT HALF A WAY OPENING

This adjustment should be made under the condition that the 3 carburetors are properly balanced in the idling speed.

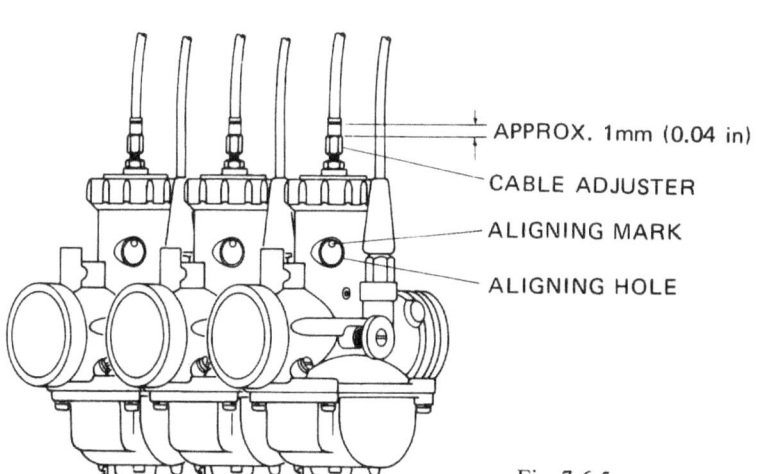

Fig. 7-6-5

Adjust all the 3 cable adjusters so that the aligning mark on side of each throttle valve comes to upper surface of the hole on respective carburetors when the throttle grip is twisted half a way and that all the 3 wires have play of approximately 1.0 mm (0.04 in) when the grip is fully returned.

7-7. STARTER SYSTEM

7-7-1. ELECTRIC STARTER

This section deals with the power transmission mechanism of the starter system and dispence with the explanation of the starter motor since it is described in the section 7-11.

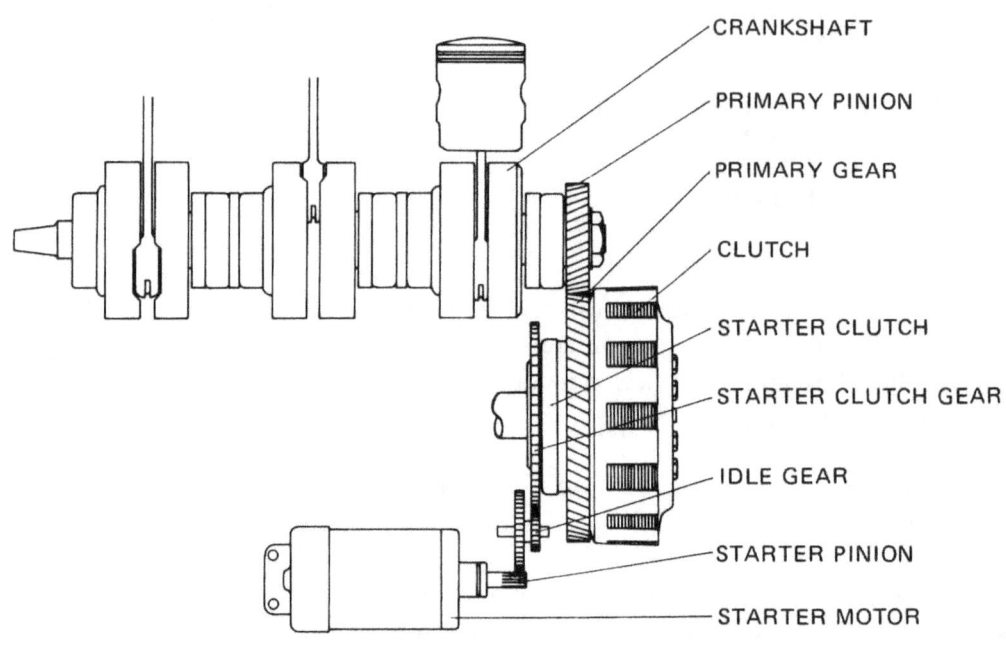

Fig. 7-7-1

Above illustration shows the electric starter system. The starting torque is transmitted to the crankshaft through the idle gear, the starter clutch gear, the starter clutch, the primary gear and the primary pinion. The starter clutch includes overrunning clutch mechanism inside and it only allows the torque to be transmitted from starter motor side to engine side. Therefore, the starter clutch slips as soon as the engine starts resulting in loading no engine power to the starter motor. Even when the transmission is in gear, needless to say, the engine starting can be done with releasing clutch.

The construction of the starter clutch (overrunning clutch) is as shown in Fig. 7-7-2.

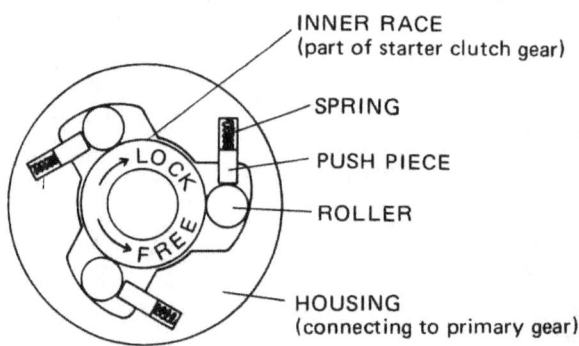

Fig. 7-7-2

NOTE ON ASSEMBLING STARTER CLUTCH

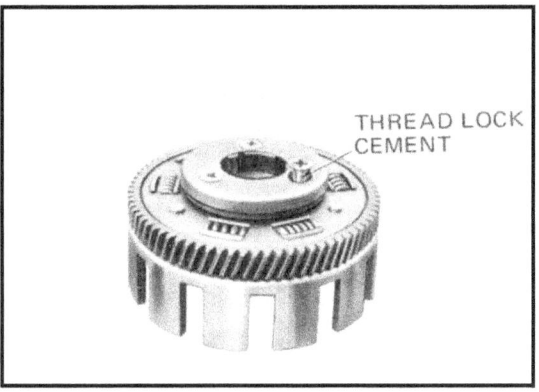

Fig. 7-7-3 Starter clutch screws

When assembling the starter clutch parts on the primary gear, apply thread lock cement (Suzuki genuine part 99000-32010) to the 3 screws shown in Fig. 7-7-3 in order to prevent the screws from coming loose.

7–7–2. KICK STARTER

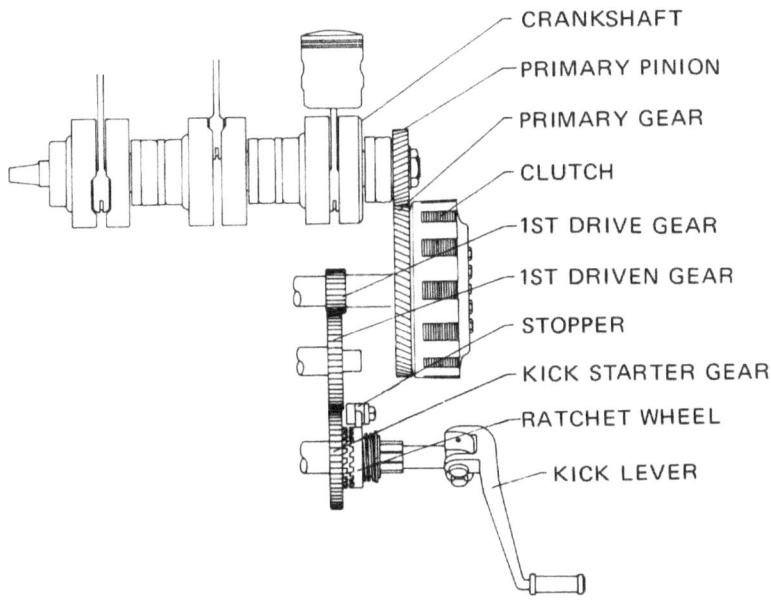

Fig. 7-7-4

Fig. 7-7-4 shows the kick starter system. The kick starting torque is transmitted to the crankshaft after the ratchet wheel is released from the stopper and engages with the kick starter gear, through the 1st driven gear, the 1st drive gear on the counter shaft, the clutch, the primary gear and the primary pinion. The movement of the ratchet wheel in axial direction is limited by the stopper when the kick lever is fully returned and it stays away from the kick starter gear, which allows the kick starter gear to turn freely together with the other gears being engaged or connected.

NOTE:
For the assembly job of the kick starter, refer to the section 7-3-13.

7-8. CLUTCH

The clutch is of wet multi-disc type and its construction is as shown in Fig. 7-8-1.

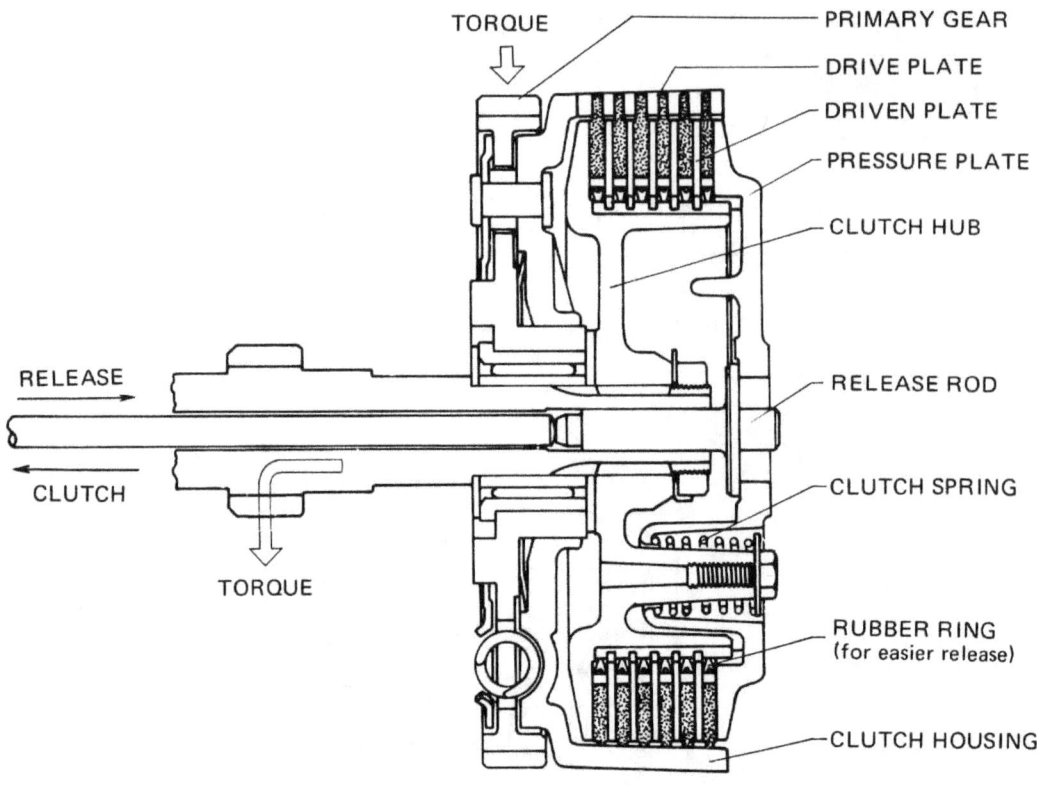

Fig. 7-8-1

7–9. TRANSMISSION

7–9–1. CONSTRUCTION

The type of the transmission is constant mesh 5 speed. The construction and working principle are explained in this section.

Engine power is transmitted to the drive shaft through the clutch, countershaft, gears on the countershaft and gears on the drive shaft. From the drive shaft to the rear wheel, the power is further transmitted through the drive sprocket, drive chain and driven sprocket. Each one set of drive and driven gears is used for each speed and these two gears are always paired so that one gear is free and the other gear is fixed on the related shaft in its turning direction. The sliding gears shown in the illustration can move axially and clutch their facing free gears with dogs, which enable the free gears to be fixed with the shaft. This movement is done by the gear shifting forks.

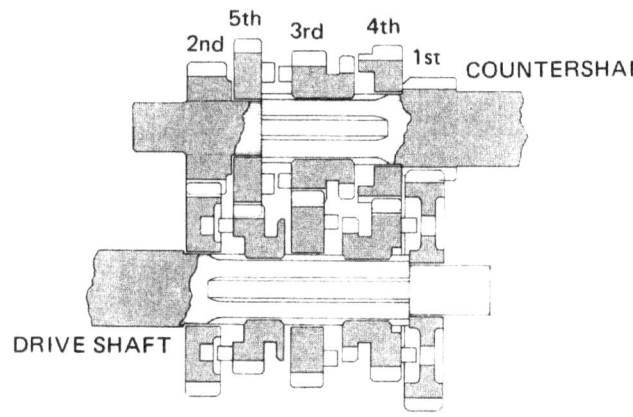

Fig. 7-9-1 Neutral position

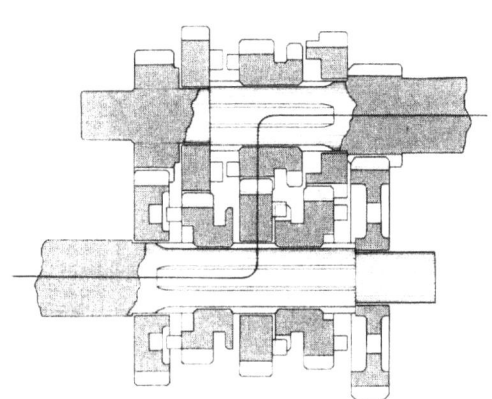

Fig. 7-9-4 3rd position

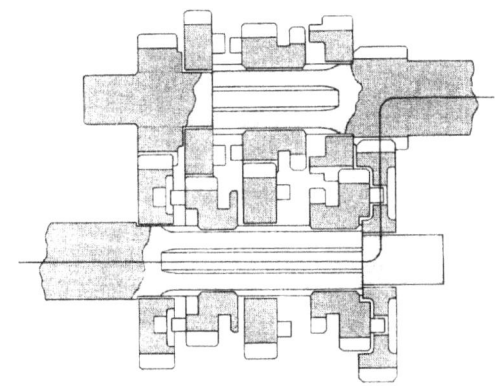

Fig. 7-9-2 1st position

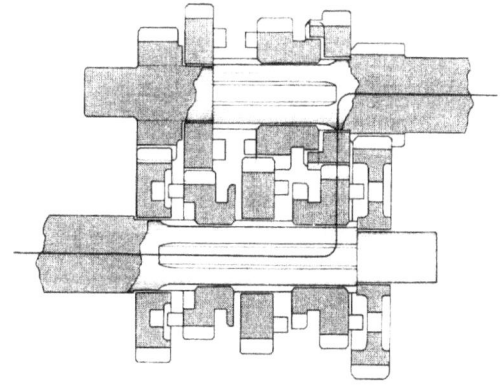

Fig. 7-9-5 4th position

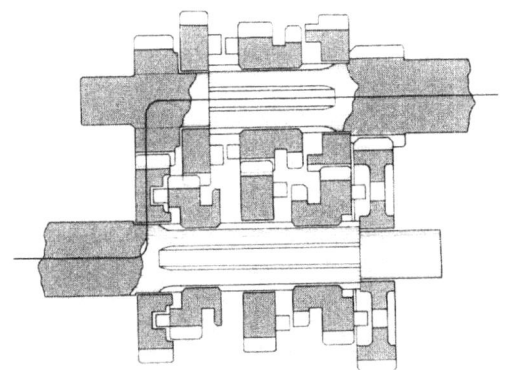

Fig. 7-9-3 2nd position

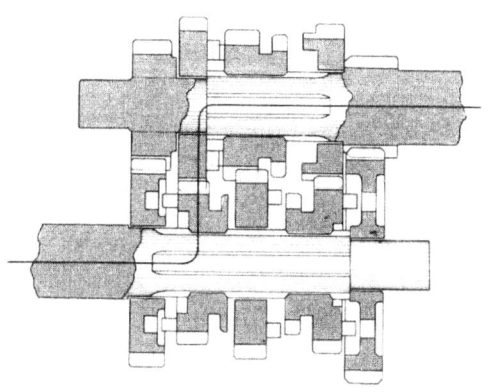

Fig. 7-9-6 5th position

7-9-2. TRANSMISSION OIL

In order to have better clutch releasing effect and reduce the oil resistance when it is stirred by the primary gear, the transmission case is so designed as to make different oil levels in the transmission and clutch chamber.

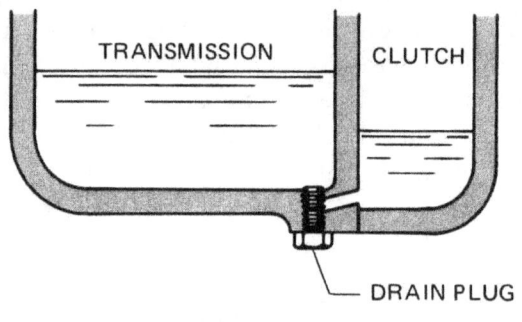

Fig. 7-9-7

Both the transmission and clutch chamber can be drained at the same time as shown in Fig. 7-9-7. However, if a shorter drain plug is used instead of original, the oil level may become the same in the two chambers. Therefore, be sure not to use the other plug than the one designed for this model.

NOTE:
At the time of the first supply of oil after the transmission is overhauled, fill with 1,600 cc of oil and with 1,500 cc whenever changed.

7-10. AIR CLEANER

7-10-1. CONSTRUCTION

The element is made of washable spongy plastics and contains oil in it so as to further prevent the dust from penetration. The construction is shown in Fig. 7-10-1.

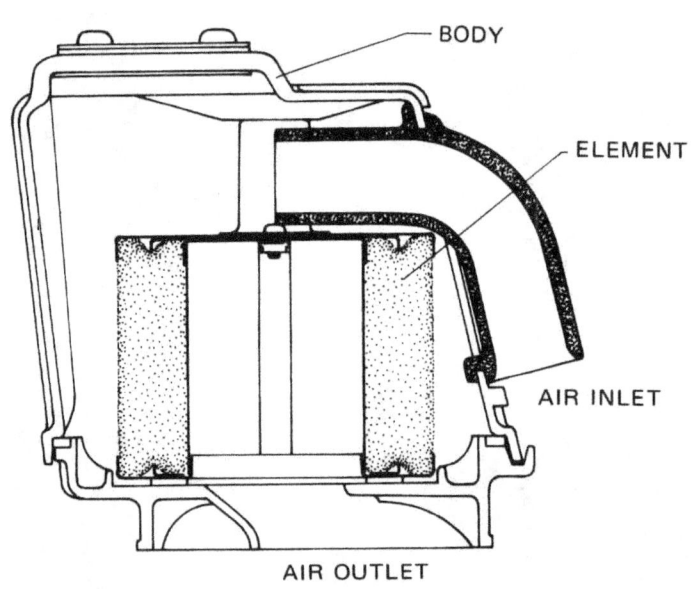

Fig. 7-10-1

7-10-2. MAINTENANCE

When cleaning the element, pull it off and wash with clean petrol. After draining the element, soak it into Suzuki CCI oil or other two-stroke oil of around SAE No.30 and squeeze oil from the element.

7–11. ENGINE ELECTRICAL

7–11–1. ELECTRIC STARTER

Since the mechanism of starting torque transmission has been explained in the section 7-7, this section only deals with the starter motor and its wirings.

I. WIRING

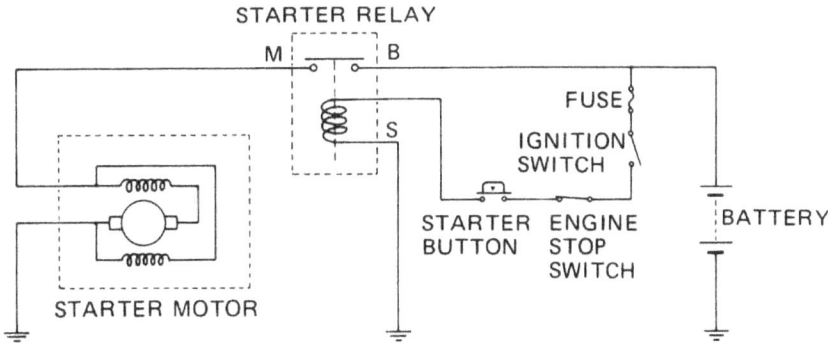

Fig. 7-11-1

II. CONSTRUCTION

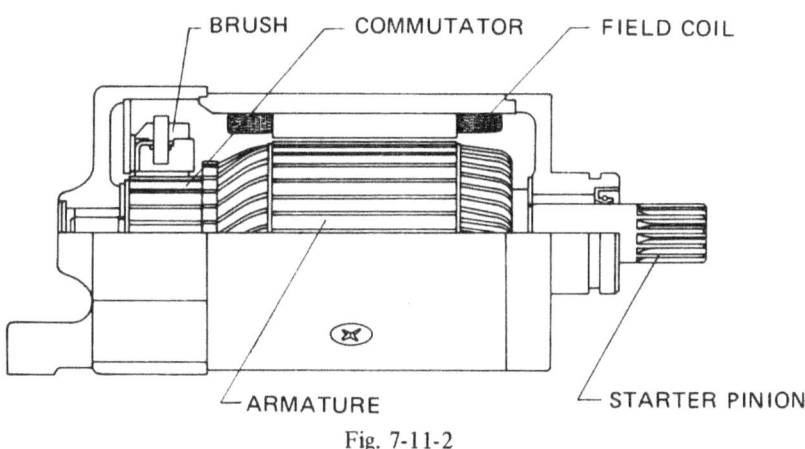

Fig. 7-11-2

The starter motor is of cumulative compound type, which has a characteristic that the motor generates large torque when loaded and limits the speed by its self-control work when the motor is released from load so as not to cause over-revolution.

III. OVERHAUL

1) ARMATURE

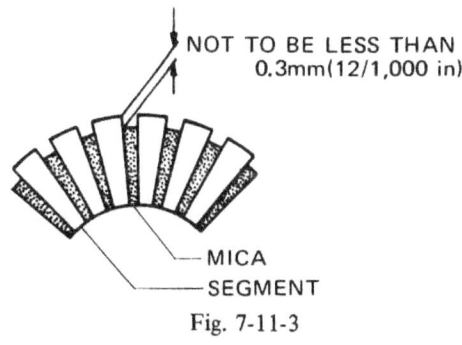

Fig. 7-11-3

* If the undercut is found to be less than 0.3 mm (12/1,000 in), increase it to 0.5 – 0.8 mm (20 – 31/1,000 in).

* Clean the undercut part whenever the motor is disassembled.

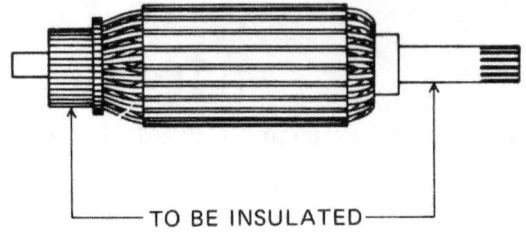

Fig. 7-11-4

* Check for the ground by a testlight or a circuit tester. If continuity is found in this test, replace the armature.

2) FIELD COILS

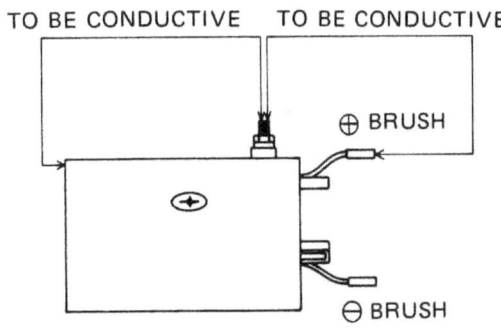

Fig. 7-11-5

Check the series and shunt coils for continuity in the state with the brushes not connected to the armature. In either test, continuity should be indicated in case these two coils are in proper condition.

3) BRUSHES

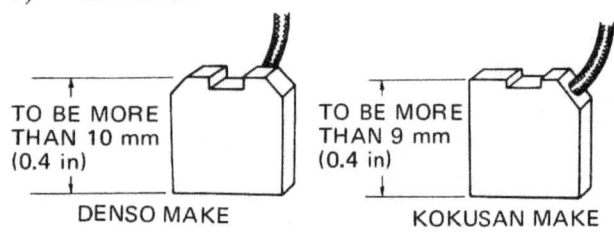

Fig. 7-11-6

Replace the brushes when the length comes to the limit shown left.

NEW BRUSH LENGTH:
DENSO MAKE – 14mm (0.55 in)
KOKUSAN MAKE – 13.5 mm (0.53 in)

7–11–2. IGNITION SYSTEM

I. WIRING

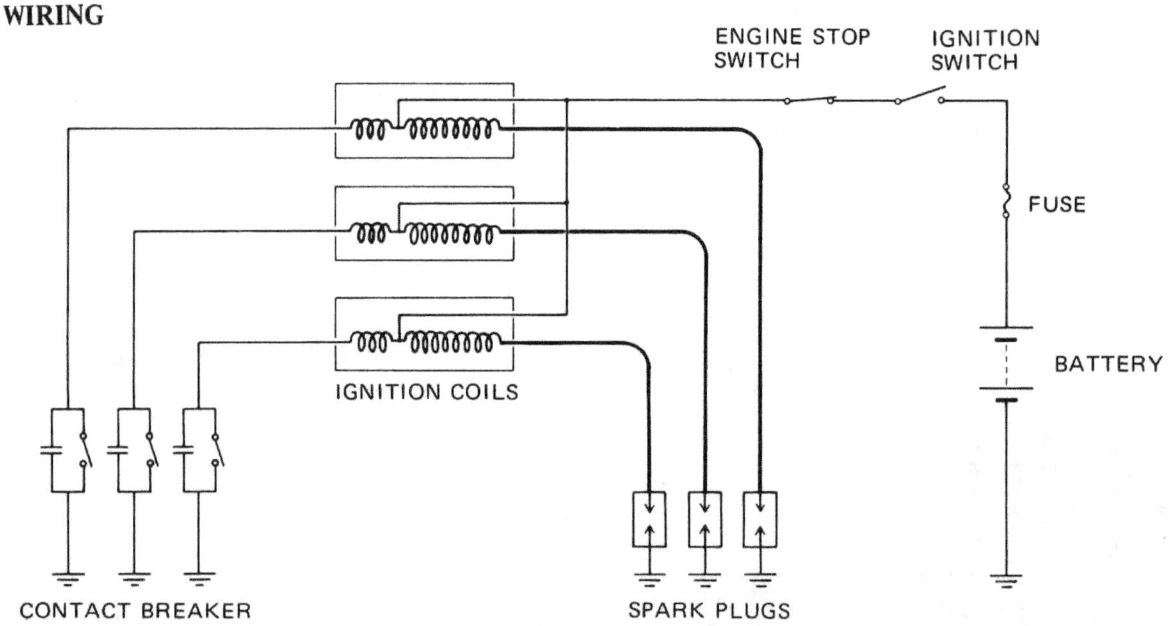

Fig. 7-11-7

II. ADJUSTING IGNITION TIMING

* When checking or adjusting the ignition timing, it is necessary that the contact point gap be checked beforehand if it is within 0.3 – 0.4 mm (12 – 16/1,000 in).
* Ignition timing for each cylinder should individually be adjusted since 3 contact points are independent and individually movable.
* Use the timing dial gauge (special tool 09931-00112) and the timing tester (special tool 09900-27002). Do not check or adjust the timing by the alignment marks on the ignition timing plate fitted at the contact breaker cam. This plate is provided for an emergency purpose.
* If the timing adjustment is to be carried out, first begin setting it with the contact point for left cylinder since this point is fitted directly on the contact breaker base on which the adjuster plates of the other two points are mounted.
* The following explains the procedure when adjusting the ignition timing.

1) Remove the spark plugs from the cylinder head and install the timing dial gauge on a spark plug hole of the left cylinder.
2) Connect one end of lead wire of the timing tester to the left contact point and the other lead wire to the ground.

Fig. 7-11-8 Attaching timing dial gauge

Fig. 7-11-9 Connecting timing tester

3) Search TDC in the dial gauge by turning the crankshaft slowly and there, set the dial to 0 position.
4) Turn the crankshaft slowly anticlockwise, that is, reverse direction of engine rotation, and stop turning the crankshaft where the sound of the timing tester just dies away.
5) Read the indication of dial gauge. This reading shows the ignition timing in piston travel from TDC.

STANDARD IGNITION TIMING: $3.37 \text{ mm } (24°) \begin{array}{c} +3° \\ -2° \end{array}$

Allowance 2.85 – 4.24 mm

6) To adjust the ignition timing, move the contact breaker base or the adjuster plate as shown in Fig. 7-11-10.

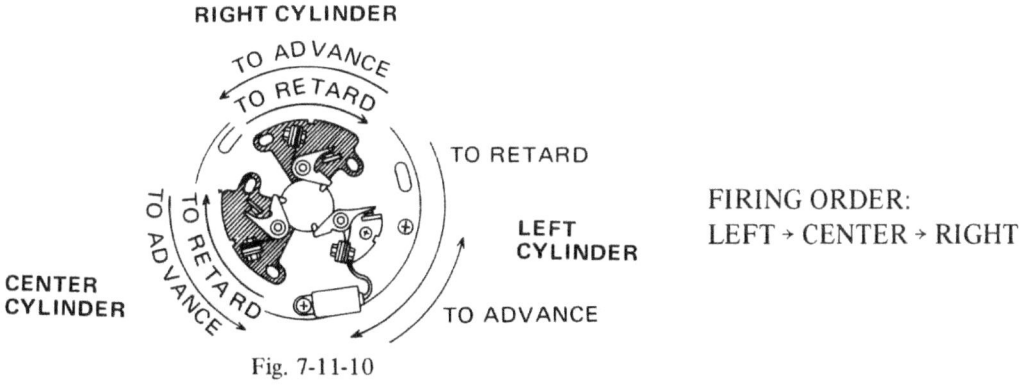
Fig. 7-11-10

FIRING ORDER:
LEFT → CENTER → RIGHT

7)   After checking or adjusting the ignition timing on the left cylinder, apply the same procedure to the other cylinders.

III. INTERCHANGEABILITY OF PARTS IN CONTACT BREAKER

Parts of DENSO and KOKUSAN makes are used in the contact breaker mechanism and there is interchangeability between them in case that the whole mechanism including the cam is replaced. However, as the component parts such as contact point, condenser, contact breaker base and cam can not be interchanged, particular attention should be paid to the difference in their shape when the parts are replaced.

1)   CONTACT BREAKER

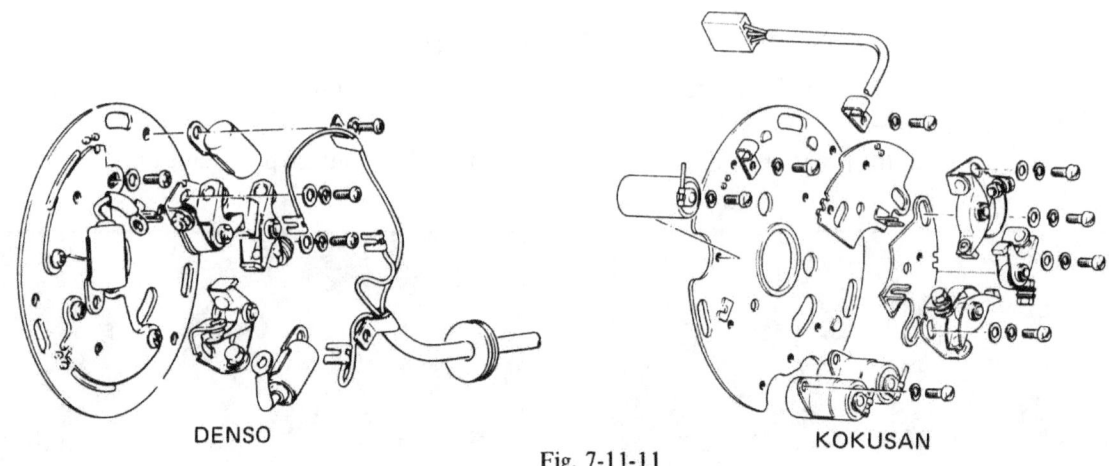

Fig. 7-11-11

2)   CONTACT BREAKER CAM

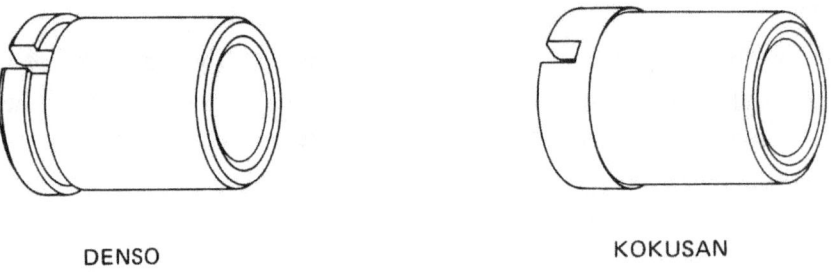

Fig. 7-11-12

7–11-3. CHARGING SYSTEM

I. WIRING

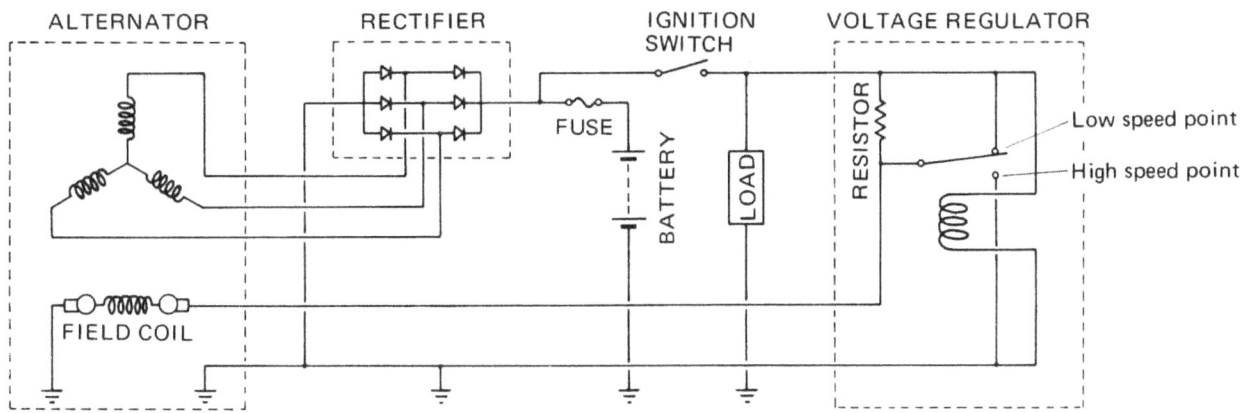

Fig. 7-11-13

Three phase AC current generated by the alternator is converted into DC current when passing through the rectifier and charges the battery through the fuse.

Voltage generated in the alternator varies according as the engine speed and as field current. Therefore, decreasing the field current when engine speed is high and increasing it when low speed, the generated voltage can be maintained regardless of any engine speed at almost constant level which a battery requires. The voltage regulator has been designed and provided in order to conform to the above condition.

The following explains the working principle of the voltage regulator.

* AT LOW SPEED

Contact point is either in contact with low speed side or making an on-and-off contact with the low speed point with vibration. When the contact point is at low speed side, the field current freely flows out from the battery through the point, and this large current consequently enables the alternator to generate the specified voltage notwithstanding at low speed. When the contact point is making an on-off contact with the low speed point with vibration, the field current flows through the point or the resistor resulting in forming a flactuating current. As the average of current formed thus is smaller than that when the point stays on low speed side, the generated voltage is slightly limited to be specified level.

* AT HIGH SPEED

Contact point vibrates on high speed side. As the field current flows intermittently, the average current becomes even smaller and the generated voltage is further limited accordingly.

II. CHECKING CHARGING SYSTEM

For checking the function of charging system, first measure the maximum terminal voltage of the battery with all the wirings properly connected when engine speed is gradually raised, that is, the regulated voltage with charging load.

STANDARD VOLTAGE: 13.5 – 14.5 with fully charged battery

If the measured voltage is not within this range, further check for the faulty carrying out the procedure explained in the next page.

* VOLTAGE OVER 14.5V

Adjust or replace the voltage regulator. For the detail, refer to the item IV in this section.

* VOLTAGE UNDER 13.5V

There may be two factors for the voltage to be under the specified level that is:

1) Voltage regulator limits the generated voltage at too low level in spite of proper function of the alternator.

2) Alternator is not able to produce specified voltage.

Therefore, it is necessary to check the system and know that the faulty falls under which case of the above. Fig. 7-11-15 shows the method to check the generated voltage of alternator separate from the work of the voltage regulator. The result will indicates where the cause lies, that is, the alternator is judged to be faulty if the voltage measured is considerably less than the figures mentioned below.

STANDARD VOLTAGE (NOT RESTRICTED):

	DENSO make	KOKUSAN make
1,500 rpm	18V	22V
2,500 rpm	31V	40V

Under the condition: with fully charged battery, alternator not heated.

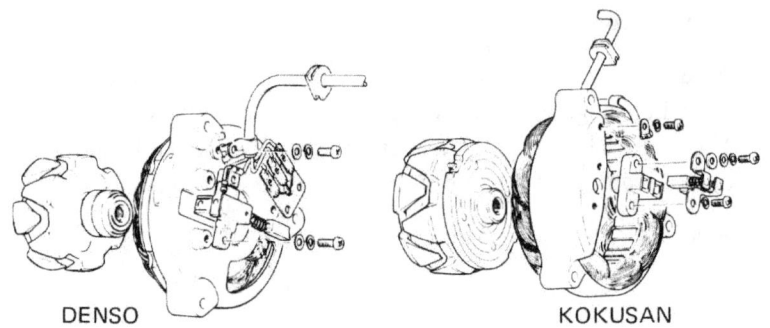

Fig. 7-11-14

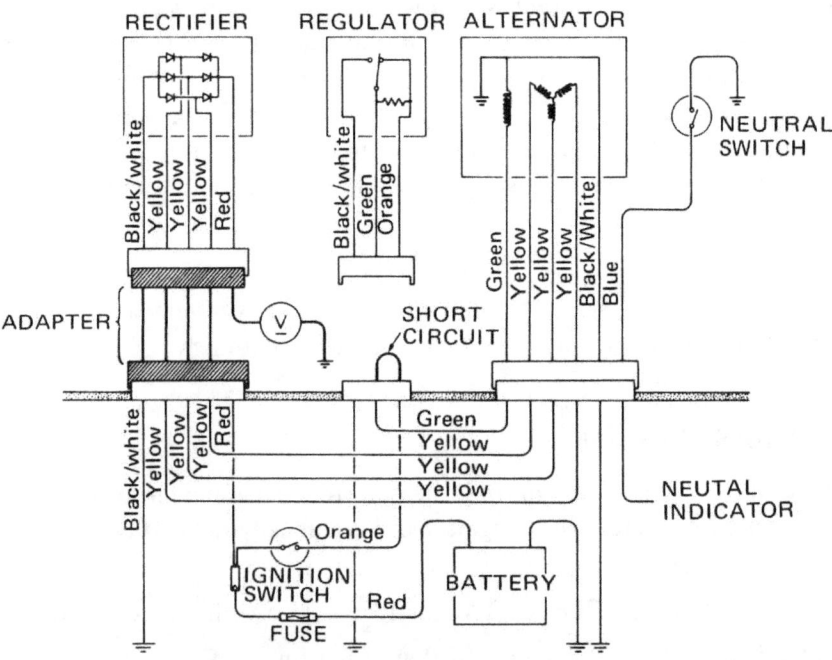

Fig. 7-11-15

III. CHECKING PARTS

1) ALTERNATOR STATOR COIL

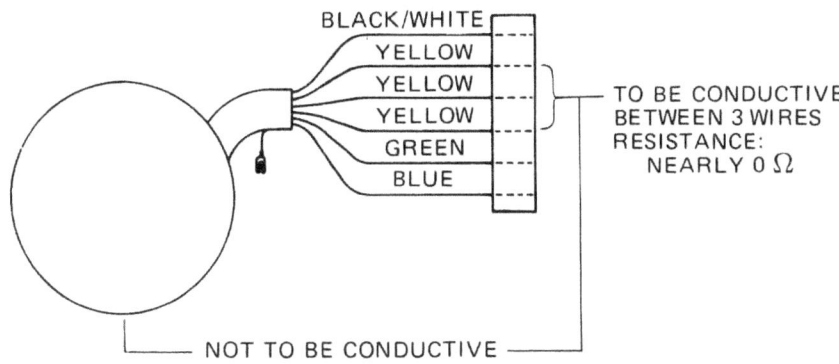

Fig. 7-11-16

2) ALTERNATOR ROTOR COIL

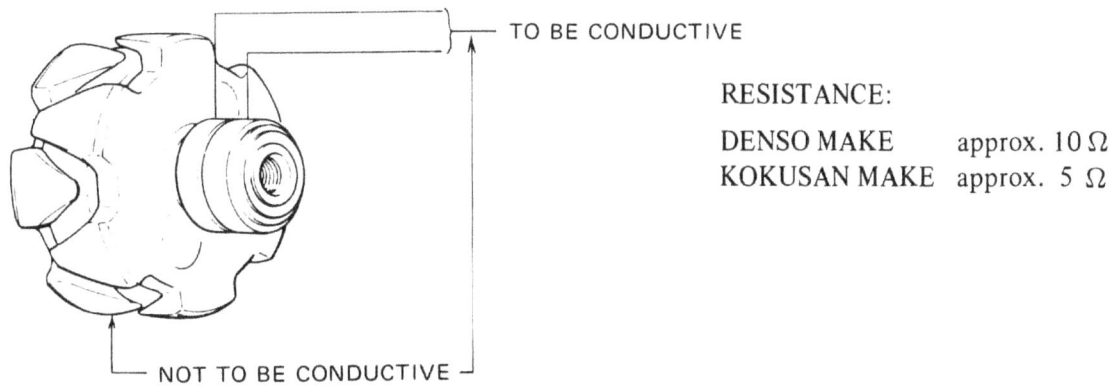

Fig. 7-11-17

3) BRUSHES

Replace the brushes when the length comes to the limit shown below.

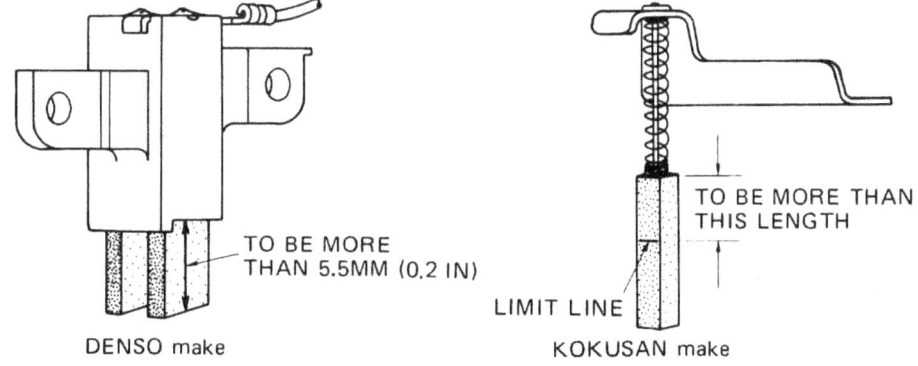

Fig. 7-11-18

4) RECTIFIER

The rectifier includes six silicon diodes and they are connected as shown in Fig. 7-11-19. Each diode has native polarity, that is, it allows current to flow only in one direction, which is the most important characteristic as a rectifier.

Check the rectifier with an ohm meter connecting its two measuring cords as shown in Fig. 7-11-19. In each connection, also do the reverse connection in order to check if there is polarity.

In case that the rectifier is in normal condition, the ohm meter indicates being conductive and not conductive respectively in all the procedure of ① to ⑥ when the meter connection is made in one way and the other way to each diode.

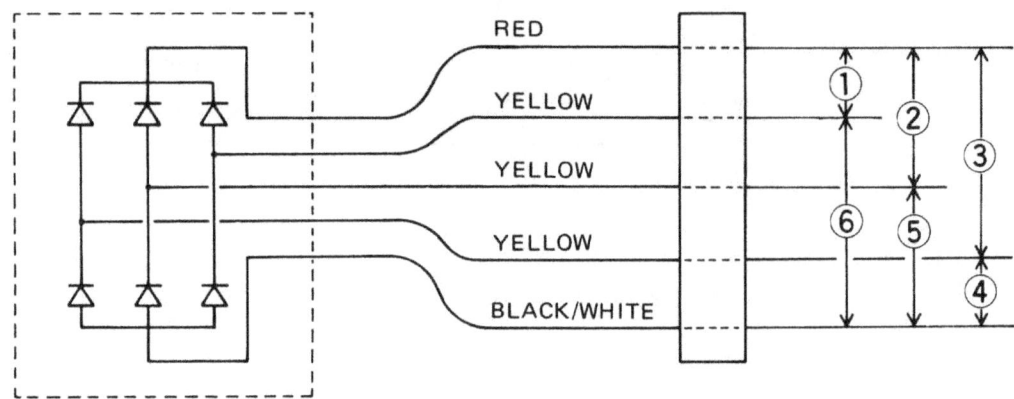

Fig. 7-11-19

Even if one of the diode is found to be defective, the whole unit should be replaced. The symptom of a damaged diode is either being or not being conductive in both directions.

NOTE:
The rectifying direction never changes from specified original state, therefore, the function can be tested by only checking if it has polarity notwithstanding its direction.

5) VOLTAGE REGULATOR

Use an ohm meter and connect it to the regulator as shown in Fig. 7-11-20.

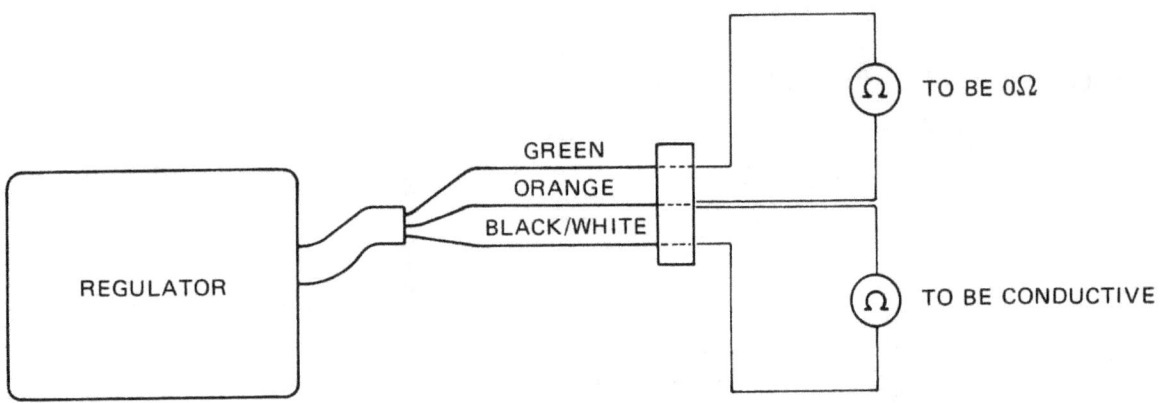

Fig. 7-11-20

IV. ADJUSTING VOLTAGE REGULATOR

When adjusting the voltage regulator, be sure to check if the following points are satisfiable.

* The alternator is generating enough voltage.
* The wirings are in proper condition.
* The battery is fully charged.
* There should not be any electrical leak being abnormal.

In case that the terminal voltage of the battery being charged by the system is not within the specified allowance. Adjust the regulator by either bending the adjuster arm or turning the adjuster screw depending on the type of the regulator.

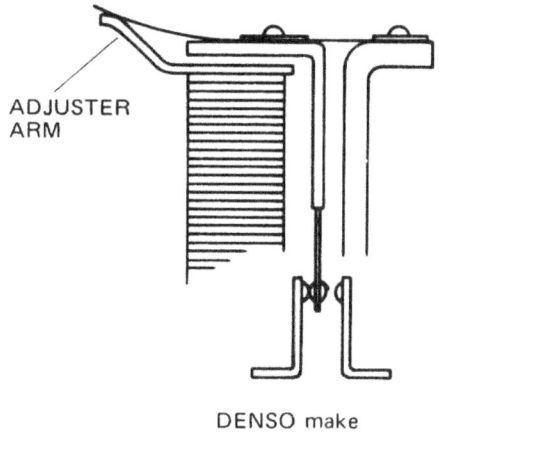
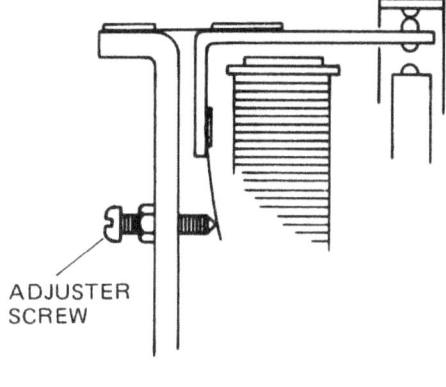

DENSO make		KOKUSAN make	
BENDING UP:	VOLTAGE RISES	SCREWING IN:	VOLTAGE RISES
DOWN:	VOLTAGE LOWERS	OUT:	VOLTAGE LOWERS

Fig. 7-11-21

NOTE:
The cover of voltage regulator is sealed in order to show that it is non-overhauled part as the readjustment may scarcely be required within the guaranty period. Therefore, breaking the seal without warrant may invalidate the warranty.

V. INTERCHANGEABILITY OF PARTS IN CHARGING SYSTEM

Parts of both DENSO and KOKUSAN makes are used in the charging system. Therefore, when replacing the parts, particular attention should be paid to the interchangeability between them.

* ALTERNATOR

  The whole sets of DENSO and KOKUSAN parts may be interchanged at the time of the assembly, however, these component parts (such as brush, rotor, stator, etc.) are not to be interchanged.

* VOLTAGE REGULATOR

  DENSO and KOKUSAN regulators are interchangeable.

8. BODY

8-1. FRONT FORK

8-1-1. CONSTRUCTION

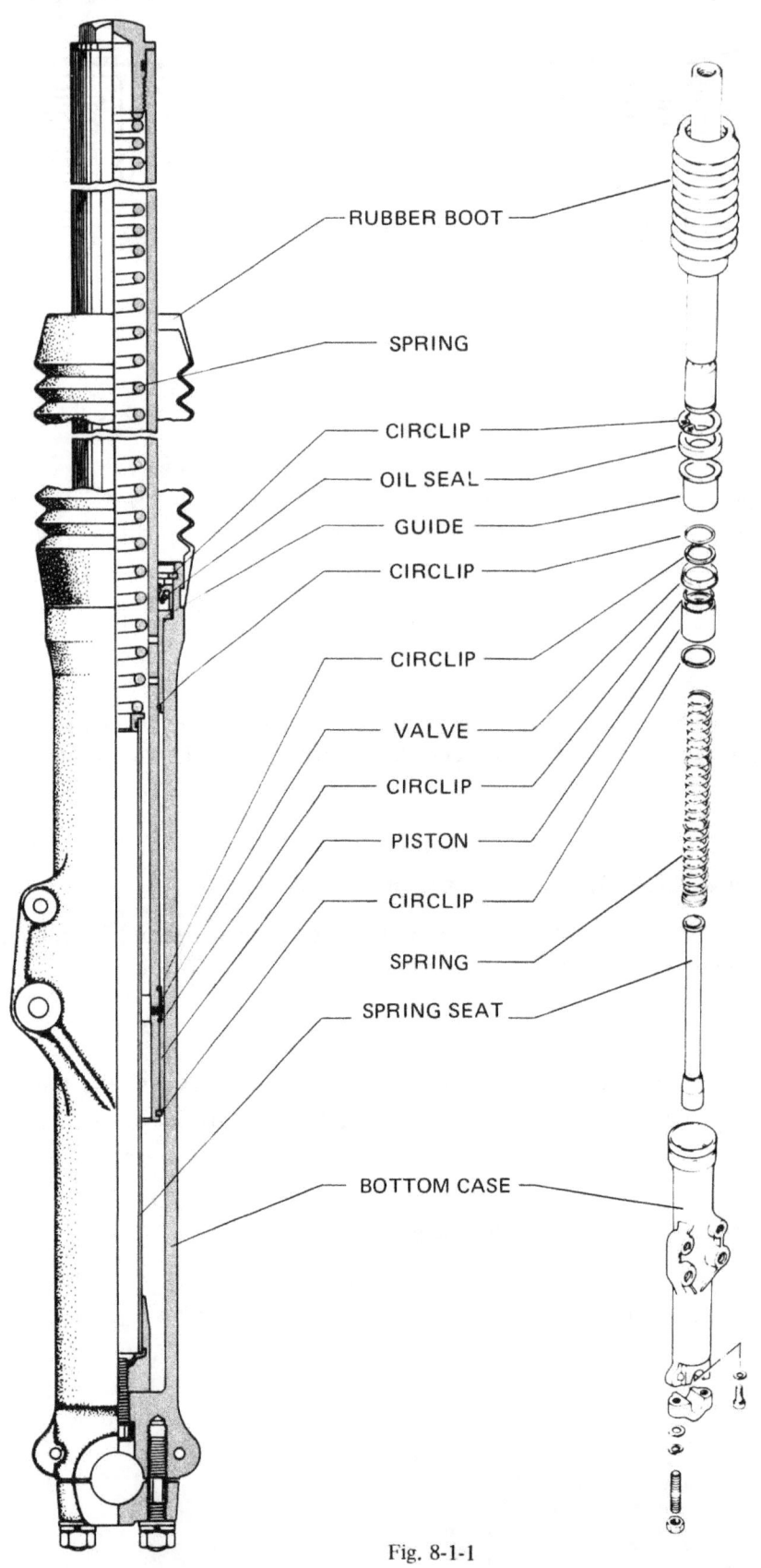

Fig. 8-1-1

8–1–2 DISASSEMBLY

Fig. 8-1-2 Disassembling front fork

After removing the front wheel and draining the front fork by the drain plug fitted on outside of the outer tube near the front axle, take off the circlip by the circlip remover (special tool 09900-06103) and the front fork outer tube can be pulled out.

8–1–3. ASSEMBLY

1) Once the bolt shown in Fig. 8-1-3 has been removed, tighten it under the condition that the front fork is completely bottomed without installing the spring, otherwise the wrong positioning of the inner part may cause an abnormal noise when operating due to collision with the end of inner tube.

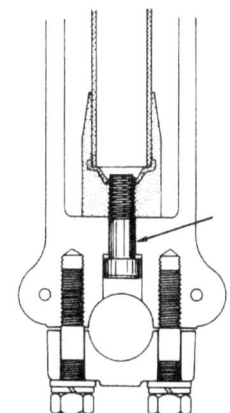

Fig. 8-1-3

2) When installing the front fork oil seal, hit it with the special tool (09940-53110) as shown in Fig. 8-1-4.

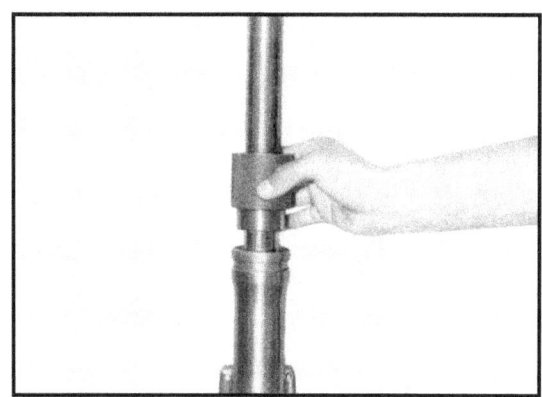

Fig. 8-1-4 Installing oil seal

3) DAMPER OIL

        CAPACITY: 230 – 240 cc in each fork
        VISCOSITY: SAE 10W/30

NOTE:
If damper oil is to be drained, be sure to pump the fork in order to throughly dry it up. Damper oil tends to remain inside the fork in the draining procedure and this may bring about excessive oil level in refilling the fork even if oil is measured to the specified amount.

4) FRONT FORK SPRING

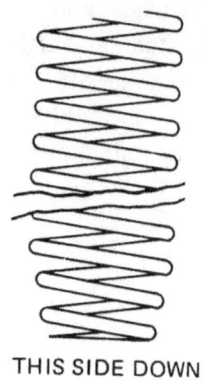

THIS SIDE DOWN

Fig. 8-1-5

When installing the front fork spring, place it with its tapered side facing down so that the spring may not block the orifice for oil passage.

8-2. REAR SHOCK ABSORBER

8-2-1. CONSTRUCTION

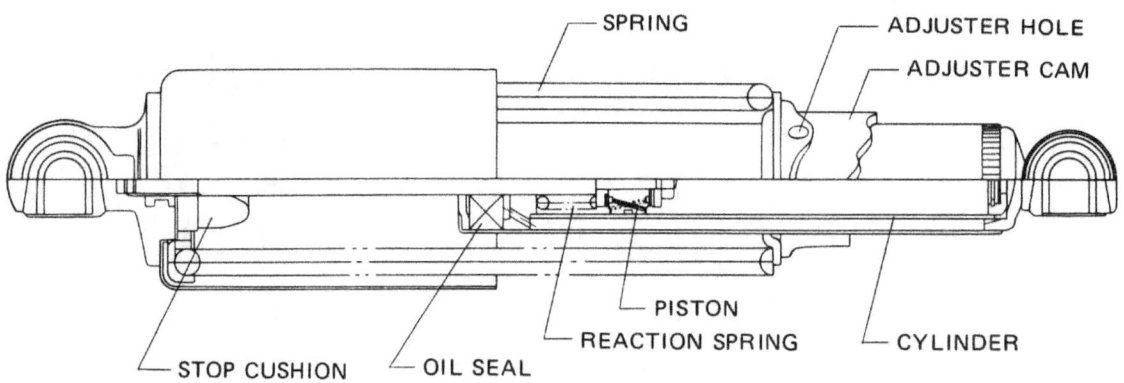

Fig. 8-2-1

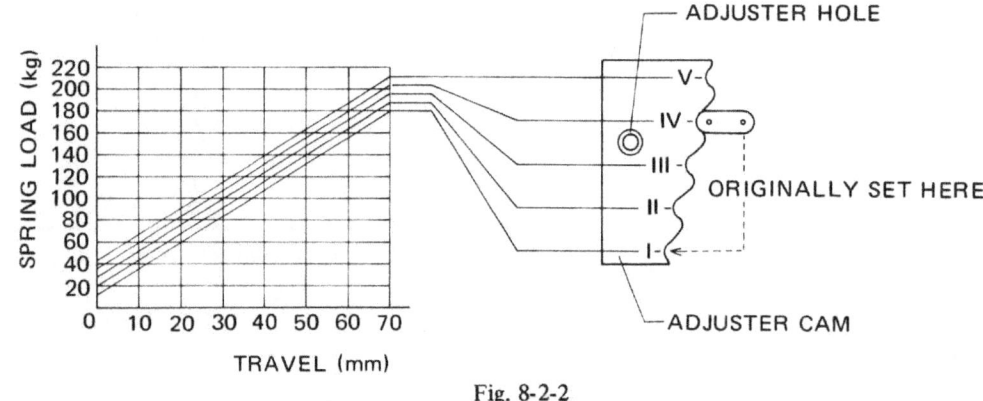

Fig. 8-2-2

The hydraulic damper is of sealed construction and works with the damping resistance of 210 and 10 kg/0.5 m/sec in its tension and compression strokes respectively.

Fig. 8-2-2 shows the spring specification and the difference of tension when the adjuster is set in its respective notches.

8–3. BRAKES

8–3–1. FRONT BRAKE

I. ADJUSTMENT

1) After loosening the lock nut, shorten the distance between two levers linked by the connecting rod so that the brake shoe operated by the lever "A" touches with the brake drum before the other brake shoe operated by the lever "B" touches with the drum as the cable is stretched.

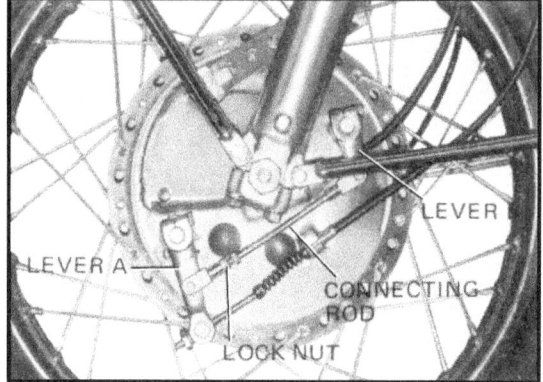

Fig. 8-3-1 Adjusting connecting rod

2) Keeping the lever "A" pushed fully toward the lever "B", extend the distance between the levers "A" and "B" by turning the connecting rod and stop turning the rod just when the lever "B" does not move any more.

3) Tighten the lock nut.

4) Adjust the other side connecting rod of the front brake in the same procedure described above.

5) Adjust the cables for both the right and left side brake pannels so that the gap between the brake lever and the throttle grip may be 20 – 30 mm (around 1 inch) and also that the equalizer may position perpendicularly to the brake lever when it is fully pulled.

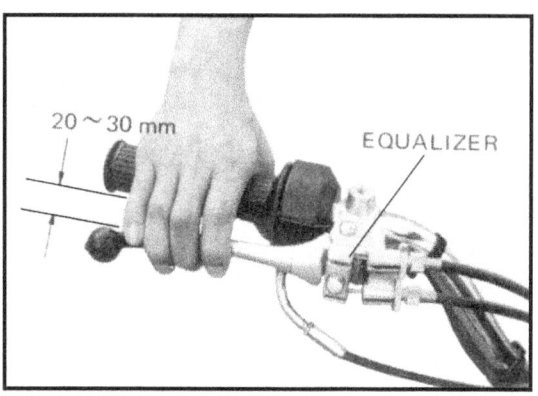

Fig. 8-3-2 Adjusting brake cable

II. INSPECTION

1) Brake shoe
   Check the outside diameter of the brake shoes as shown in Fig. 8-3-3. If the measurement is less than 194 mm (7.64 in), replace both the brake shoes.

2) Brake drum
   If the inside diameter of the brake drum exceeds 200.7 mm (7.90 in) due to the wear, replace with new brake drum.

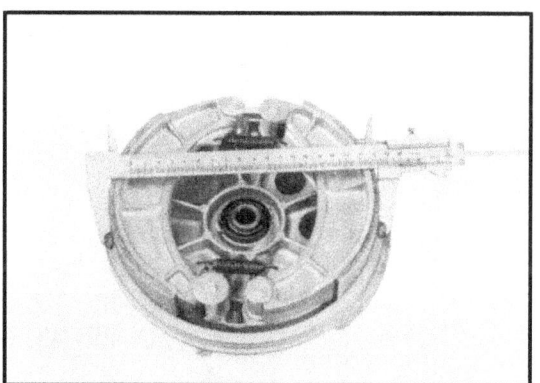

Fig. 8-3-3 Checking wear

III. VENTILATION

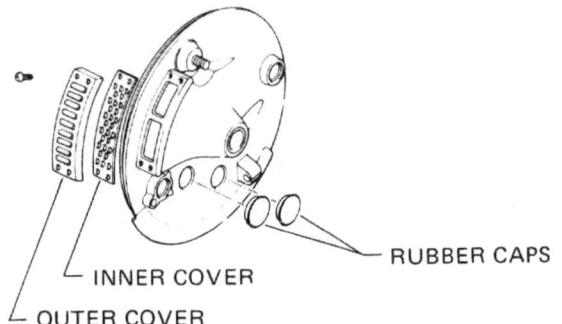

Fig. 8-3-4

For better cooling effect on the front brake, the air ventilation is provided and its air intake and outlet holes are originally closed by the covers in order to avoid the penetration of dust or other foreign substances. The air ventilation is not required in normal use for the brake is so designed as to cool itself by only heat radiation.

In case that the further cooling is necessarily required, the brake may be modified as follows.

1) Remove the outer cover and fit the inner cover by 4 screws which have fixed the outer cover.

2) Remove two rubber caps to make the air outlet passage.

8-3-2. REAR BRAKE

I. ADJUSTMENT

1) Brake pedal position
   Set the adjuster shown in Fig. 8-3-5 so that the brake pedal stays at proper position when it is not pressed.

2) Brake wire
   Adjust the wire length at its wheel side end as shown in Fig. 8-3-6 so that the proper pedal travel can be obtained.

Fig. 8-3-5 Adjusting pedal position

Fig. 8-3-6 Adjusting pedal travel

II. INSPECTION

Check the wear of the brake shoes and the brake drum in the same manner as that in the section 8-3-1.

WEAR LIMIT: IN BRAKE SHOE DIAMETER   176 mm (6.93 in)
             IN BRAKE DRUM INSIDE DIAMETER 180.7 mm (7.11 in)

8-4. WHEELS

8-4-1. CONSTRUCTION

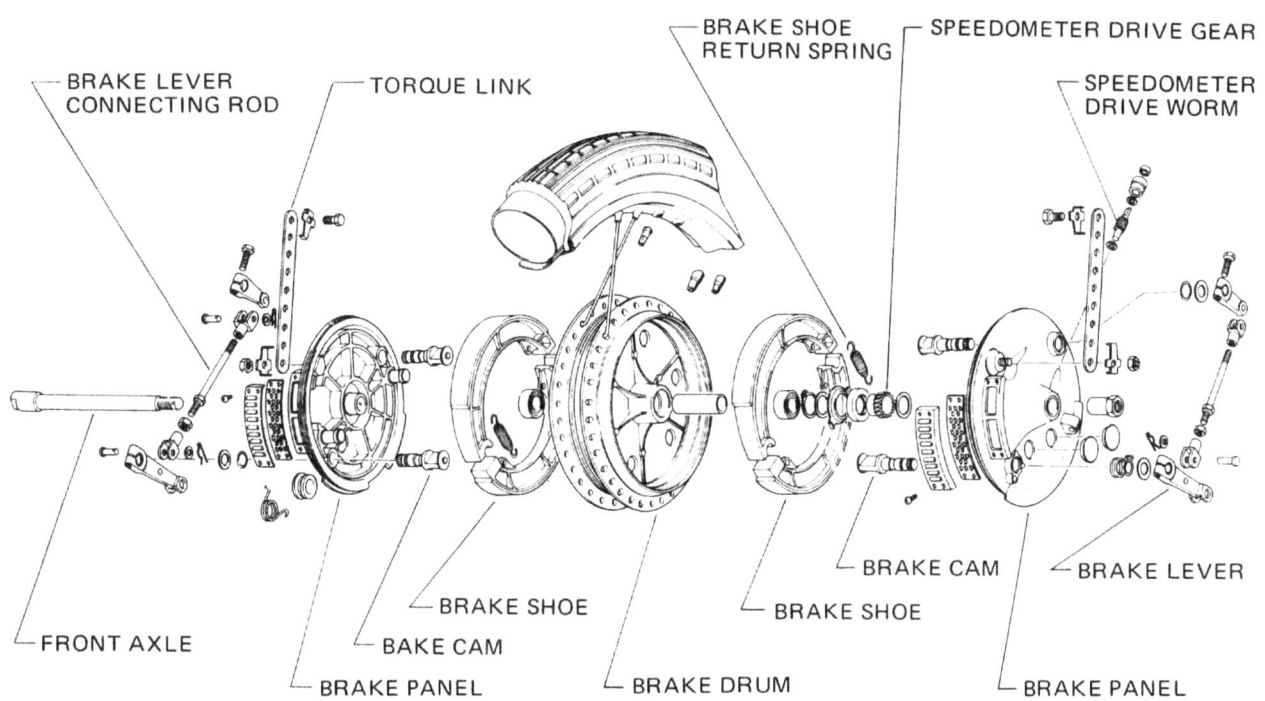

Fig. 8-4-1 Front wheel

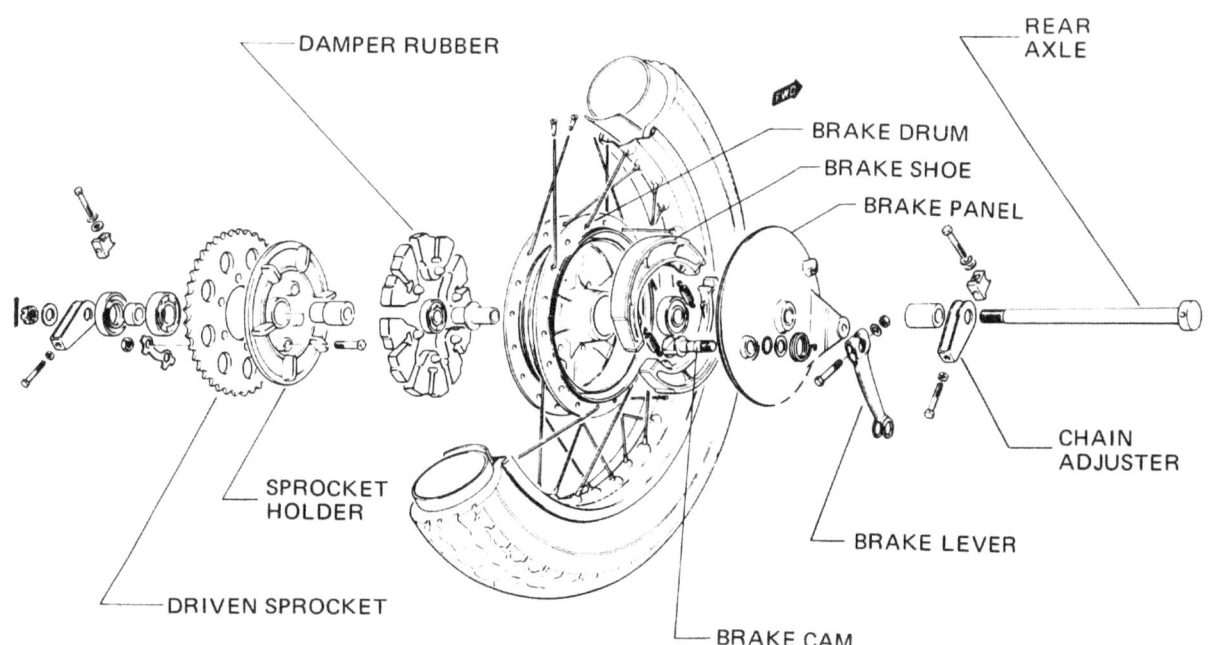

Fig. 8-4-2 Rear wheel

8-4-2. REMOVAL AND INSTALLATION

I. FRONT WHEEL

1) REMOVAL

Fig. 8-4-3

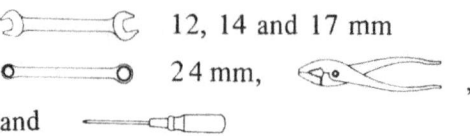

Required tool:

12, 14 and 17 mm

24 mm,

and

The wheel can be easily stripped off by removing the axle holders after disconnecting the torque links, brake cables and speedometer cable. The brake pannel can be removed from the brake drum by unscrewing the axle nut.

2) INSTALLATION

When installing the front wheel, pay attention to the following points.

① To identify the installing direction of the brake drum, refer to the shapes of both the right and left bosses at center part. Cut-way on the boss indicates the left side which engages with the speedometer driving gear.

② The axle shaft should be inserted from right side. The reverse insertion is undesirable since it may cause improper positioning of the wheel bearings.

③ When installing the torque links, tighten their fitting nut under the condition that the axle is not tightened firmly and that the brake is kept working.

④ The axle nut may be tightened in only case the axle holders are not secured.

TIGHTENING TORQUE:

Front axle shaft .... 360 – 520 kg-cm (26 – 38 lb-ft)
Axle holder .... 150 – 250 kg-cm (11 – 18 lb-ft)
Torque link bolt and nut .... 200 – 300 kg-cm (14 – 22 lb-ft)

II. REAR WHEEL

1) REMOVAL

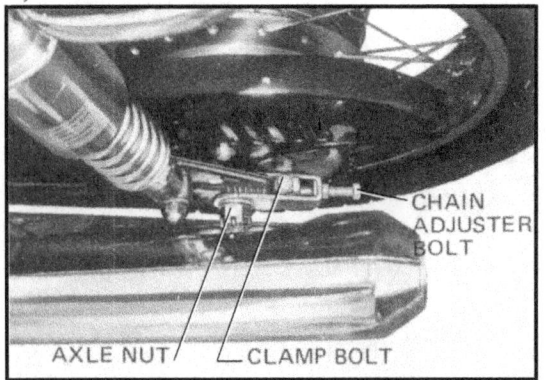

Fig. 8-4-4

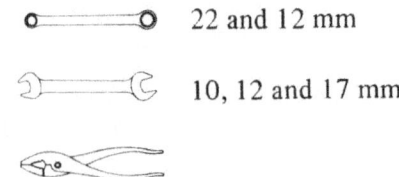

Required tool:

22 and 12 mm

10, 12 and 17 mm

When removing the rear wheel, carry out the job according to the following procedure.

① Remove the brake wire.
② Disconnect the torque link.
③ Loosen the axle nut after removing the cotter pin.
④ Remove the chain cover for easier job.
⑤ Loosen the chain adjuster bolts to its end.
⑥ Remove the clamp bolts
⑦ Move the wheel forward to its end.
⑧ Remove the drive chain from the driven sprocket. It is not necessary to disconnect the chain link.
⑨ Pull the wheel backward.

2) INSTALLATION

To install the rear wheel, follow the reverse procedure of the removal. When tightening the axle, the drive chain slack and the wheel alignment should be adjusted at the same time.

TIGHTENING TORQUE:

Axle .... 500 – 800 kg-cm (36 – 58 lb-ft)
Clamp bolts .... 130 – 230 kg-cm (9.5 – 17 lb-ft)
Chain adjuster lock nut ...... 90 – 140 kg-cm (6.6 – 10 lb-ft)
Torque link nut .... 200 – 300 kg-cm (14 – 18 lb-ft)

* DRIVE CHAIN SLACK

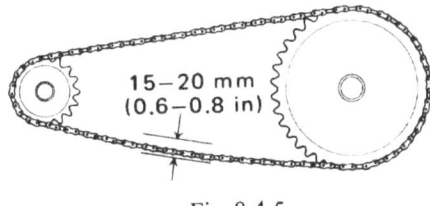

Fig. 8-4-5

Slack of the drive chain should be within 15 – 20 mm (0.6 – 0.8 in) as shown in Fig. 8-4-5 when the axle is firmly tightened.

* WHEEL ALIGNMENT

For adjusting the rear wheel alignment with the front wheel, carry out the job according to the following procedure.

NOTE:
The notched lines are provided on both the left and right swinging arm ends which indicate that the axle is to be set perpendicularly to the straight running direction if the center of the axle is set at the same notched line on both the left and right sides. However, due to slight inaccuracy made by the mechanical play in this mechanism and by the designed construction itself, the exact alignment may not be obtained by this method. Therefore, to get the accurate alignment, adopt the method explained hereunder and do not use the notched lines except when the adjustment is made on the user's level or for an emergency purpose.

VISUAL CHECK

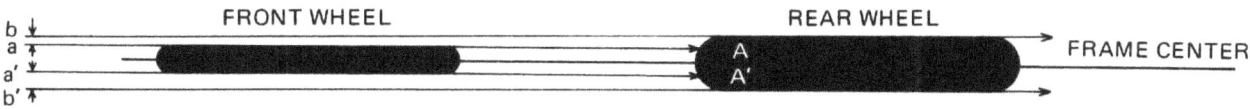

Fig. 8-4-6

To check the alignment visually, first set the front wheel so that the center line of the front wheel faces that of the rear tire surface, that is, in Fig. 8-4-6, points "A" and "A'" positioned by the visual axes "a" and "a'" when seen along the front tire side surfaces leave the same width of the visible areas on left and right side respectively on the rear tire surface.

Keeping the front wheel in this state, view one side of the rear tire from forward so that the visual axis is along the side surface and do the same to the other side. The visual axes "b" and "b'" in Fig. 8-4-6 are thus made.

If the alignment is properly adjusted, the distance between "a" and "b" must be the same as that between "a'" and "b'". In case of Fig. 8-4-6, the rear wheel should be adjusted so that the axle may turn the wheel slightly to the right since the distance of "a − b" is smaller than that of "a' − b'".

MECHANICAL CHECK

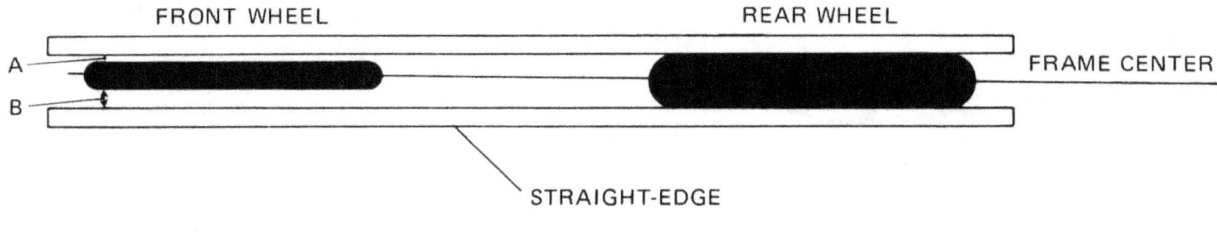

Fig. 8-4-7

Put a straight-edge to the side of the rear wheel evenly and setting the front wheel in parallel with the straight-edge, measure the clearance "A" shown in Fig. 8-4-7. Measure the clearance "B" in the same way and compare it with "A".

If the alignment is properly adjusted, A and B thus measured must be the same. In case of Fig. 8-4-7, the rear wheel is to be turned slightly to the right in order to have both the front and rear wheel being in line.

8–4–3. CHECKING WHEEL

I. RIM RUNOUT

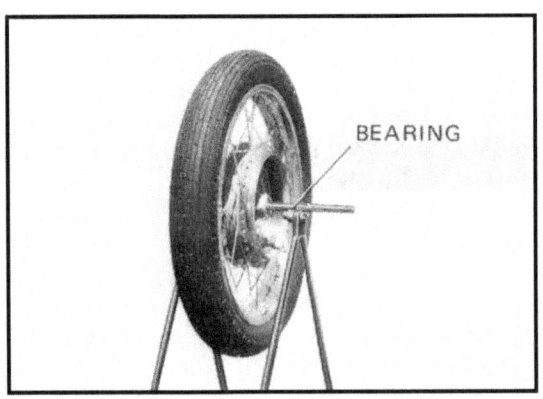

Fig. 8-4-8

Measure the lateral and radial runout by a dial gauge or a surface gauge using a wheel stand as shown in Fig. 8-4-8. If the either lateral or radial runout exceeds 2 mm (0.08 in), correct or replace the rim.

II. WHEEL BALANCE

Put the wheel on the stand as shown in Fig. 8-4-8 and leave it free. If the wheel always stops at a certain particular position, install the balancer weight on the spokes located at around the highest position in this state. Two kind of the balancers are provided as genuine parts and these weight are written as follow.

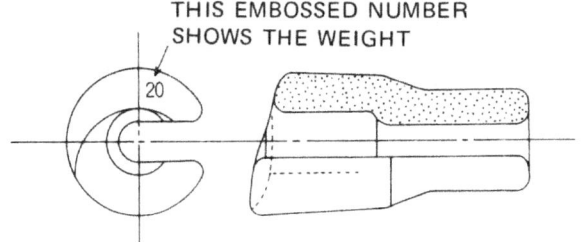

Fig. 8-4-9 Balancer weight

PART NUMBER	WEIGHT
55411-11000	20 g
55412-11000	30 g

If the weight other than 20 or 30 g is required, the balancer may be adjusted in weight by cutting it.

8-4-4. TIRES

I. WEAR LIMIT

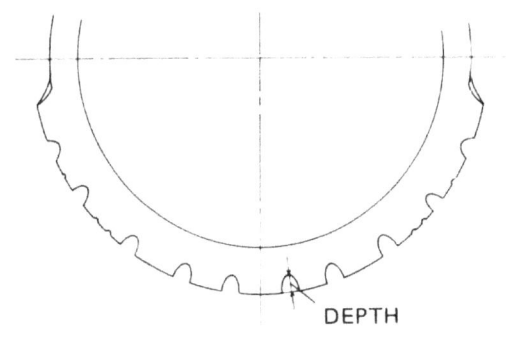

Fig. 8-4-10

To ensure the braking effect and the stability at high speed, the tire should keep enough depth in the grooves shaped on the tread surface.

When the depth of the tire shown in Fig. 8-4-10 reaches the wear limit given below, replace with new tire.

WEAR LIMIT IN DEPTH:
    Front   1.6 mm (0.06 in)
    Rear   2.0 mm (0.08 in)

TIRE USED ON THIS MODEL:
    Front .... BRIDGESTONE SUPER SPEED-21FS
    Rear .... BRIDGESTONE SUPER SPEED-21R2 CA

II. RECOMMENDED TIRE PRESSURE

Since tire pressure affects the durability and safety in driving to a great extent, it is necessary that the pressure be always kept properly. The following list shows the recommended tire pressure for this model.

DRIVING CONDITION	FRONT				REAR			
	SOLO RIDING		DUAL RIDING		SOLO RIDING		DUAL RIDING	
	kg/cm^2	lb/in^2	kg/cm^2	lb/in^2	kg/cm^2	lb/in^2	kg/cm^2	lb/in^2
NORMAL RIDING	1.6	23	1.6	23	1.8	26	2.0	28
HIGH SPEED CRUISING	1.8	26	1.8	26	2.0	28	2.0	28

In order to have the tire properly settled in the rim, first inflate it with the pressure of 5 kg/cm^2 (71 lb/in^2) and then adjust the pressure by deflating it.

NOTE:
When mounting the rear tire on the rim, be sure to observe the specified installing direction. The embossed arrow on the side surface of the tire shown in Fig. 8-4-11 indicates that the tire should be driven toward the arrow, in other words, the rotational direction.

Fig. 8-4-11

8–5. DRIVE CHAIN

In order to secure the chain from disconnection which might take place by any chance when it is given a heavy load or an impact during the acceleration or the gear shifting procedure, the chain used on this model is constructed as an endless type unlike those equipped on small capacity motorcycles. Because of this particularity, it is necessary on servicing the drive chain that special attention be paid to the point explained in this section.

8–5–1. MAINTENANCE

The drive chain must be checked and serviced at the time of every 800 km (500 miles) and lubrication is indispensable at this time of the service. In case the motorcycle is used at sustained high speed or under the condition of frequent rapid acceleration, it is recommended to shorten the service interval to 500 km (300 miles).

For adjusting procedure of the drive chain, refer to the section 8-4-2.

8–5–2. INSPECTION

Check the drive chain for any of the following conditions. The sprockets should also be checked at the same time since the wear of the sprockets are subsequent to that of the chain.

DRIVE CHAIN
* Damaged rollers
* Loose pins
* Dry or rusted links
* Kinked or bent links
* Excessive wear
* Improper adjustment

SPROCKETS
* Excessive wear
* Broken or damaged teeth
* Loose sprocket nuts

For checking the wear, measure the distance between a span of 20 pins, from pin center to pin center, with the chain held taut and any stiff joints straightened in order to determine if the chain is worn beyond its service limit. The distance of the new drive chain is 11-7/8 in (301.6 mm), and if the distance exceeds 12-1/8 in (308.0 mm), the chain ends its service life and must be replaced.

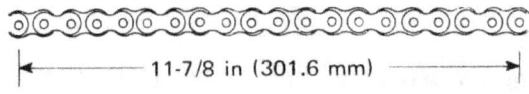

Fig. 8-4-12

8-5-2. DISJOINING AND REJOINING CHAIN

These jobs may be required if the optional sprockets larger than STD size are to be used since these sprockets may need longer drive chain. Following sprockets are provided for this model as optional parts.

DRIVE SPROCKET		DRIVEN SPROCKET	
Number of teeth	Part number	Number of teeth	Part number
		38	64511-33760
15	27511-33600	(40) STD	64511-33751
		42	64511-33741
(16) STD	27511-34000	44	64511-33770
		46	64511-33001

To extend the length of the drive chain, use following genuine parts.

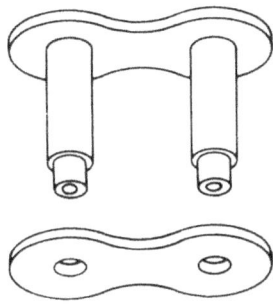

Fig. 8-4-13 Chain joint

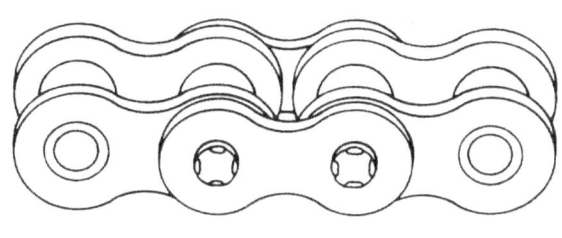

Fig. 8-4-14 Chain extension

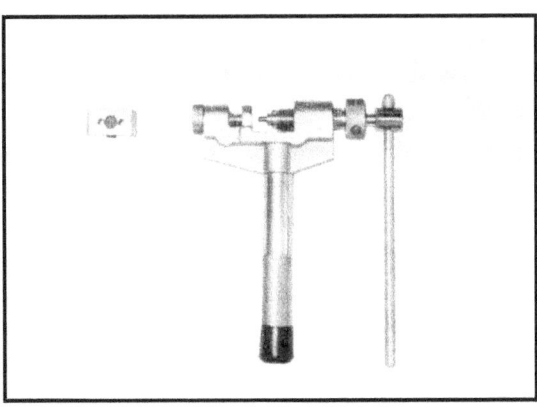

Fig. 8-4-15 Drive chain joint tool

The chain extension includes 3 links while its required length depends on the choice of the sprocket size and also on the wear of the drive chain being serviced. Therefore, adjust the length of the extension by cutting it so that the proper chain length is obtained for the changed sprocket size. When connecting the chain extension to the drive chain, use two sets of the chain joints shown in Fig. 8-4-13 on the both ends of the extension and caulk the pins by the special tool shown in Fig. 8-4-15. For the usage of the special tool, follow the instruction supplied with the tool.

NOTE:
1) If the connection is made on the chain with the chain joint as explained above, this particular part may not easily be disjointed because of wide flare of the pins. Therefore, in case of this chain, disjoint at any other part.

2) From the safety point of view, the snap type joint widely used for small motorcycles should not be used on this model.

3) The sprocket of 15 teeth is the smallest possible size for this motorcycle in strength point of view of the chain, therefore, do not use the sprocket of less than 14 teeth though it is available as optional for other models.

8-6. BODY ELECTRICAL

8-6-1. SWITCHES

This section explains the inside wiring of the switches. When checking their functions, connect a circuit tester to the switches referring to the inside wiring given below.

I. IGNITION SWITCH

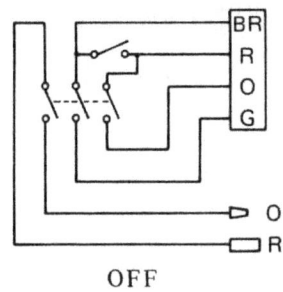
OFF

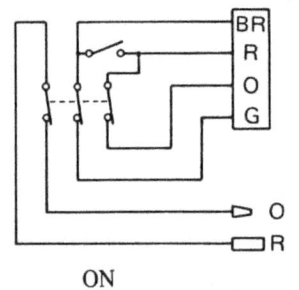
ON

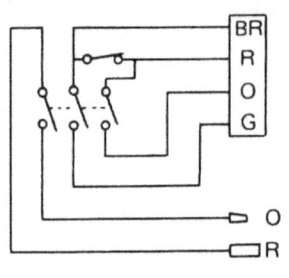

BR: BROWN   O: ORANGE
R : RED   G: GRAY

Fig. 8-6-1

II. HANDLE RIGHT SWITCH BOX

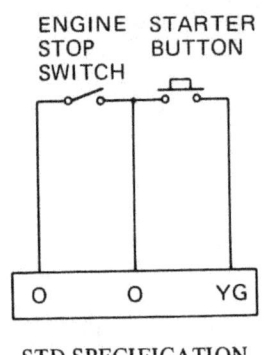
STD SPECIFICATION

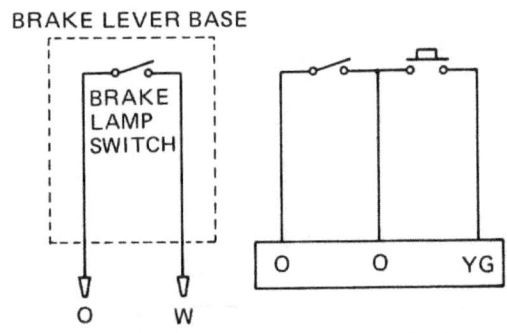
USA & CANADA SPECIFICATION

O : ORANGE
YG: YELLOW GREEN
W : WHITE

Fig. 8-6-2

III. HANDLE LEFT SWITCH BOX

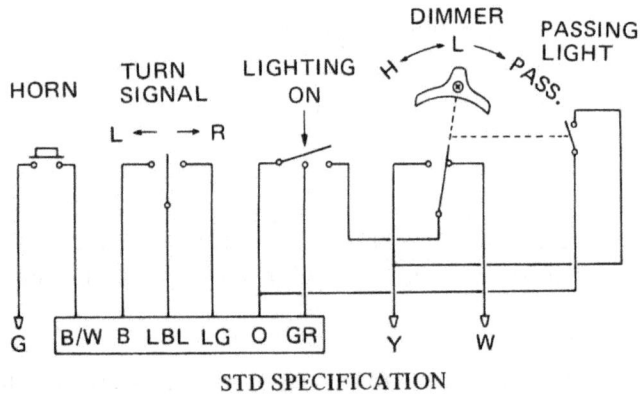
STD SPECIFICATION

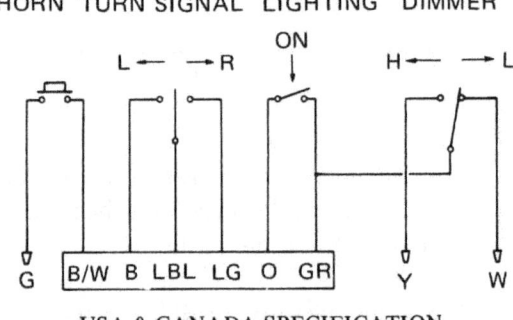
USA & CANADA SPECIFICATION

G   : GREEN   GR : GRAY
B   : BLACK   Y : YELLOW
LBL : LIGHT BLUE   W : WHITE
LG : LIGHT GREEN   B/W: BLACK WITH
O   : ORANGE   WHITE TRACER

Fig. 8-6-3

8-6-2. **TURN SIGNAL RELAY**

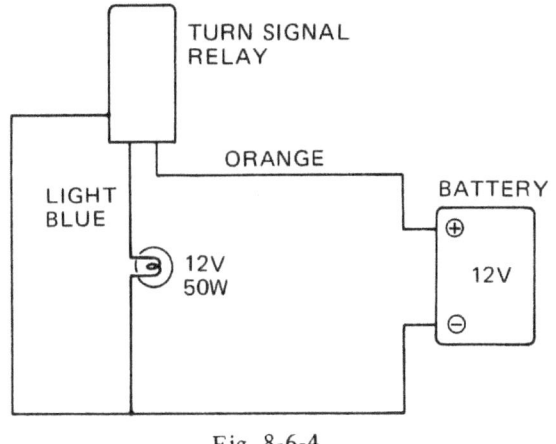

Fig. 8-6-4

If the turn signal relay is to be checked separately from the original wiring, connect a bulb of 12V 50W as shown in Fig. 8-6-4. If the turn signal relay functions properly, the bulb must blink continuously with constant frequency.

8-6-3. **BATTERY**

The battery used on this model is either of **YUASA** or **FURUKAWA** make. Both of them are of same type, 12V, 11AH, 12N11-3A-1, and there is interchangeability between them.

I. **INITIAL CHARGE**

The battery is of dry-charged type unlike that of a large capacity battery, however, it necessitates the initial charging with the specified rate before the battery is put in use since the plates may be oxidized to a certain extent during the storage.

* INITIAL CHARGING RATE : 1.1A   15 – 20 Hours
* SPECIFIC GRAVITY OF ELECTROLYTE : 1.280 at 20°C (68°F)

II. **RECHARGE**

To check the battery condition in capacity, measure the specific gravity of electrolyte by means of hydrometer and refer to the following list.

SPECIFIC GRAVITY at 20°C (68°F)	CONDITION	NECESSARY MEASURE
1.250 – 1.280	OK	
1.220 – 1.250	Under charged	Recharge
Below 1.220	Run down	Replace or recharge

Recharging rate: 1.1A   12 – 15 Hours

NOTE:
When recharging the battery, be sure to remove it from the motorcycle in order to prevent the rectifier from being damaged due to excessive voltage given by any chance.

III. **BATTERY EXHAUST PIPE**

Since the battery exhaust pipe is fixed on the motorcycle body by a clamp, the battery should be dismounted disconnecting the pipe at the joint and leaving the pipe on the body.

If the piping is to be required, place the exhaust pipe as shown in Fig. 8-6-5.

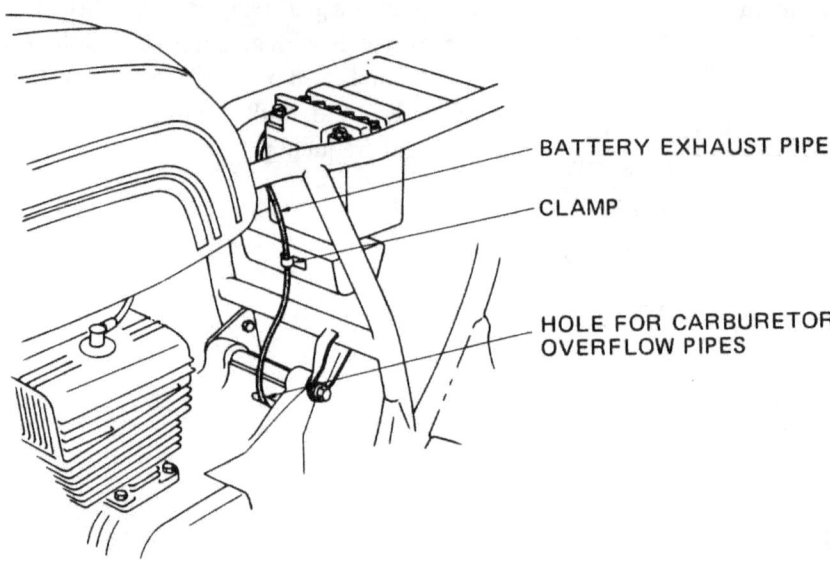

Fig. 8-6-5

NOTE:
If the battery acid is put to the drive chain, the chain may break when loaded. Therefore, set the outlet of the pipe so as not to face the drive chain.

9. SPECIFICATIONS FOR INSPECTION AND REPAIR

9-1. ENGINE

PART	CHECK ITEM	STANDARD	LIMIT	OPERATION	REMARKS
CYLINDER	Wear		0.1 mm (4/1,000 in)	Rebore	Measurement is the difference between largest and smallest diameter of the bore.
	Cylinder-piston clearance	0.045 mm (1.8/1,000 in)			Measure the piston diameter at 26 mm (1.02 in) above the piston skirt in the direction perpendicular to the piston pin hole. MEASUREMENT BY THICKNESS GAUGE SHOWS ENTIRELY DIFFERENT FIGURE.
PISTON RING	End gap	0.15 – 0.35 mm (6 – 14/1,000 in)	0.7 mm (28/1,000 in)	Replace	Measure with a thickness gauge when the ring is inserted into the lower part of the cylinder.
CRANK-SHAFT	Con-rod small end shake		3 mm (0.12 in)	Repair or replace	Check the shake at at TDC with a dial gauge.
	Radial Runout	Below 0.05 mm (2/1,000 in)			Measure with a dial gauge when both the ends are held.
CLUTCH DRIVE PLATE	Thickness	3.5 mm (0.138 in)	3.2 mm (0.126 in)	Replace	
CLUTCH DRIVEN PLATE	Warp		0.4 mm (16/1,000 in)	Replace	Measure with a thickness gauge placing the plate on the surface plate.

9-2. ELECTRICAL

PART	CHECK ITEM	STANDARD	LIMIT	OPERATION	REMARKS
CONTACT BREAKER	Contact Point gap	0.3 – 0.4 mm (12–16/1,000 in)	Under or over STD.	Adjust	
	Ignition Timing	3.37 mm (24 degree)	Under or over 2.85–4.24 mm (22° – 27°)	Adjust	In piston travel from TDC.
	Firing Order	L → C → R			
	Condenser capacity	0.16 – 0.20 µF			
IGNITION COIL	Continuity in Primary coil		If 0 or ∞ Ω	Replace	Resistance: approx. 4 – 6Ω
	Continuity in secondary coil		If 0 or ∞ Ω	Replace	Resistance: approx. 15 – 25kΩ
ALTERNATOR	Continuity in stator coils		If ∞ Ω	Replace	Refer to page 55.
	Ground in stator coils		If grounded	Replace	Refer to page 55.
	Continuity in field coil		If 0 or ∞ Ω	Replace	Approx. resistance: Denso 10Ω Kokusan 5Ω
	Wear of brushes	DENSO: 14 mm (0.6 in) from holder	5.5 mm (0.22 in)	Replace	Refer to page 55.
		KOKUSAN: 5 mm (0.2 in) from end to limit line	Until the limit line		
VOLTAGE REGULATOR	Regulated voltage	13.5 – 14.5 V	Under or over STD.	Adjust or replace	With fully charged battery. Refer to page 53, 56 and 57.
STATER MOTOR	Mica undercut	0.5 – 0.8 mm (20–30/1,000 in)	0.3 mm (12/1,000 in)	Rectify	
	Brushes	DENSO: 14 mm (0.55 in)	10 mm (0.4 in)	Replace	
		KOKUSAN: 13.5 mm (0.53 in)	9 mm (0.4 in)	Replace	
BATTERY	Specific Gravity	1.280 when 20°C (68°F)	Below 1.250	Recharge	

9-3. BODY

PART	CHECK ITEM	STANDARD	LIMIT	OPER-ATION	REMARKS
FRONT FORK	Damper oil	SAE 10W/30 230 – 240 cc in each fork			
BRAKE SHOE	Wear		Front: 194 mm (7.64 in)	Replace	Measure the diameter when the shoes are installed on the pannel.
BRAKE SHOE	Wear		Rear: 176 mm (6.93 in)	Replace	Measure the diameter when the shoes are installed on the pannel.
BRAKE DRUM	Wear	Front: 200 mm (7.87 in)	Front: 200.7 mm (7.90 in)	Replace	
BRAKE DRUM	Wear	Rear: 180 mm (7.09 in)	Rear: 180.7 mm (7.11 in)	Replace	
DRIVE CHAIN	Slack	15 – 20 mm (0.6–0.8 in)			
DRIVE CHAIN	Wear	11-7/8 in (301.6 mm)	12-1/8 in (308.0 mm)	Replace	Distance between 20 pins.
TIRE	Wear in Depth		Front: 1.6 mm (0.06 in) Rear: 2.0 mm (0.08 in)		

10. TIGHTENING TORQUE

PART	TIGHTENING TORQUE	
	kg-cm	lb-ft
Front axle nut	360 – 520	26 – 38
Front axle holder nut	150 – 250	11 – 18
Front torque link bolt & nut	200 – 300	14 – 22
Handlebars clamp bolt	120 – 200	9 – 14
Front fork lower bracket bolt	200 – 300	14 – 22
Steering stem nut	600 – 1000	43 – 72
Front fork upper bracket bolt (R & L)	200 – 300	14 – 22
Front fork upper bracket bolt (center)	150 – 250	11 – 18
Brake cam lever fitting nut	50 – 80	4 – 6
Engine mounting nut	250 – 400	18 – 29
Rear swinging arm pivot shaft nut	500 – 750	36 – 54
Front footrest bolt	300 – 450	22 – 33
Rear torque link nut	200 – 300	14 – 18
Rear shock absorber nut	200 – 300	14 – 18
Rear axle	500 – 800	36 – 58

TIGHTENING TORQUE FOR GENERAL BOLTS

BOLT DIAMETER (mm)	TIGHTENING TORQUE			
	Usual bolt		"S" marked bolt	
	kg-cm	lb-ft	kg-cm	lb-ft
5	20 – 40	1.5 – 2.9	30 – 60	2.2 – 4.4
6	40 – 70	2.9 – 5.1	60 – 100	4.4 – 7.3
8	90 – 140	6.6 – 10	130 – 230	9.5 – 17
10	180 – 280	13 – 20	250 – 400	18 – 29

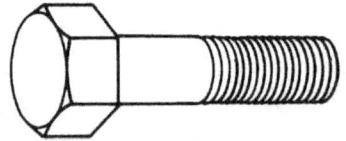

USUAL BOLT

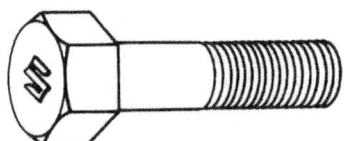

"S" MARKED BOLT

11. IMPORTANT FUNCTIONAL PARTS

For safety driving of motorcycle, it is highly requested to check up the important items in accordance with following check list at the time of the periodical inspection.

Check list of important functional parts for safety driving.

SYSTEM	ITEM	CHECK FOR
FUEL SUPPLY	Carburetor	Uneven movement of throttle valve, Fuel leakage
	Fuel hose Fuel tank Fuel cock	Fuel leakage
SUSPENSION	Front fork	Crack, Welding faulty of parts
	Front fork lower and upper bracket	Crack, Welding faulty
	Front and rear axle	Crack
	Rear swinging arm	Crack, Welding faulty
STEERING	Handlebars Handlebar clamp	Crack
BRAKES	Front hub drum Rear hub drum Front hub panel Rear hub panel	Crack
	Front torque link Rear torque link	Crack
	Front brake shoe Rear brake shoe	Crack, Peeling off of lining
	Front brake cam shaft Rear brake cam shaft	Crack, Deformation of serration
	Rear brake cable	Insecure connection of cable end
	Brake pedal	Crack, Welding faulty
	Brake lever	Crack
	Front brake cable	Insecure connection of cable end
FRAME	Frame	Crack, Welding faulty

NOTES

PERIODICAL INSPECTION LIST

The chart below indicates time when inspections, adjustments and maintenance are required based on the distance the motorcycle runs, that is first 1,000 km (750 mi), and every 3,000 km (2,000 mi), 6,000 km (4,000 mi) and 12,000 km (8,000 mi) thereafter. According to the chart, advise users to have the motorcycle checked and serviced at your shop. See the appropriate section for instructions on making the inspection.

Service	Distance (km) / Distance (mi)	1,000 km / 750 mi	Every 3,000 km / Every 2,000 mi	Every 6,000 km / Every 4,000 mi	Every 12,000 km / Every 8,000 mi
Oil pump		Check operation, adjust control lever aligning marks	Check operation, adjust control lever aligning marks		
Spark plug		Clean	Clean and adjust gap		
Gearbox oil		Change	Change	Replace	
Throttle and brake cables		Adjust play	Adjust play	Lubricate	
Carburetor		Adjust with throttle valve screw and pilot air screw	Adjust with throttle valve screw and pilot air screw		Overhaul and clean
Contact breaker		Check contact point gap and ignition timing	Check contact point gap and ignition timing, Lubricate contact breaker cam oil felt		Replace contact point
Cylinder head and cylinder		Retighten cylinder and cylinder head nuts	Retighten cylinder and cylinder head nuts		
Battery		Check and service electrolyte	Check and service electrolyte		
Fuel cock		Clean fuel strainer		Clean fuel strainer	
Drive chain		Adjust	Adjust and lubricate	Wash	
Brakes		Adjust play	Adjust play		
Air cleaner			Clean		
Throttle grip				Put grease in throttle grip	
Exhaust pipe and Muffler		Retighten exhaust pipe flange fitting screw	Retighten exhaust pipe flange fitting screw	Remove carbon	
Steering stem		Check play / Retighten stem nut		Check play / Retighten stem nut	
Bolts, Nuts and Spokes		Retighten		Retighten	

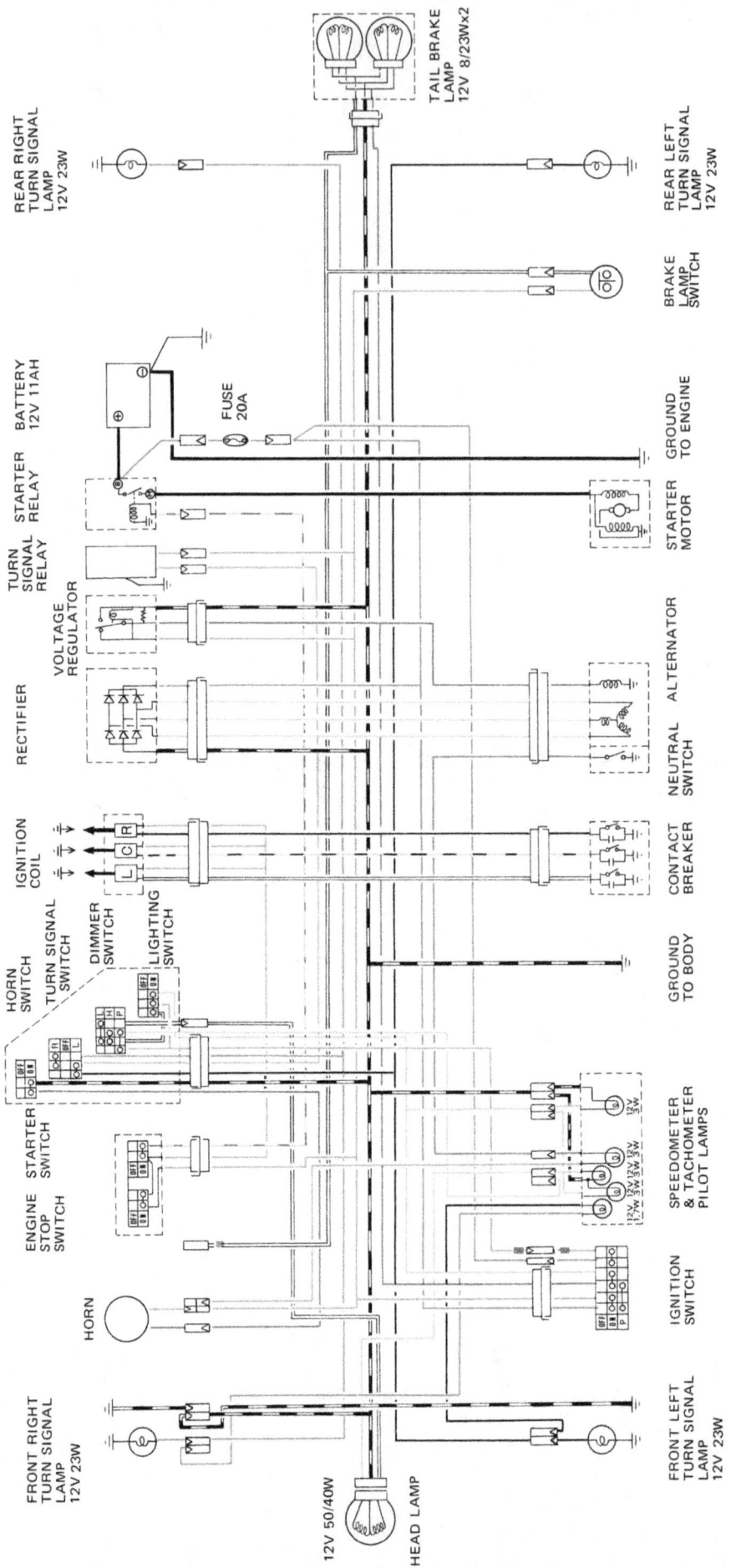

WIRING DIAGRAM (Standard specification)

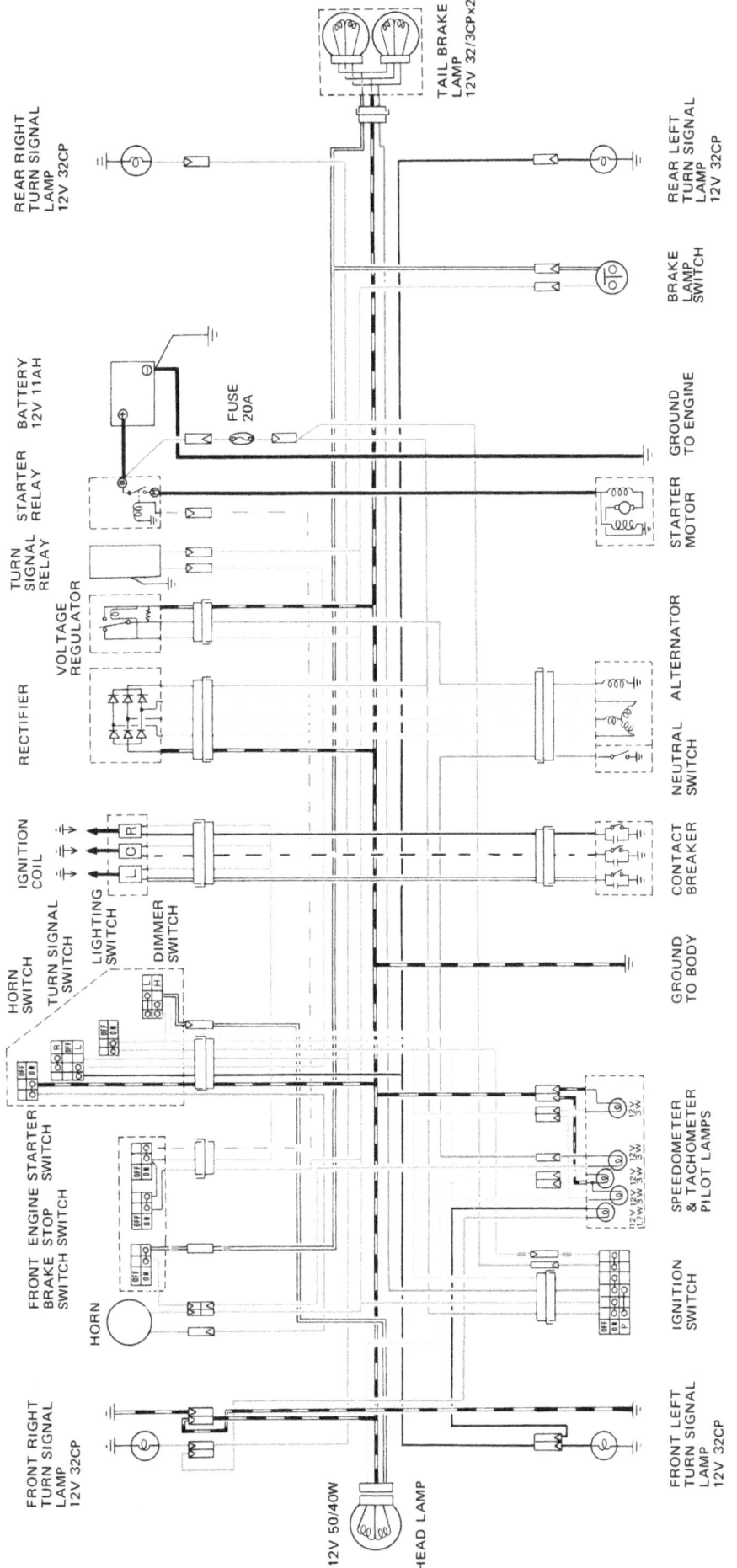

WIRING DIAGRAM (USA & CANADA specification)

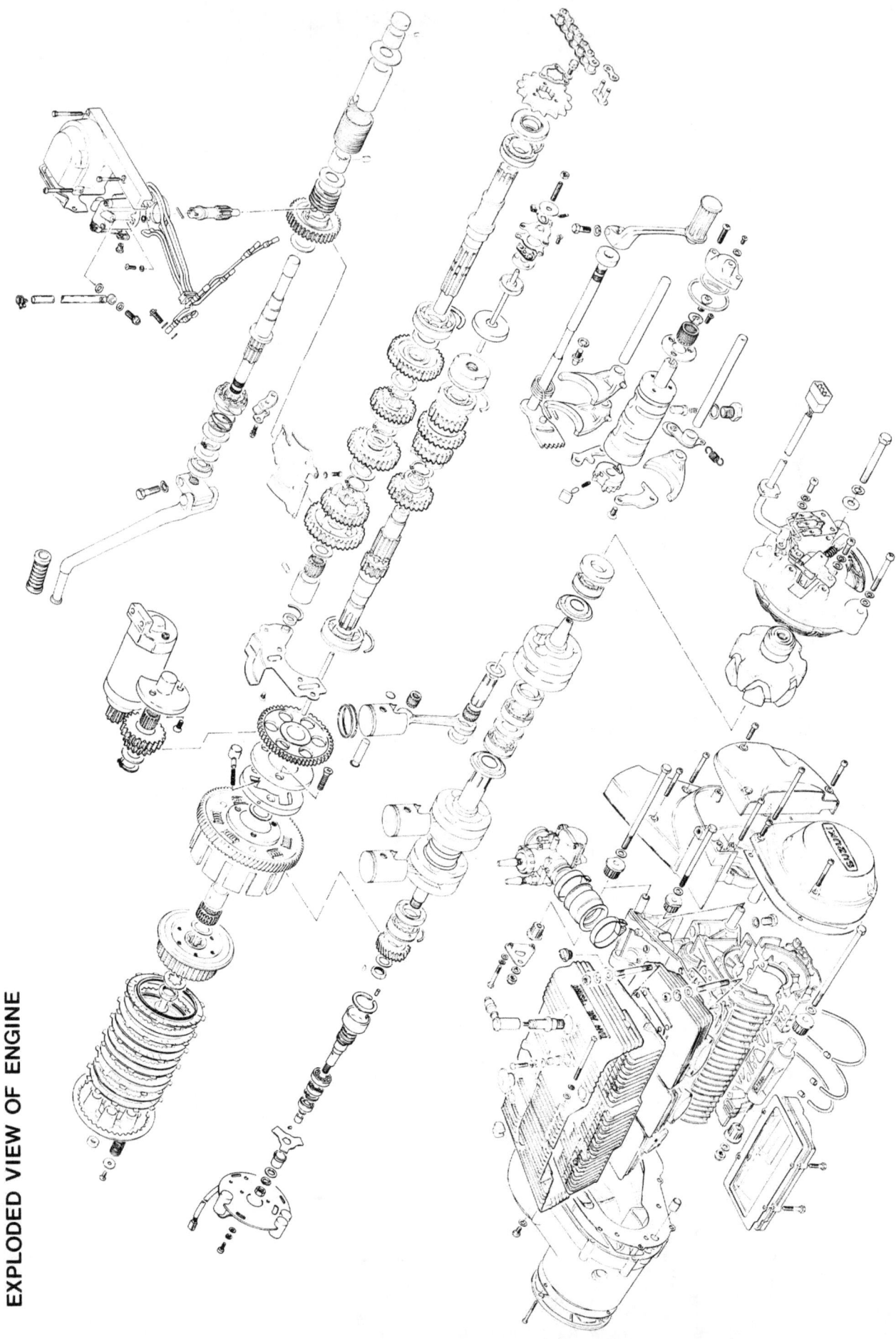

EXPLODED VIEW OF ENGINE

NOTES

SUZUKI MOTOR CO., LTD.

SUZUKI SERVICE MANUAL

MODEL

DISC BRAKE

FOREWORD

The purpose of this service manual is to provide a detailed description on the construction, operating principles, and adjusting and operating methods of the hydraulic disc brakes which have been recently adopted to Models GT125, GT185, GT250, GT380, GT550 and GT750.

To ensure a safe operation of these models capable of high-speed performance, an adequate maintenance of the brakes is vital. This manual is presented in the simplest possible manner so that the materials included are easily comprehensive to you. We hope that correct maintenance of these disc brakes will be facilitated most effectively by utilization of this manual.

Because this manual has been compiled on the models of the motorcycles available as of December, 1973, it is possible that the contents of this manual may not necessarily correspond to the motorcycles delivered to you due to possible changes of their specifications.

International Service Department
$ SUZUKI MOTOR CO ,LTD
December, 1973

FEATURES OF DISC BRAKE

Compared with the conventional drum-type brakes, the hydraulic disc brake has the following features:

- *Heat radiation from the friction surfaces is quite effective since the discs rotate in direct contact with the air. Therefore, stable brake power can always be provided, even if the disc brake is used repeatedly at high speeds.*

- *A brake lever stroke remains always constant since none of the disc brake parts is subjected to any deformation due to elevated temperatures.*

- *Replacement of pads is simple and no troublesome adjustment is required.*

- *Steady brake performance is ensured, since, even if the disc is wet during running in rainy weather or on muddy road, the restoring ability of brake power is excellent due to the extreme pressure characteristics for pushing pads.*

- *It has a smooth operation, since it has little portion to be mechanically abrased.*

INDEX

1. SPECIFICATION AND SERVICE DATA 4
2. TROUBLE SHOOTING 5
3. OUTLINE OF HYDRAULIC DISC BRAKE 6
   - 3-1 General 6
   - 3-2 Operation of Master Cylinder 7
   - 3-3 Operation of Caliper 8
4. INSPECTION AND REPAIR 9
   - 4-1 Brake Fluid and Its Handling 9
   - 4-2 Inspection and Replacing Method of Pads 10
   - 4-3 Master Cylinder, Brake Hose and Brake Pipe . 13
   - 4-4 Caliper 19
   - 4-5 Brake Disc 22
   - 4-6 Periodic Replacement Parts 23
5. TIGHTENING TORQUE 24
6. SPECIAL TOOLS FOR DISC BRAKE 25
   - 6-1 Special Tools 25
   - 6-2 Necessary Materials 25

1. SPECIFICATION AND SERVICE DATA

Item	GT125 GT185 S.T.D. figure	GT125 GT185 Limit	GT250 GT380 S.T.D. figure	GT250 GT380 Limit	GT550 S.T.D. figure	GT550 Limit	GT750 S.T.D. figure	GT750 Limit
Disc thickness, front brake	5.00 mm (0.197 in.)	under 4.00 mm (0.157 in.)	7.00 mm (0.276 in.)	under 6.00 mm (0.236 in.)	7.00 mm (0.276 in.)	under 6.00 mm (0.236 in.)	7.00 mm (0.276 in.)	under 6.00 mm (0.236 in.)
Disc runout front brake	max. 0.1 mm (0.004 in.)	over 0.3 mm (0.012 in.)	max. 0.1 mm (0.004 in.)	over 0.3 mm (0.012 in.)	max. 0.1 mm (0.004 in.)	over 0.3 mm (0.012 in.)	max. 0.1 mm (0.004 in.)	over 0.3 mm (0.012 in.)
Outer diameter brake disc	250 mm (9.843 in.)		275 mm (10.827 in.)		295 mm (11.614 in.)		295 mm (11.614 in.)	
Inner diameter, master cylinder	14.00 to 14.04 mm (0.551 to 0.553 in.)	over 14.05 mm (0.553 in.)	14.00 to 14.04 mm (0.551 to 0.553 in.)	over 14.05 mm (0.553 in.)	14.00 to 14.04 mm (0.551 to 0.553 in.)	over 14.05 mm (0.553 in.)	15.87 to 15.91 mm (0.625 to 0.626 in.)	over 15.92 mm (0.627 in.)
Piston diameter, master cylinder	13.96 to 13.98 mm (0.550 to 0.551 in.)	under 13.94 mm (0.549 in.)	13.96 to 13.98 mm (0.550 to 0.551 in.)	under 13.94 mm (0.549 in.)	13.96 to 13.98 mm (0.550 to 0.551 in.)	under 13.94 mm (0.549 in.)	15.83 to 15.85 mm (0.623 to 0.624 in.)	under 15.81 mm (0.622 in.)
Inner diameter caliper cylinder	38.18 to 38.20 mm (1.503 to 1.504 in.)	over 38.22 mm (1.504 in.)	38.18 to 38.20 mm (1.503 to 1.504 in.)	over 38.22 mm (1.504 in.)	38.18 to 38.20 mm (1.503 to 1.504 in.)	over 38.22 mm (1.504 in.)	38.18 to 38.20 mm (1.503 to 1.504 in.)	over 38.22 mm (1.504 in.)
Piston diameter caliper cylinder	38.15 to 38.18 mm (1.502 to 1.503 in.)	under 38.10 mm (1.500 in.)	38.15 to 38.18 mm (1.502 to 1.503 in.)	under 38.10 mm (1.500 in.)	38.15 to 38.18 mm (1.502 to 1.503 in.)	under 38.10 mm (1.500 in.)	38.15 to 38.18 mm (1.502 to 1.503 in.)	under 38.10 mm (1.500 in.)
Effective diameter, front brake disc	199 mm (7.835 in.)		224 mm (8.819 in.)		244 mm (9.606 in.)		244 mm (9.606 in.)	
Effective brake lining area	19cm² x 2 pcs. (2.95 in² x 2 pcs.)		19cm² x 2 pcs. (2.95 in² x 2 pcs.)		19cm² x 2 pcs. (2.95 in² x 2 pcs.)		19cm² x 4 pcs. (2.95 in² x 4 pcs.)	
Type, front brake	Right-hand, hydraulic, single disc brake		Right-hand, hydraulic, single disc brake		Right-hand, hydraulic, single disc brake		Right-hand, hydraulic, double disc brake	
Type, caliper	Floating caliper, single cylinder		Floating caliper, single cylinder		Floating caliper, single cylinder		Floating caliper, single cylinder	

2. TROUBLE SHOOTING

Symptom and possible cause	Countermeasure
1. Insufficient brake power	
1) Leakage of brake fluid from hydraulic system	Repair or replace
2) Worn pads	Replace
3) Oil adhesion on engaged surface of pads	Clean disc and pads
4) Worn disc	Replace
5) Instruded air in hydraulic system	Bleed air
2. Brake squeaking	
1) Carbon adhesion on pad surface	Repair surface with sandpaper
2) Tilted pad	Modify pad fitting
3) Damaged wheel bearing	Replace
4) Loosened front-wheel axle	Tighten with regular torque
5) Worn pads	Replace
6) Intruded foreign substance into brake fluid	Replace brake fluid
7) Clogged return port of master cylinder	Disassemble and clean master cylinder
3. Excessive brake lever stroke	
1) Intruded air into hydraulic system	Bleed air
2) Worn brake lever cam	Replace brake lever
3) Insufficient brake fluid	Replenish fluid to normal level; bleed air
4) Improper quality of brake fluid	Replace by proper one
4. Leakage of brake fluid	
1) Insufficient tightening of connection joints	Tighten with regular torque
2) Cracked pipe	Replace
3) Worn piston and/or cup	Replace piston and/or cup

3. OUTLINE OF HYDRAULIC DISC BRAKE

3-1 General

The hydraulic disc brake adopted in Suzuki's models GT125, GT185, GT250, GT380, GT550 and GT750 consists of four main portions, i.e., brake discs mounted on a front wheel hub, a master cylinder for pressurizing, a brake hose line for fluid pressure, and a caliper which presses pads to brake disc by means of hydraulic pressures.

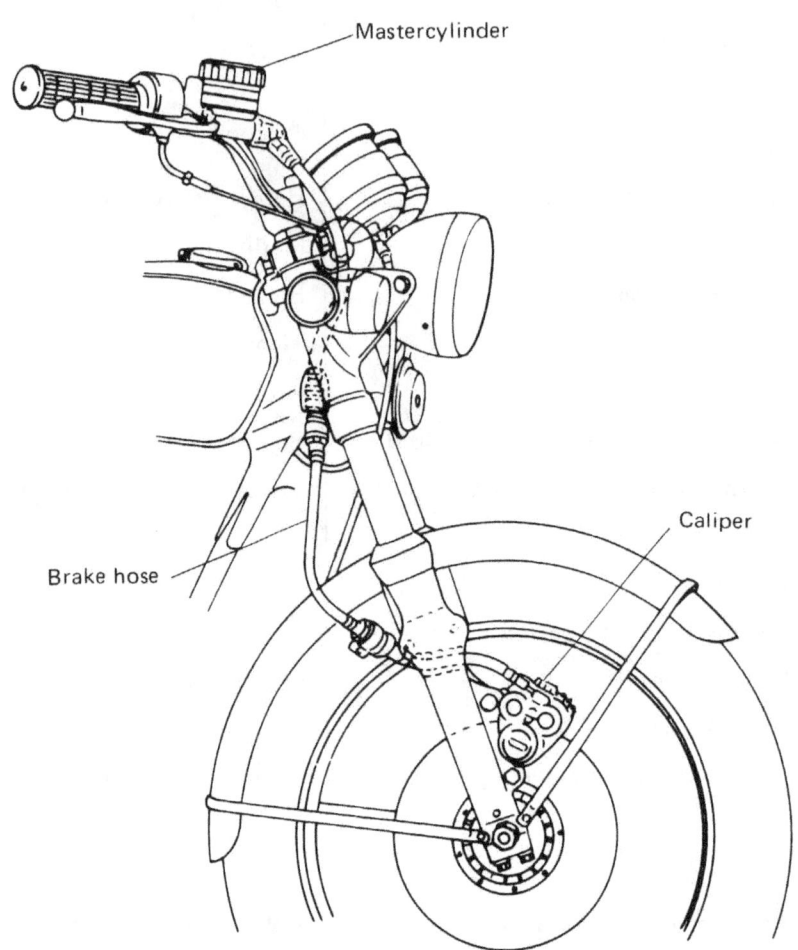

Fig. 3-1-1

3-2 Operation of Master Cylinder

3-2-1 Squeezing brake lever

The piston ③ is pushed in the direction of arrow by the brake cam ② when the brake lever is squeezed. The primary cup ④ also moves together with the piston and when it closes the return port ⑤ which is provided at the master cylinder body, brake fluid in front of the primary cup begins to be pressurized and delivered to the caliper by opening the check valve ⑥ with its pressure.

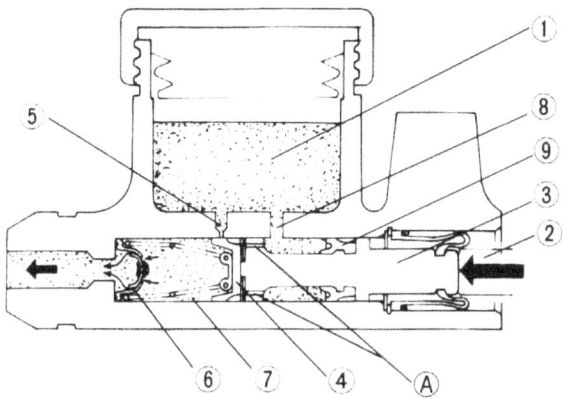

1 Reservoir
2 Brake lever cam
3 Piston
4 Primary cup
5 Return port
6 Check valve
7 Spring
8 Inlet port
9 Secondary cup

Fig. 3-2-1

3-2-2 Releasing brake lever

As soon as the brake lever is released, the piston is pushed back by the spring ⑦. Because the brake fluid from the caliper may not return to the master cylinder immediately due to its flow resistance, hydraulic pressure inside the cylinder is reduced momentarily and fluid flows from the reservoir to the front section of the primary cup through the inlet port ⑧, three small holes Ⓐ on the piston flange and the circumference of the primary cup.

Then high pressure brake fluid from the caliper releases the check valve body from its contact with the outlet part allowing to have the clearance for a fluid passage. A small amount of the fluid returns from the caliper to the master cylinder through the clearance thus made by the movement of the check valve body.

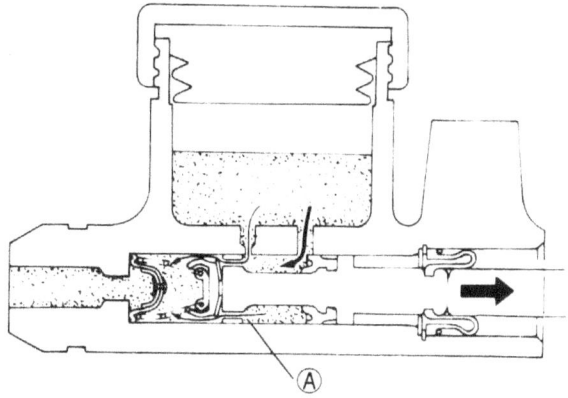

Fig. 3-2-2

3-2-3 After completing return stroke of brake lever

A large amount of the brake fluid having been delivered to the caliper returns to the reservoir through the clearance behind the check valve base and the return port on the master cylinder body.

As the brake fluid from the caliper returns to the reservoir, hydraulic pressure in the brake hose is reduced gradually and the spring tension surmounts the hydraulic pressure of the brake hose resulting in closing the clearance behind the check valve base. However, some fluid pressure still remains in the brake hose because of the initial tension of the spring. Brake fluid continues to flow into the reservoir through a small notch provided around the periphery of the check valve body and the return port. The master cylinder completes its operation when residual pressure in the brake hose vanishes completely.

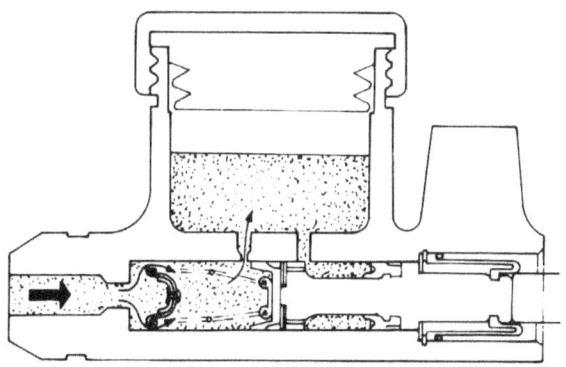

Fig. 3-2-3

3-3 Operation of Caliper

3-3-1 Squeezing brake lever

Brake fluid from the master cylinder delivered under pressure flows into the caliper cylinder through inlet portion Ⓐ of the caliper and pushes piston ① in the direction of arrow.

The pushed piston moves together with the pad No.1 (moving side) ② in this direction until it can not move any further forward due to the pad No.1 hitting brake disc ③.

As soon as the pad No.1 touches the brake disc so that the piston may not move any further, the caliper body floating on the caliper axle is pushed in reverse direction by the fluid pressure in the cylinder and moves in the right side direction as shown in Fig. 3-3-2.

Since the pad No.2 (stationary side) ④ is mounted to the caliper body, the disc is subjected to a powerful braking force with pads Nos.1 and 2 depressing the disc from opposite directions respectively.

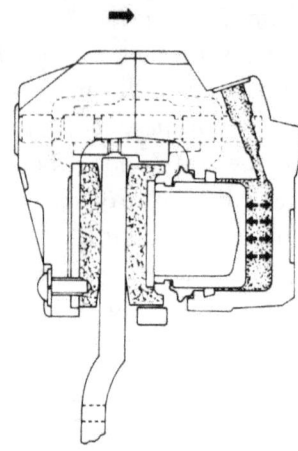

Fig. 3-3-2

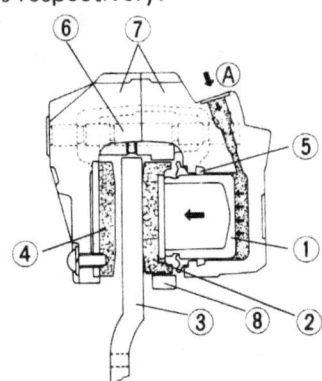

1 Piston	5 Piston seal
2 Pad No. 1	6 Caliper axle
3 Brake disc	7 Caliper body
4 Pad No. 2	8 Caliper holder

Fig. 3-3-1

3-3-2 Releasing brake lever

When the brake lever is released and fluid pressure in the caliper cylinder vanishes, the piston moves in the direction of arrow in Fig. 3-3-3, being pushed by piston seal ⑤ which was pressed onto the piston by fluid pressure and is now restoring its original shape with fluid pressure released. Therefore, the pads pressed to the disc part from the disc since the piston moves as much as the piston seal displacement, thus setting the brake disc free.

3-3-3 Self adjusting of clearance between pads and disc

If the traveling distance of piston exceeds the displacement of the piston seal, the piston is moved as far as the braking stroke while the piston slides between itself and the piston seal, whereas a return stroke of the piston due to the piston seal restoration after brake release is always constant and the returned position of the piston relatively varies with the wear of pads.

Consequently, clearance between the pads and the piston, or between the pads and the brake disc is always kept constant regardless of the condition of pad wear.

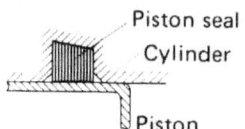

When brake lever is released

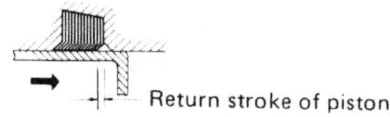

When brake lever is squeezed

Fig. 3-3-3

4. INSPECTION AND REPAIR

4-1 Brake Fluid and Its Handling

4-1-1 Inspecting brake fluid level

Be sure to check brake fluid level in the reservoir. In inspecting brake fluid, first mount your motorcycle firmly onto the center stand with its handlebar kept straight up without fail. If the level is found to be lower than the level mark ① provided on the reservoir, replenish the reservoir with one of the brake fluid graded below.

Spacification & Classification	Remarks
DOT 3	in U.S.A.
DOT 4	in U.S.A.
SAE J1703a	
SAE J1703b	
SAE J170c	
SAE 70R3	A classification in obsolete specification of SAE J70b.

Note: Since the brake system of these motorcycles is filled with a glycol base brake fluid by the manufacturer, do not use or mix different types of fluid such as silicone-based and petroleum-based fluid for refilling the system, otherwise damage sustained will be serious.

Do not use any brake fluid taken from old or used, or unsealed containers.

Do not squeeze the brake lever while the reservoir cap is removed, otherwise brake fluid will sometimes spout out. Do not put the removed reservoir cap on the speedometer or tachometer. Brake fluid will damage the paint surface and instrument gauge lenses.

Take due care especially so that water may not enter brake fluid on rainy day particularly during replacement or in handling a brake fluid container, because brake fluid has hygroscopic property, and its boiling point falls excessively if water is mixed with it.

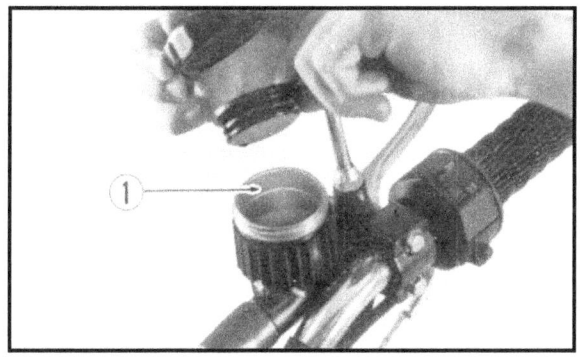

(All "K" models)   Fig. 4-1-1

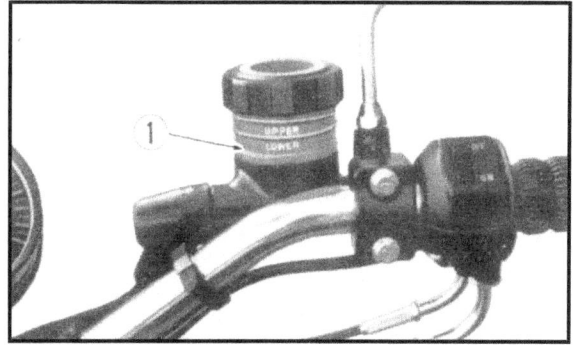

(All "L" models)   Fig. 4-1-2

4-1-2 Air bleeding from brake system

If the brake lever travel becomes excessive or the lever feels a soft or spongy feeling, you must carry out air bleeding from the brake system in the following procedure:

It is best if two persons perform this.

1) Attach the bleeder tube to the bleeder valve after removing the bleeder valve dust cap as shown in Fig. 4-1-3. A transparent tube is useful in finding air bubble expelled from the system.
2) The tube must be submerged in a clean container partially filled with brake fluid.
3) Fill the reservoir with the aforementioned brake fluid.

Note: Keep at least one half full of fluid in the reservoir during the bleeding procedure.

Fig. 4-1-3

4) Screw in the cap on the reservoir to prevent a spout of brake fluid and entry of dust.
5) Allow the pressure in the hydraulic system by squeezing rapidly the brake lever several times and then holding the lever tight.
6) Unscrew (open) the bleeder valve by one half turn and squeeze the lever all the way down. Do not release the lever until the bleeder valve is screwed in (closed) again.
7) Repeat steps 5) and 6) until air bubbles disappear in the bleeder tube or container and screw in (close) the bleeder valve securely.
8) Remove the tube and install the bleeder valve dust cap.
9) Check the fluid level in the reservoir and replenish if necessary, after the bleeding operation has been completed.
10) Reinstall the diaphragm and the diaphragm plate and tighten the reservoir cap securely.

Caution: Do not reuse the brake fluid drained from the system.

For model GT750, bleed air at first from the left-hand side caliper and then from the right according to the aforementioned procedure.

4-1-3 Changing brake fluid

Boiling point of brake fluid falls considerably with absorption of moisture which may take place during a long period of use. Therefore, it is recommended to exchange old brake fluid with new one periodically.

Exchange interval: One year

On changing brake fluid, extreme attention should be paid so as not to mix any foreign materials because they would block the return port of the master cylinder resulting in the brake dragging or squeaking.
When brake fluid is to be changed, perform the following procedure.
1) Attach a bleeder tube to the bleeder valve. Drain out old brake fluid by squeezing the brake lever with the bleeder valve opened until the brake fluid disappears in the bleeder tube.
2) After old brake fluid is drained out from the system completely, carry out the same procedure as described in "4-1-2 Air bleeding".

4-2 Inspection and Replacing Method of Pads

4-2-1 Inspection of pads

Check worn condition of the friction pads. If any of the friction pads is worn out up to the red limit line ① marked on its circumference, replace it following the procedure of "4-2-2" or "4-2-3".

Caution: Wash mud and dust off around the front wheel and/or caliper prior to the replacing operation.

Fig. 4-2-1

4-2-2 Replacing of pads for models GT125, GT185, GT250, GT380 or GT550

1) Set up the center stand and load at the rear portion to let the front wheel free.
2) Remove the front wheel assembly.
3) Unscrew the pad fastening screw, and take off pad No. 2 (stationary side).

Fig. 4-2-2

4) Squeeze the brake lever two or three times gradually to force out pad No. 1 by fluid pressure while observing the motion of pad.

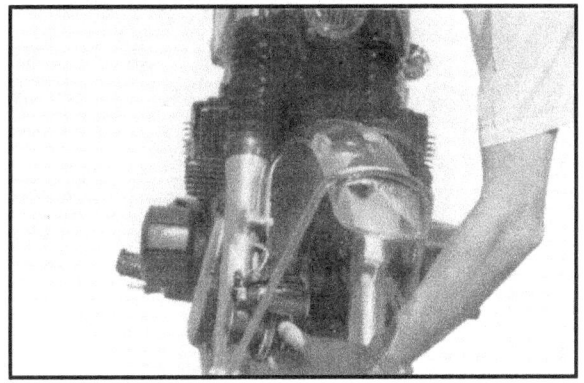

Fig. 4-2-3

5) Apply "Brake Pad Grease", which is provided as a component of Pad Set as shown in Fig. 4-2-4, onto the periphery and back plate of pad No. 1 as illustrated in Fig. 4-2-5 in a very thin layer.

Caution: Do not use another grease.
Apply grease thinly so as not to flow out, otherwise resulting in reduced brake performance.

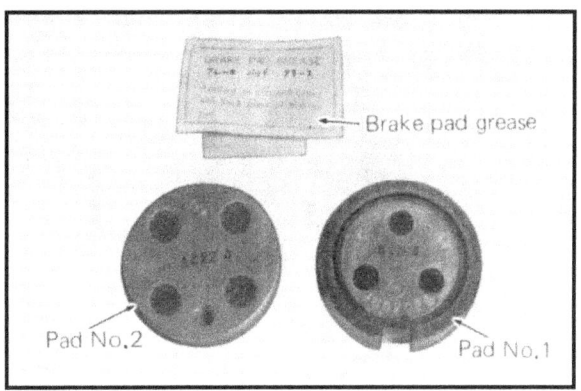

Fig. 4-2-4

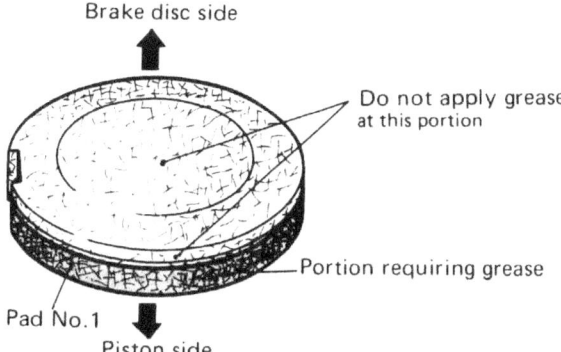

Fig. 4-2-5

Note: The pad set supplied as a repair part is classified into three types according to the shape of Pad No. 1. The following table shows part numbers and the shapes of Pad No. 1. When replacing this part, refer to this table and be careful not to assemble erroneously.

Shape of pad	Parts No.	Model to which pad is applicable
Flat	59100–36830	GT125L, GT185L
Identification mark "A" Depth 1.5mm (0.06 in.)	59100–18840	Models GT250L, GT380L, GT550L and GT550K with engine serial numbers 32292 and thereafter, and models GT750L and GT750K with engine serial numbers 38591 and thereafter.
Depth 2.8 mm (0.11 in.)	59100–31830	Models GT250K, GT380K and GT550K with engine serial numbers 32291 and before, and model GT750K with engine serial numbers 38590 and before.

6) Push in pad No. 1 into the caliper holder.

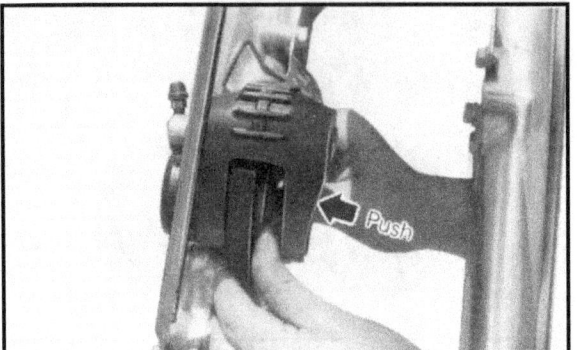

Fig. 4-2-6

7) Mount pad No. 2 to the caliper body.

Caution: Do not apply any grease to the pad No. 2, and take care not to mount it inclined.

8) Install the front wheel assembly to the front fork.
9) Squeeze the brake lever two or three times to confirm its operation, and bleed air if necessary.

4-2-3 Replacing of pad for model GT750

1) Take off the left brake pipe cover ① and pipe guide ②.

Fig. 4-2-7

2) Loosen the two left caliper fitting bolts ③.

Fig. 4-2-8

3) Detach the left caliper with the brake pipe connected and fix it on the front fork by string or hold it unmoved so as not to bend the brake pipe.

Fig. 4-2-9

4) Take off the front wheel assembly.
5) Mount the removed left caliper to the front fork
6) Insert a spacer ④ between pads Nos. 1 and 2 of the right caliper to stop piston movement and clip it with an elastic rubber ring ⑤ to prevent it from falling.

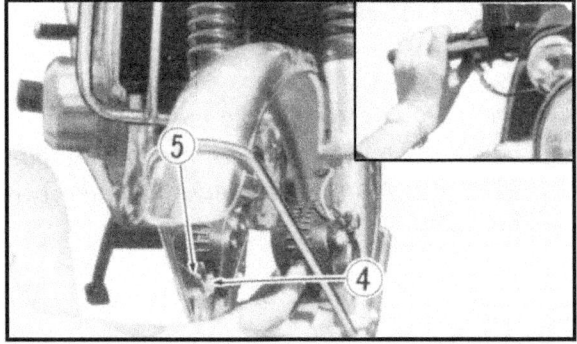

Fig. 4-2-10

7) Replace pads Nos. 1 and 2 of the left caliper in the same manner as for models GT125, GT185, GT250, GT380 and GT550.
8) Remove the spacer from the right caliper, and insert it in the left caliper.
9) Replace pads Nos. 1 and 2 of the right caliper.
10) Take off the left caliper and hold it.
11) Install the front wheel assembly to the front fork.
12) Mount the left caliper to the front fork.
13) Mount the left brake pipe cover and guide.
14) Squeeze the brake lever two or three times to confirm its operation, and bleed air if necessary.

Note: When replacing the front tire or repairing puncture, it is necessary to remove the left caliper before removing the front wheel assembly.

4-3 Master Cylinder, Brake Hose and Brake Pipe

4-3-1 General

Always check the master cylinder, brake hose and the brake pipe for operation and leakage of brake fluid since they are very important parts for safe riding.
If any abnormal condition is found, repair or replace. Though every part is made of material rigidly selected under high degree quality control, periodically replace the master cylinder piston cup and its related parts in order to always keep the motorcycle in its best condition.

Index No.	Description
1	Master cylinder assembly
2	Check valve
3	Spring
4	Primary cup
5	Secondary cup
6	Piston
7	Stop plate
8	Circlip
9	Boot
10	Boot plate
11	Boot stopper
12	Diaphragm
13	Diaphragm plate
14	Reservoir cap
15	Washer
16	Bolt
17	Master cylinder boot
18	Union bolt
19	Washer
20	Front brake hose
21	Brake hose guide
22	Grommet
23	Brake pipe
24	Brake hose guide
25	Grommet
26	Brake hose
27	Grommet

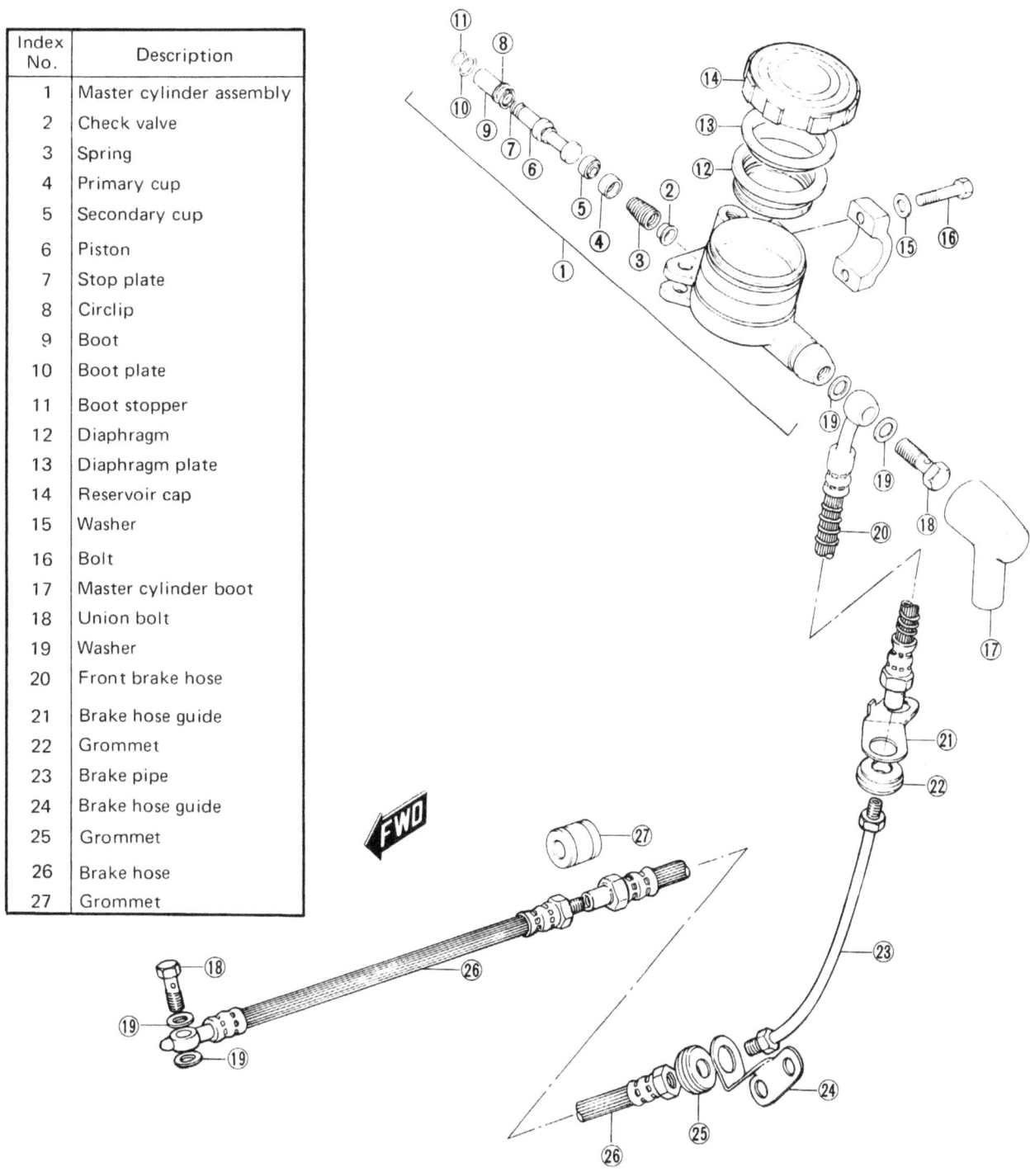

(GT125, GT185)

Fig. 4-3-1

102

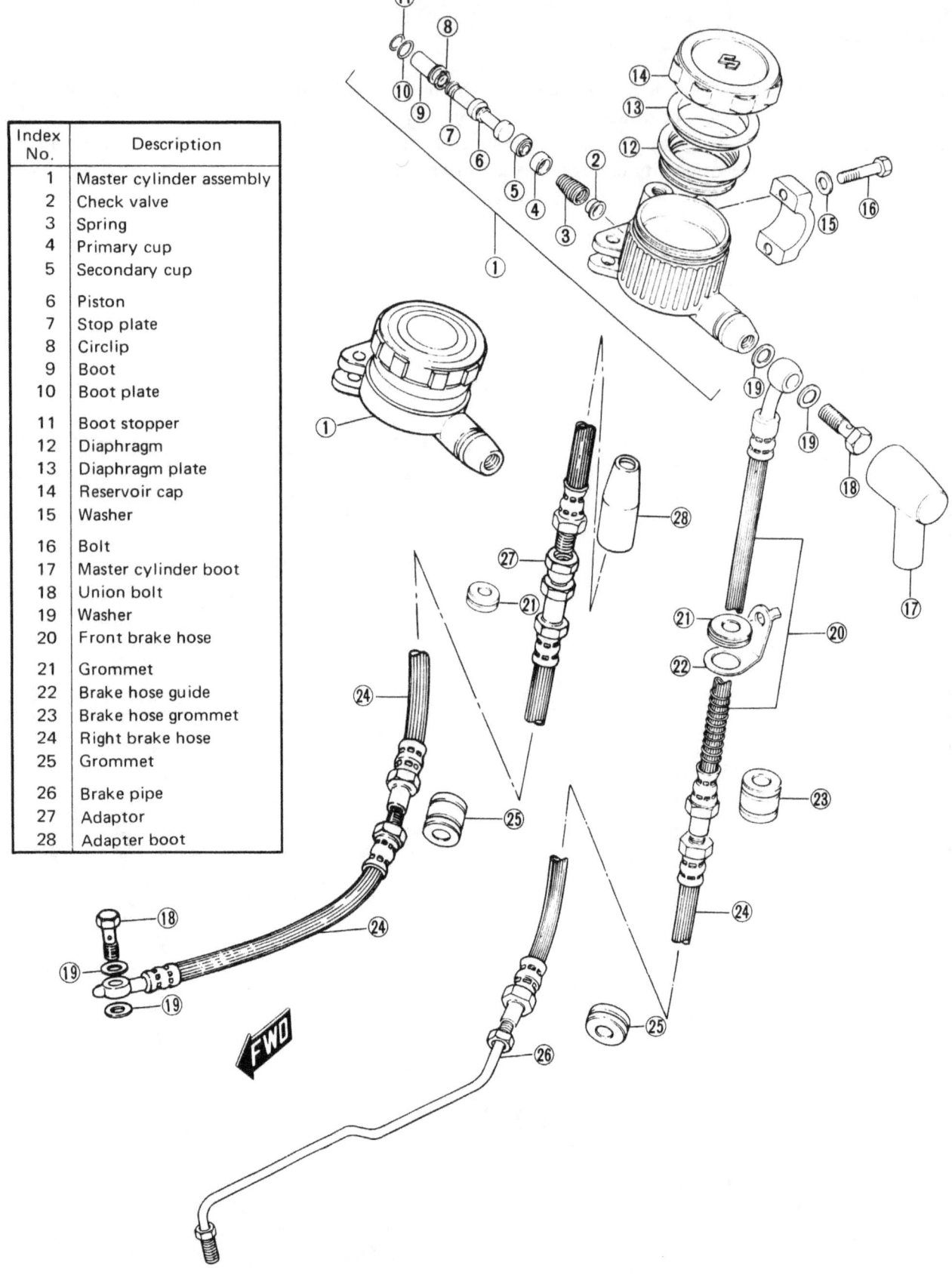

Index No.	Description
1	Master cylinder assembly
2	Check valve
3	Spring
4	Primary cup
5	Secondary cup
6	Piston
7	Stop plate
8	Circlip
9	Boot
10	Boot plate
11	Boot stopper
12	Diaphragm
13	Diaphragm plate
14	Reservoir cap
15	Washer
16	Bolt
17	Master cylinder boot
18	Union bolt
19	Washer
20	Front brake hose
21	Grommet
22	Brake hose guide
23	Brake hose grommet
24	Right brake hose
25	Grommet
26	Brake pipe
27	Adaptor
28	Adapter boot

(GT250, GT380 & GT550) Fig. 4-3-2

14

Index No.	Description
1	Master cylinder assembly
2	Check valve
3	Spring
4	Primary cup
5	Secondary cup
6	Piston
7	Plate stop
8	Circlip
9	Boot
10	Boot plate
11	Boot stopper
12	Diaphragm
13	Diaphragm plate
14	Reservoir cap
15	Bolt
16	Washer
17	Master cylinder boot
18	Union bolt
19	Washer
20	Grommet
21	Brake hose guide
22	Front brake hose
23	RH & LH brake hose
24	Three way joint
25	Grommet
26	RH brake pipe
27	LH brake pipe
28	Adapter
29	Adapter boot

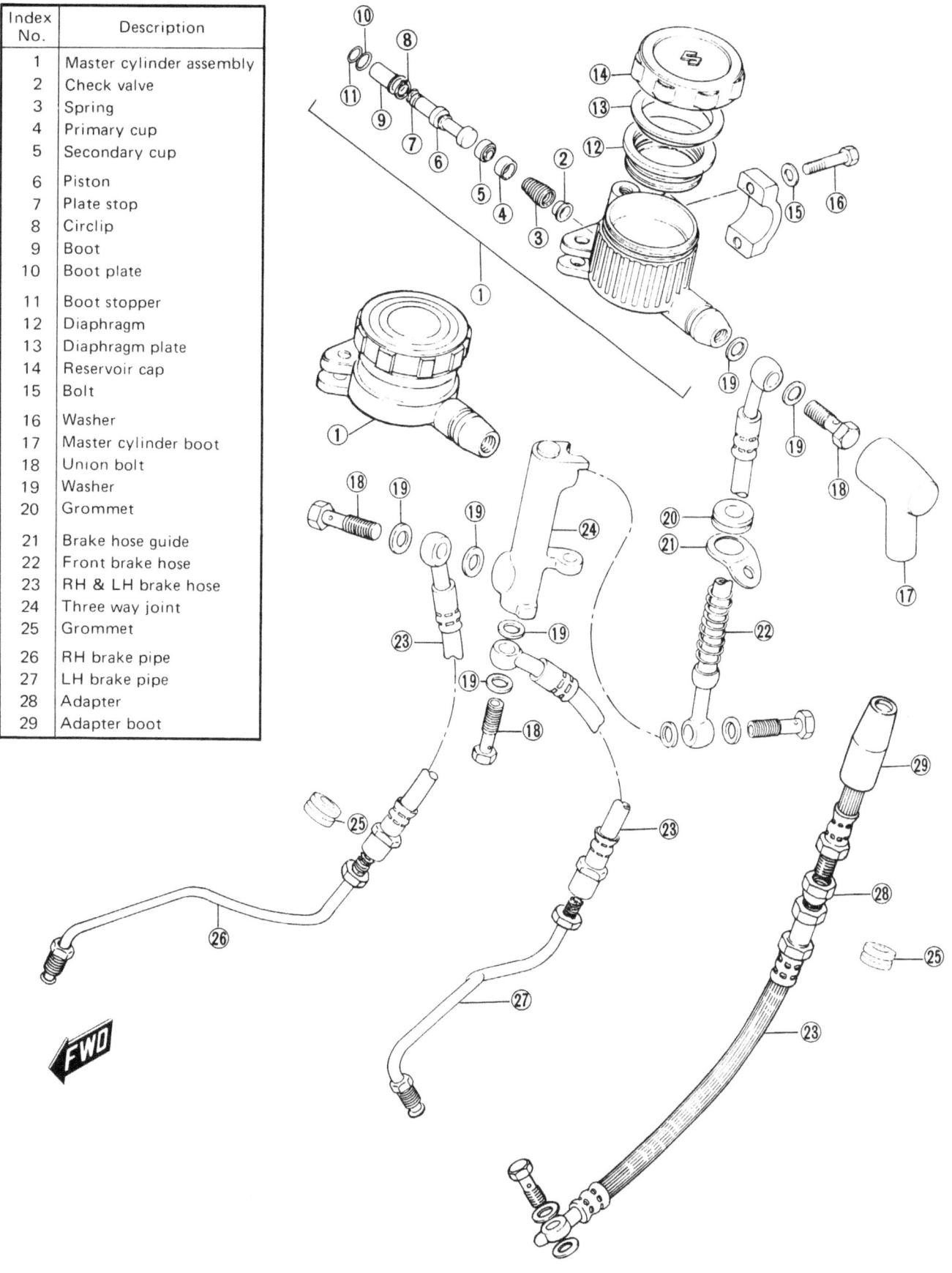

(GT750) Fig. 4-3-3

4-3-2 Removing master cylinder

1) Remove the stop switch from the master cylinder (only for U.S.A. and Canadian specifications).

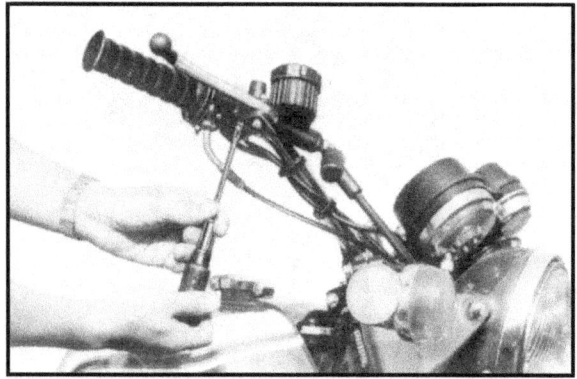

Fig. 4-3-3

2) Put a piece of rag beneath the union bolt on the master cylinder to catch drops of brake fluid. Unscrew the union bolt and disconnect the connection between the brake hose and the master cylinder.

Fig. 4-3-4

3) Unscrew two master cylinder fastening bolts and remove the master cylinder body from the handlebar.
4) Empty brake fluid out of the reservoir.

4-3-3 Disassembling master cylinder

1) Remove the brake lever.
2) Remove the boot stopper while taking care not to damage the boot and then remove the boot.

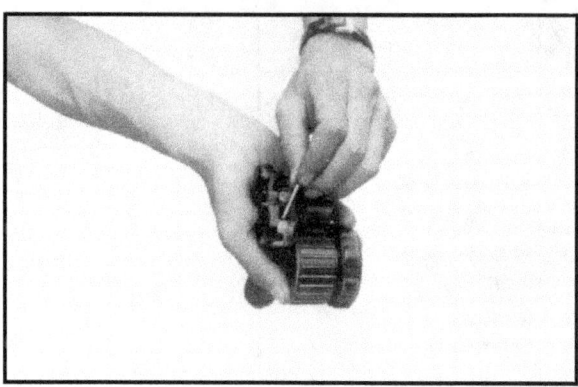

Fig. 4-3-5

3) Remove the circlip with the special tool (Circlip remover ① 19920 - 73110).

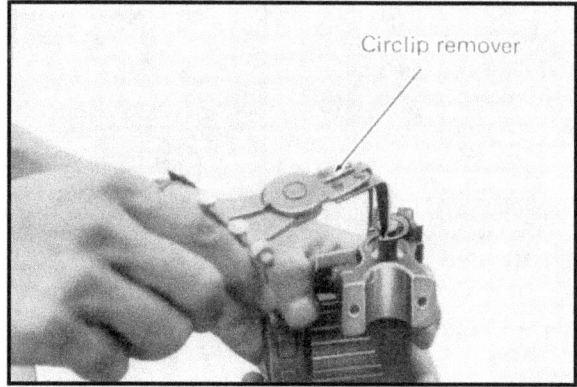

Fig. 4-3-6

4) Remove the piston, primary cup, spring and check valve.
5) Put the removed parts into a clean container and wash them in new brake fluid.

Caution: Never wash them in gasoline or petroleum; otherwise such fluid will damage rubber parts.

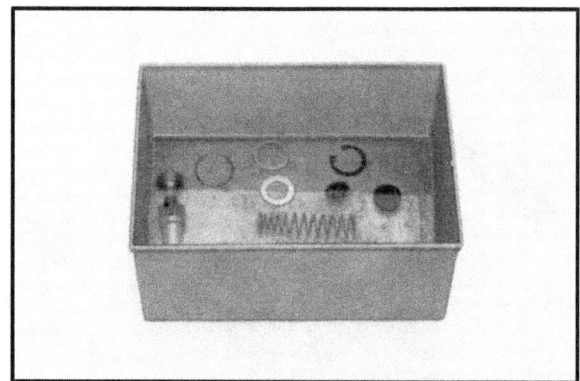

Fig. 4-3-7

4-3-4 Checking master cylinder

Replace the following parts with new one if any abnormality is found.

1) Master cylinder: Measure inner diameter of the master cylinder with an inside dial indicator.

Standard	Limit	Model
14.00 to 14.04 mm (0.551 to 0.553 in.)	Over 14.05 mm (0.553 in.)	GT125 GT185 GT250 GT380 GT550
15.87 to 15.91 mm (0.625 to 0.626 in.)	Over 15.92 mm (0.627 in.)	GT750

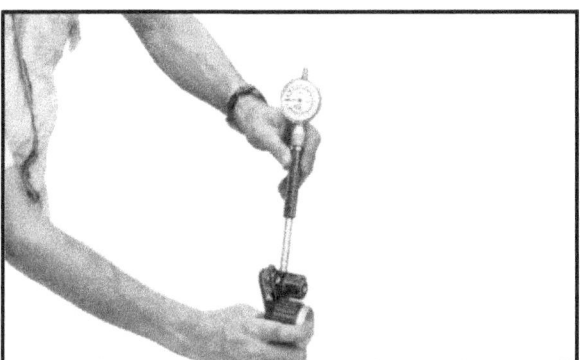

Fig. 4-3-8

2) Piston: Measure outer diameter of the piston.

Standard	Limit	Model
13.96 to 13.98 mm (0.550 to 0.551 in.)	Under 13.94 mm (0.549 in.)	GT125 GT185 GT250 GT380 GT550
15.83 to 15.85 mm (0.623 to 0.624 in.)	Under 15.81 mm (0.622 in.)	GT750

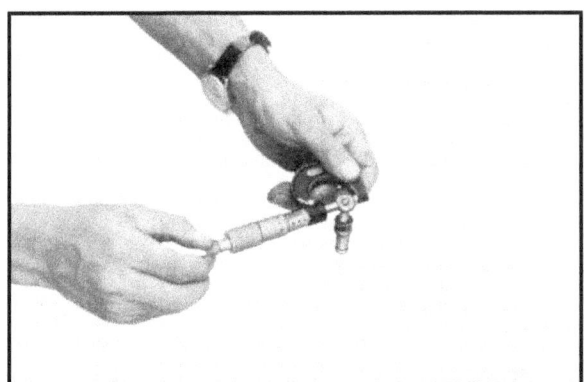

Fig. 4-3-9

3) Check valve: Inspect the check valve for operation.
4) O-ring (For models GT125L, GT185L, GT250L, GT380L, GT550L and GT750L):

Check the mating surfaces of the plastic reservoir and master cylinder proper for oil leaking.

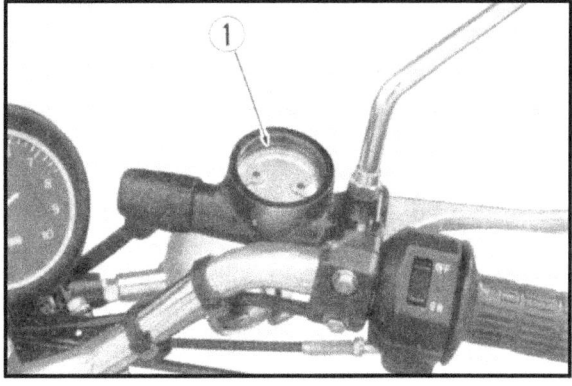

Fig. 4-3-10

4-3-5 Assembling master cylinder

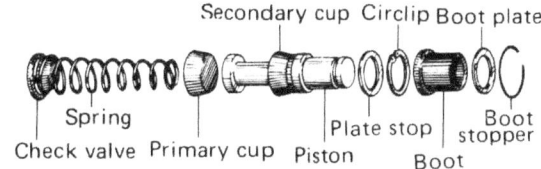

Fig. 4-3-11

Follow the removal procedures in the reverse order. When assembling them, pay attention to the following points.

1) Do not confuse the directions of assembling the primary cup. Refer to Fig. 4-3-11.
2) Replace a cotter pin of the brake lever pivot nut with new one and fit it securely.
3) Mount the master cylinder to the handlebar so that a gap between it and the switch box is about 2 mm (0.08 in.) and the reservoir becomes horizontal when the motorcycle is held on the center stand and steering is kept in a straight-on direction. Refer to Fig. 4-3-12.

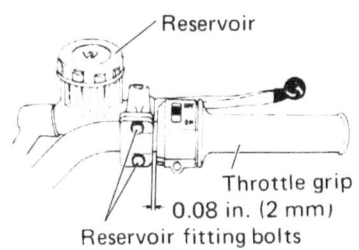

Fig. 4-3-12

4-3-6 Master cylinder identification mark

Cylinder bore of the master cylinder for model GT750 is larger than that for model GT125, GT185, GT250, GT380 or GT550. In order to easily distinguish the master cylinder for model GT750 from those for other models, an identification mark "D" is punched on the back of the reservoir.

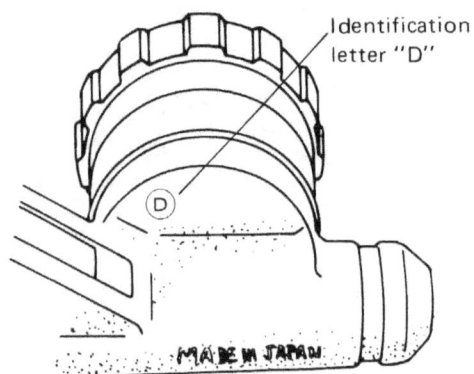

Fig. 4-3-13

4-3-7 Checking brake hose and pipe

Always check for the following items and replace immediately if any abnormality is found.
1) Damage to or swell of brake hose and/or pipe.
2) Traces of wear on the brake hose and/or pipe in contact with other parts.
3) Rusty brake pipe.
4) Fluid leakage at any joint of brake pipes and/or hose.

Note: If leakage should be found at any joint, retighten the bolts and nuts to the specified tightening torque. (Refer to page 24.)

4-3-8 Assembling brake hose and pipe

When connecting the brake hose and pipe, pay attention to the following points.
1) Be sure to use new brake pipe at all times when the brake pipe is assembled, because the cut end of the used brake pipe has been flared along the shape of the caliper inlet or the brake hose outlet as shown in Fig. 4-3-14. If the used pipe is reinstalled as it is, the air-tightness of the connection decreases, causing the brake fluid leakage.

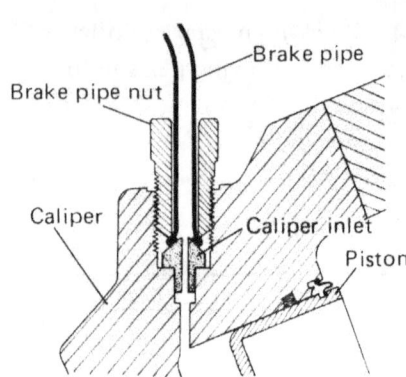

Fig. 4-3-14

2) When tightening two brake hose adapters, make sure that the hoses are free and not twisted. For models GT125L, GT185L, GT250K, GT380K, GT550K and GT750K which use brake pipe rather than hose, tighten the brake pipe adapter last of all. For models GT250L, GT380L, GT550L, and GT750L, first of all, remove twist from the hose, and then, tighten the hose joint with the brake hose adapter shown in Fig. 4-3-15.

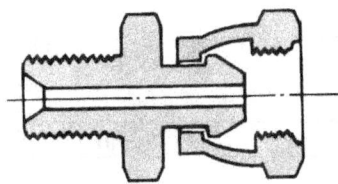

Fig. 4-3-15

3) When connecting the brake pipe to the caliper body, screw the nut in with your fingers to prevent stripping the threads, and then tighten it with a wrench to the specified torque.
4) Check that there is a generous space between each of them and the fuel tank, the front fork or other parts, and correct if any abnormality is found. Check that the hose or pipe does not contact any other parts particularly when the handlebar is turned fully to the right or left or when the front fork is brought down to the bottom.
5) After the assembling, check for no brake fluid leakage at any connection while holding the brake lever tightly.

4-4 Caliper

4-4-1 General

Index No.	Description
1	Caliper assembly
2	Caliper holder
3	Caliper stopper
4	Stopper rubber
5	Piston
6	Piston seal
7	Pad No.1 (moving side)
8	Pad No.2 (stationary side)
9	Screw
10	Lock washer
11	Caliper axle
12	Axle dust cover
13	Caliper axle "O" ring
14	Piston boot
15	Bleeder cap
16	Bleeder
17	Bolt
18	Washer
19	Lock washer
20	Caliper emblem

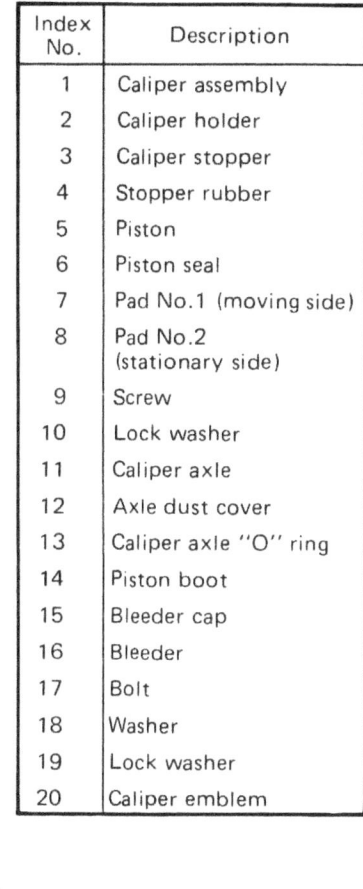

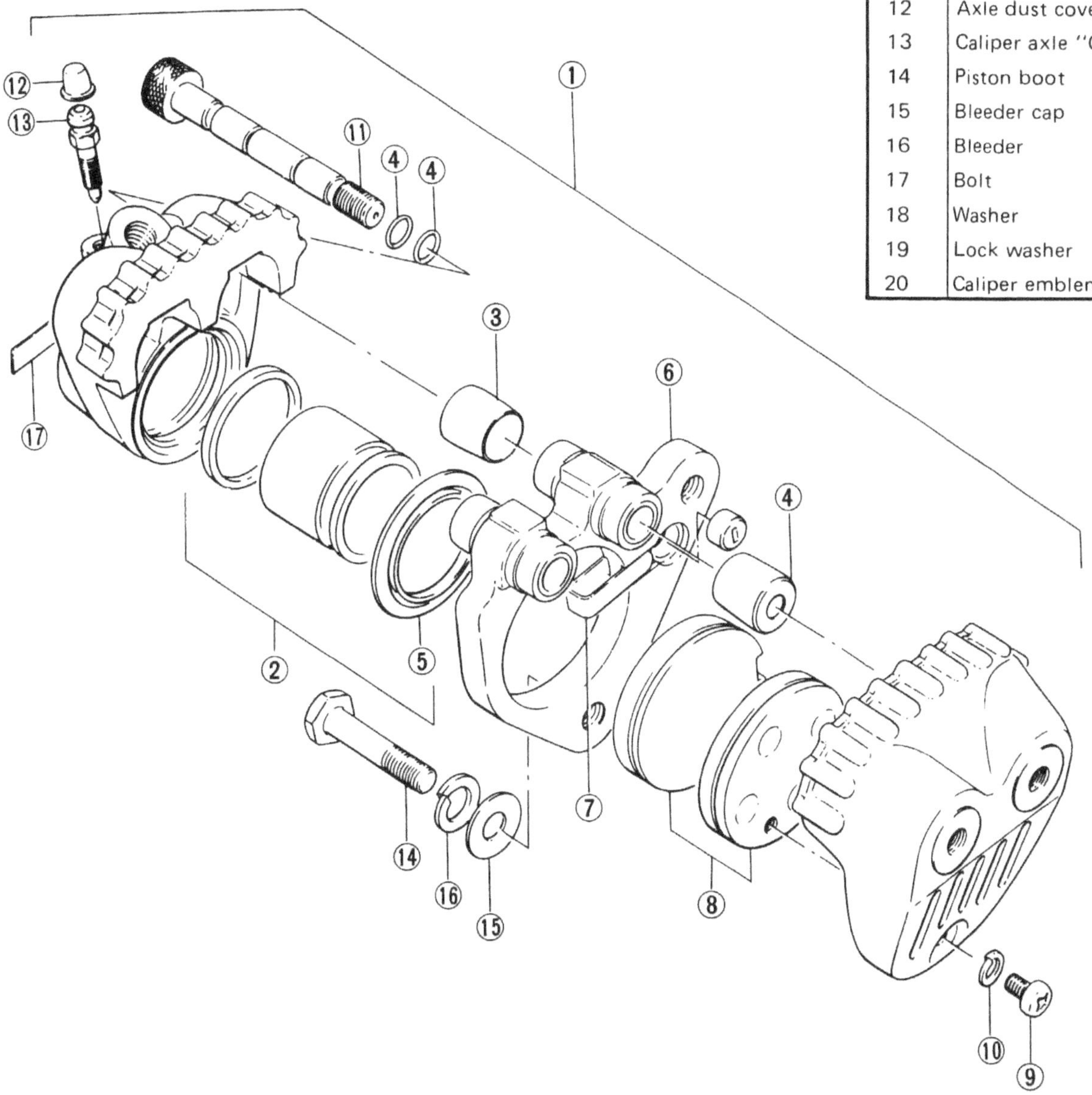

Fig. 4-4-1

4-4-2 Removing
1) Unscrew the brake pipe nut and caliper fastening bolts.
2) Pull out the caliper body from the disc plate.

4-4-3 Disassembling
1) Unscrew the caliper axle bolts with a special tool (8 mm hexagon L-type wrench 09900-06904) and separate the inner caliper body from the outer body.

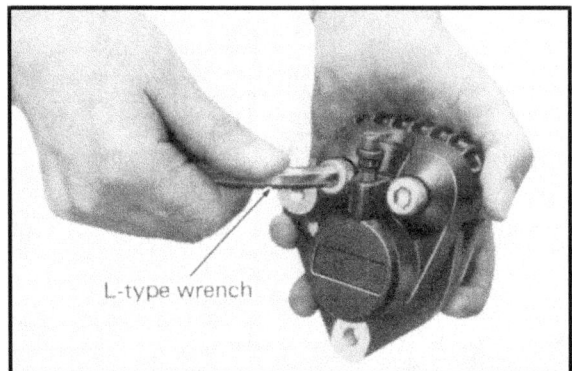

Fig. 4-4-2

2) Remove the caliper holder.
3) Remove "O" rings on the caliper axle.
4) Remove the caliper axles.
5) Remove the piston boot.
6) Push out the piston with compressed air while holding it with finger to prevent it from blowing out.

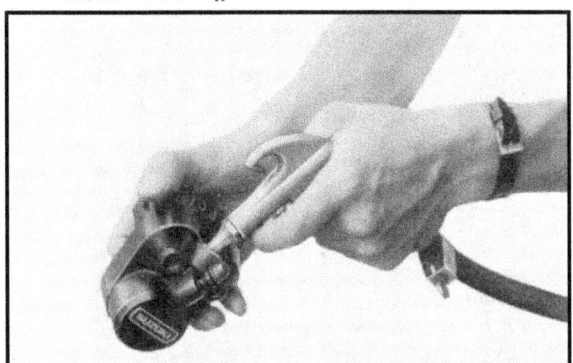

Fig. 4-4-3

7) Remove the piston seal as shown in Fig. 4-4-4.
8) Wash the piston, piston boot, piston seal and "O" rings of the caliper axles with new brake fluid. See Fig. 4-4-5.

Caution: Never use gasoline or petroleum; otherwise rubber parts will be damaged.
Do not wash the pads and also take care that brake fluid is not splashed onto the pads.

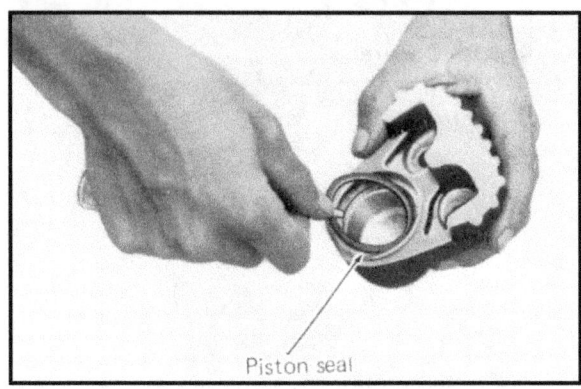

Fig. 4-4-4

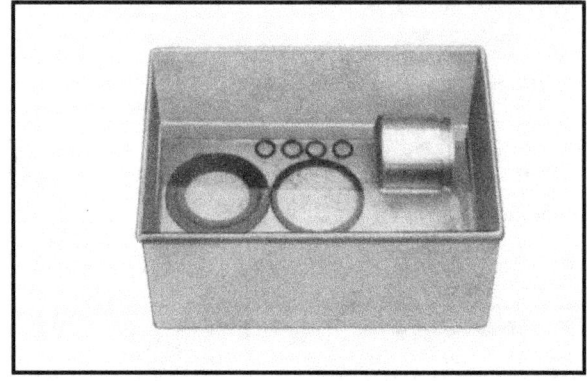

Fig. 4-4-5

4-4-4 Checking
When disassembling the caliper, check the following points and replace if any abnormality is found.

1) Cylinder: Its inner diameter is not worn out of its limit.

Standard	Limit	Model
38.18 to 38.20 mm (1.503 to 1.504 in.)	Over 38.22 mm (1.504 in.)	GT125 GT185 GT250 GT380 GT550 GT750

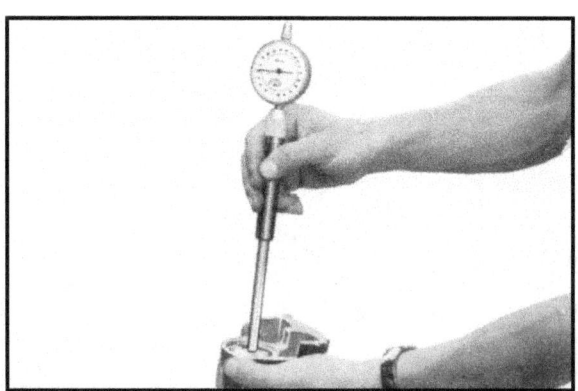

Fig. 4-4-6

2) Piston: Its outer diameter is not worn out of its limit.

Standard	Limit	Model
38.15 to 38.18 mm (1.502 to 1.503 in.)	Under 38.10 mm (1.500 in.)	GT125 GT185 GT250 GT380 GT550 GT750

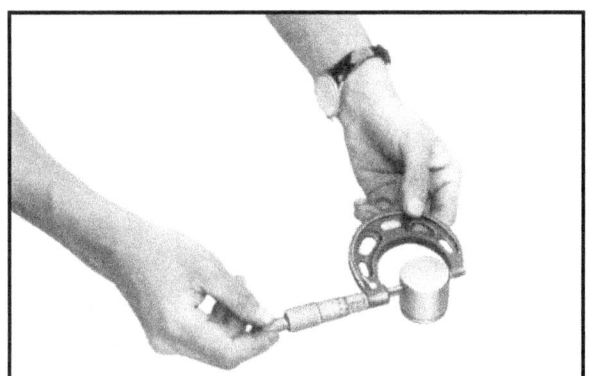

Fig. 4-4-7

3) Piston seal: No damage nor excessive wear
4) Piston boot: No damage nor settling
5) Pads Nos. 1 and 2: Not worn out of its limit (refer to "4-2-1 Inspecting of Pads").
6) Caliper body: No crack

4-4-5 Assembling

Follow the removal procedure in the reverse order. When assembling them, pay attention to the following points.

1) Apply "Suzuki Caliper Axle Grease" with property of high heat resistance onto the caliper axle.

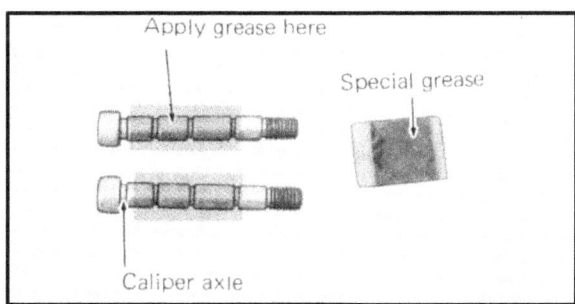

Fig. 4-4-8

2) Apply a generous amount of brake fluid onto the inner surface of the cylinder and periphery of the piston and then assemble.
3) Do not assemble the piston seal with it inclined or twisted. See Fig. 4-4-9.

4) In installing the piston, push it slowly into the cylinder while taking care not to damage the piston seal.

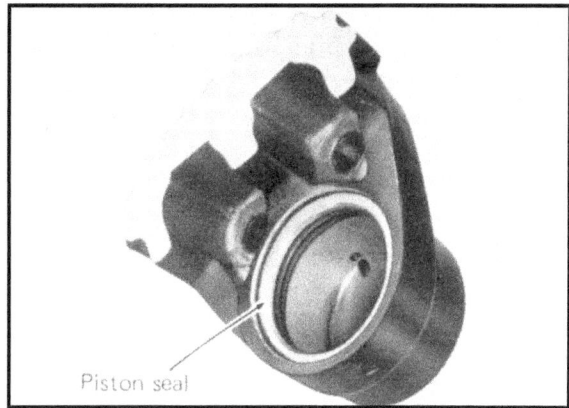

Fig. 4-4-9

5) Apply "Suzuki Brake Pad Grease" shown in Fig. 4-4-10 onto the periphery of pad No. 1 (refer to "4-2-2 Replacing of Pads").

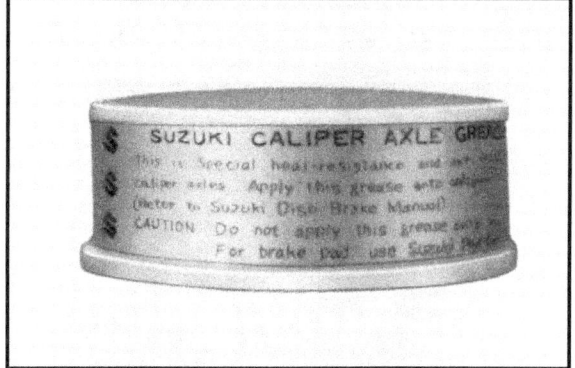

Fig. 4-4-10

6) Bleed air after assembling (refer to "4-1-2 Air bleeding from brake system").
7) After bleeding air, check for brake fluid leakage while holding the brake lever tightly.
8) After a test run, check the pads and brake disc do not press each other excessively by turning the front wheel by hand.

4-5 Brake Disc

4-5-1 General
The brake disc, made of stainless steel having excellent heat-resistance and abrasion-proof properties, is fastened to the front hub with six high tensile strength bolts.

4-5-2 Checking
1) Runout of the brake disc should not be greater than the limit. Measure brake disc runout with a dial indicator as shown in Fig. 4-5-1. If the runout is over the limit on the largest periphery of the disc plate, check whether the cause lies in the front wheel bearing or the brake disc itself, and replace defective parts.

Standard	Limit	Model
0.1 mm (0.004 in.)	0.3 mm (0.012 in.)	GT125 GT185 GT250 GT380 GT550 GT750

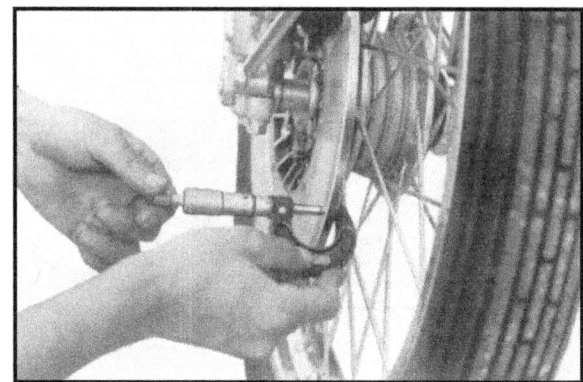

Fig. 4-5-2

Fig. 4-5-1

2) Thickness of the brake disc should not be less than the limit. Measure its worn portion with a micrometer as shown in Fig. 4-5-2 and replace the brake disc if the thickness is less than the limit.

Standard	Limit	Model
5.00 mm (0.197 in.)	Under 4.00 mm (0.157 in.)	GT125 GT185
7.00 mm (0.276 in.)	Under 6.00 mm (0.236 in.)	GT250 GT380 GT550 GT750

3) Surface of the brake disc should be free from oil. Take care that no oil is adhered on the brake disc surface, since oil adhesion there is very dangerous. If oil is placed on the disc by mistake, wipe off the oil with a soft waste-cloth soaked with alcohol.
4) The brake disc fitting bolts should be securely tightened to the specified torque and should be secured with lock washers.

Fig. 4-5-3

4-6 Periodic Replacement Parts

The component parts of the master cylinder assembly and the caliper assembly may be worn and deteriorated in function in long period of use. However, it is generally difficult to foresee how long each component will further work with proper function thereafter, since deterioration of function much depends upon usage of brake by individual motorcycle.
Then, from safety points of view, the following is defined as periodic replacement parts in order to prevent unforeseen trouble caused by wearing of component.
Replace all the following parts at a time with Suzuki genuine parts sets.

Exchange interval: Two years

1. Components of master cylinder assembly
   (Use Suzuki Genuine parts: Master cylinder cup set)

   1. Primary cup
   2. Spring
   3. Piston
   4. Check valve
   5. Circlip
   6. Boot plate
   7. Boot
   8. Stop plate
   9. Boot stopper

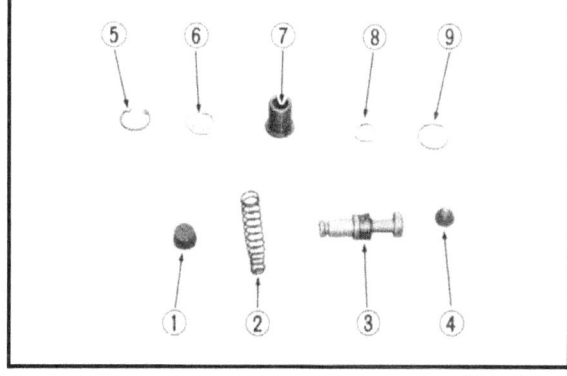

Fig. 4-6-1

2. Component of caliper assembly
   (Use Suzuki Genuine parts: Pad and piston set)

   1. "O" ring
   2. Stopper
   3. Piston seal
   4. Boot
   5. Piston
   6. Suzuki Caliper Axle Grease
   7. Axle shaft dust cover
   8. Pad No. 1
   9. Pad No. 2
   10. Suzuki Brake Pad Grease

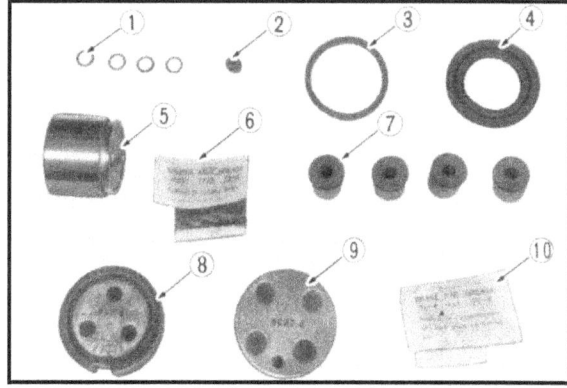

Fig. 4-6-2

Note: Pad and piston set includes two kinds of grease packed in pouch. Grease in the pouch printed "Caliper Axle Grease" should be used for the caliper axle and printed "Brake Pad Grease" for the pad No. 1.

Caution: Be sure to wash all component parts in the above sets with clean brake fluid before installing them into the master cylinder or caliper.

5. TIGHTENING TORQUE

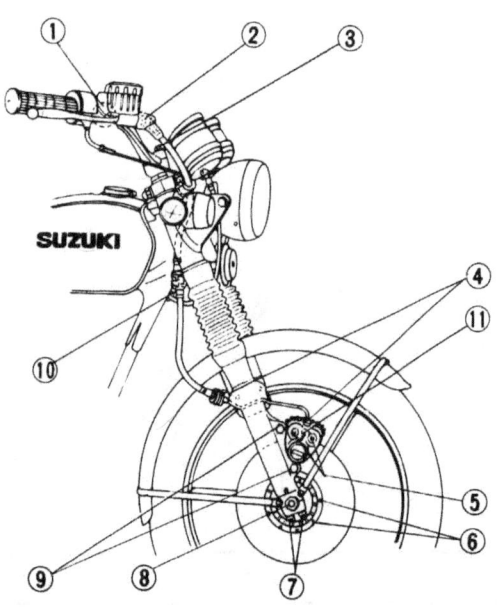

Fig. 5-1-1

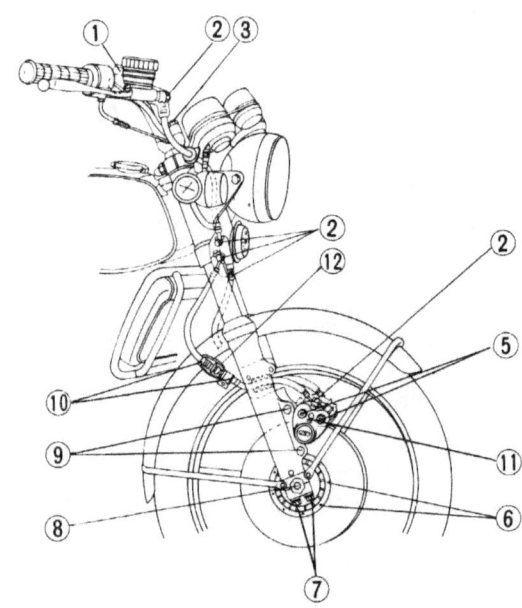

Fig. 5-1-2

Item No.	Description	Bolt-and nut diameter	Tightening torque	
		mm	kg-cm	ft-lb
1	Master cylinder clamp bolt	6	50 to 80	3.6 to 5.8
2	Union bolt	10	150 to 250	11 to 18
3	Handlebar clamp bolt	8	120 to 200	9 to 14
4	Brake pipe nut	10	130 to 180	9.5 to 13
5	Caliper axle bolt	10	250 to 350	18 to 25
6	Brake disc fitting bolt	8	150 to 250	11 to 18
7	Front axle holder nut	8	150 to 250	11 to 18
8	Front axle shaft nut	12	360 to 520	26 to 38
9	Caliper fitting bolt	10	250 to 400	18 to 29
10	Brake hose joint	10	250 to 350	18 to 25
11	Bleeder bolt	7	60 to 90	4.3 to 6.5
12	Adaptor	10	250 to 300	18 to 22

6. SPECIAL TOOLS FOR DISC BRAKE

6-1 Special tools

The following special tools are necessary for disassembling and reassembling disc brakes. Please use these special tools to ensure your operation.

Part No.	Description	Used for
09920-73110	Special circlip opener	Disassembling master cylinder
09900-06904	8 mm hexagon L-type wrench	Disassembling caliper

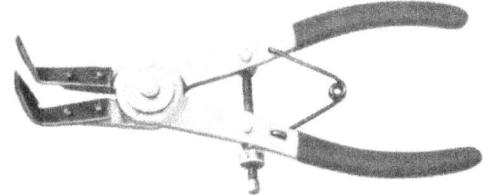

Special circlip opener   Fig. 6-1-1

8 mm hexagon L-type wrench   Fig. 6-1-2

6-2 Necessary materials

The two types of grease shown in the following table are applied to the moving parts when overhauling the disc brake. These grease feature their high lubrication and pressure withstanding performances even at a high temperature, and further, they do not affect rubber parts. When overhauling the disc brake, do not use other grease but these two types only.

Part No.	Description	Use
99000-25100	Suzuki brake pad grease	Lubrication of pad No.1
99000-25110	Suzuki caliper axle grease	Lubrication of caliper axle

Suzuki brake pad grease   Fig. 6-2-1

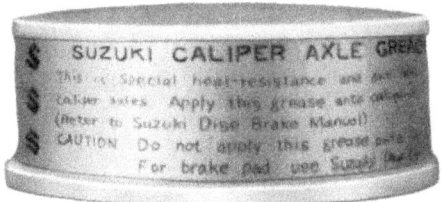

Suzuki caliper axle grease   Fig. 6-2-2

≋ SUZUKI MOTOR CO., LTD.

SUZUKI SERVICE MANUAL

MODEL
GT550
VM28SC CARBURETOR

FOREWORD

This manual is published for the information and use of the personnel who are concerned in the maintenance of the VM24SC and VM28SC Carburetors used on the 1974 Suzuki GT380L and GT550L. The manual applies only to the carburetors and is prepared for use with the manuals published for the motorcycles.

It has its own index and contains a description of the major components and their functions as well as maintenance.

All information, illustrations and specifications contained in this manual are based on the products manufactured before Nov., 1974. Any changes, deletions or additions to this manual will be followed by the Service Bulletin.

Feb., 1974

SUZUKI MOTOR CO., LTD.

INDEX

SUZUKI TYPE VM CARBURETOR FOR GT380 & GT550

CHAPTER 1. DESCRIPTION 1
    1. Operation 2
    2. Specifications 7
    3. Troubleshooting Guide 7
    4. Special Tools, Adhesive and Grease 8

CHAPTER 2. REPAIR AND ADJUSTMENT 9
    1. Disassembly 9
    2. Inspections 11
    3. Assembly and Adjustment 12
    4. Carburetor Adjustment 18

CHAPTER 1. DESCRIPTION

The Model VM24SC and VM28SC Carburetors currently used on the Suzuki GT380L and GT550L are of an AMAL type carburetor with an independent starting circuit. It also includes an additional system of linkage to force the throttle valve to the closed position to provide for sticky valve or broken valve return spring.

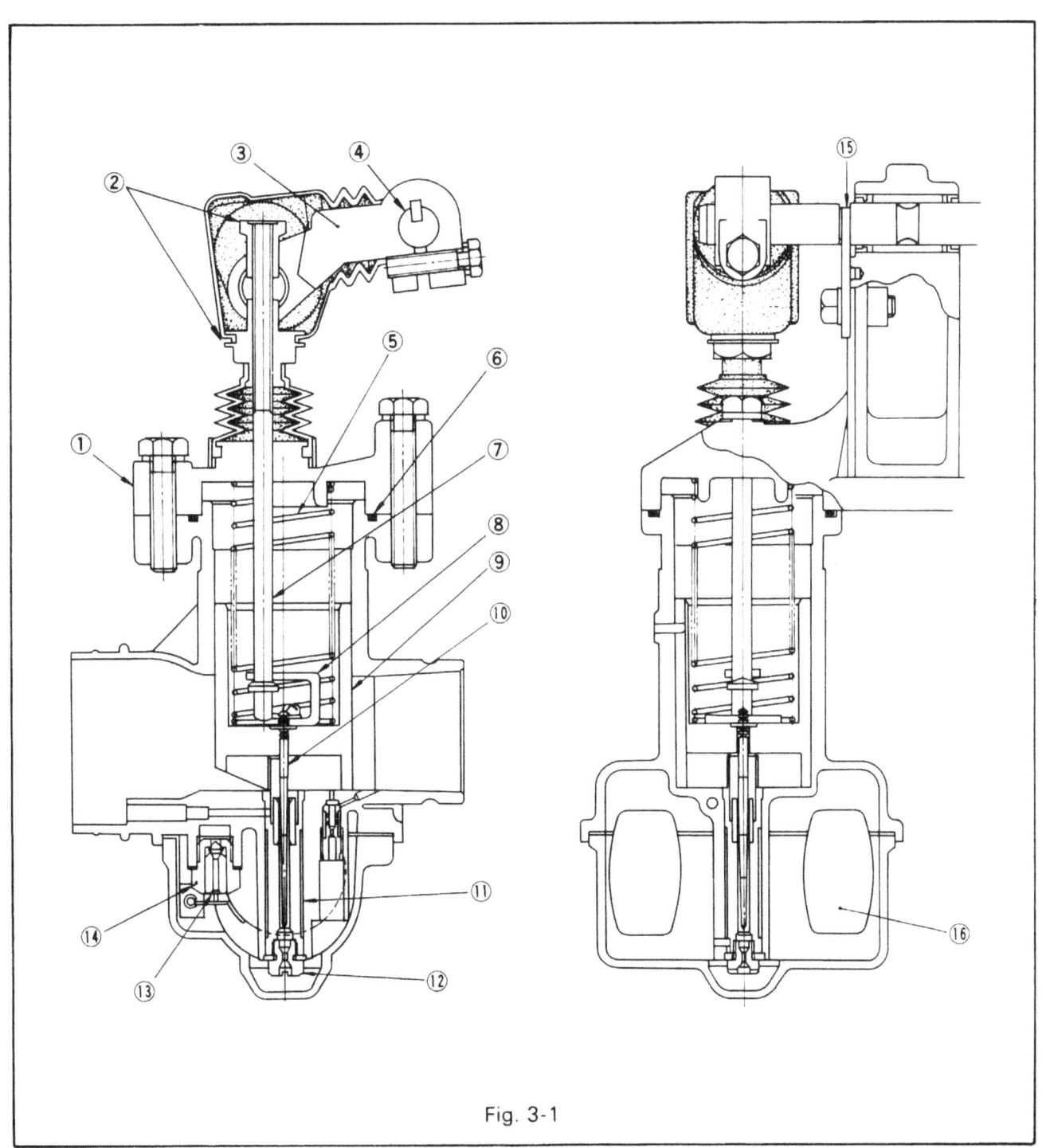

Fig. 3-1

1. Mixing chamber top
2. Throttle valve adjust nut
3. Throttle valve arm
4. Throttle valve shaft
5. Throttle valve spring
6. O-ring
7. Throttle valve rod
8. Jet needle set plate
9. Throttle valve
10. Jet needle
11. Needle jet
12. Main jet
13. Needle valve
14. Valve seat
15. Shaft stop plate
16. Float

1. Operation

a) Forced throttle-return system

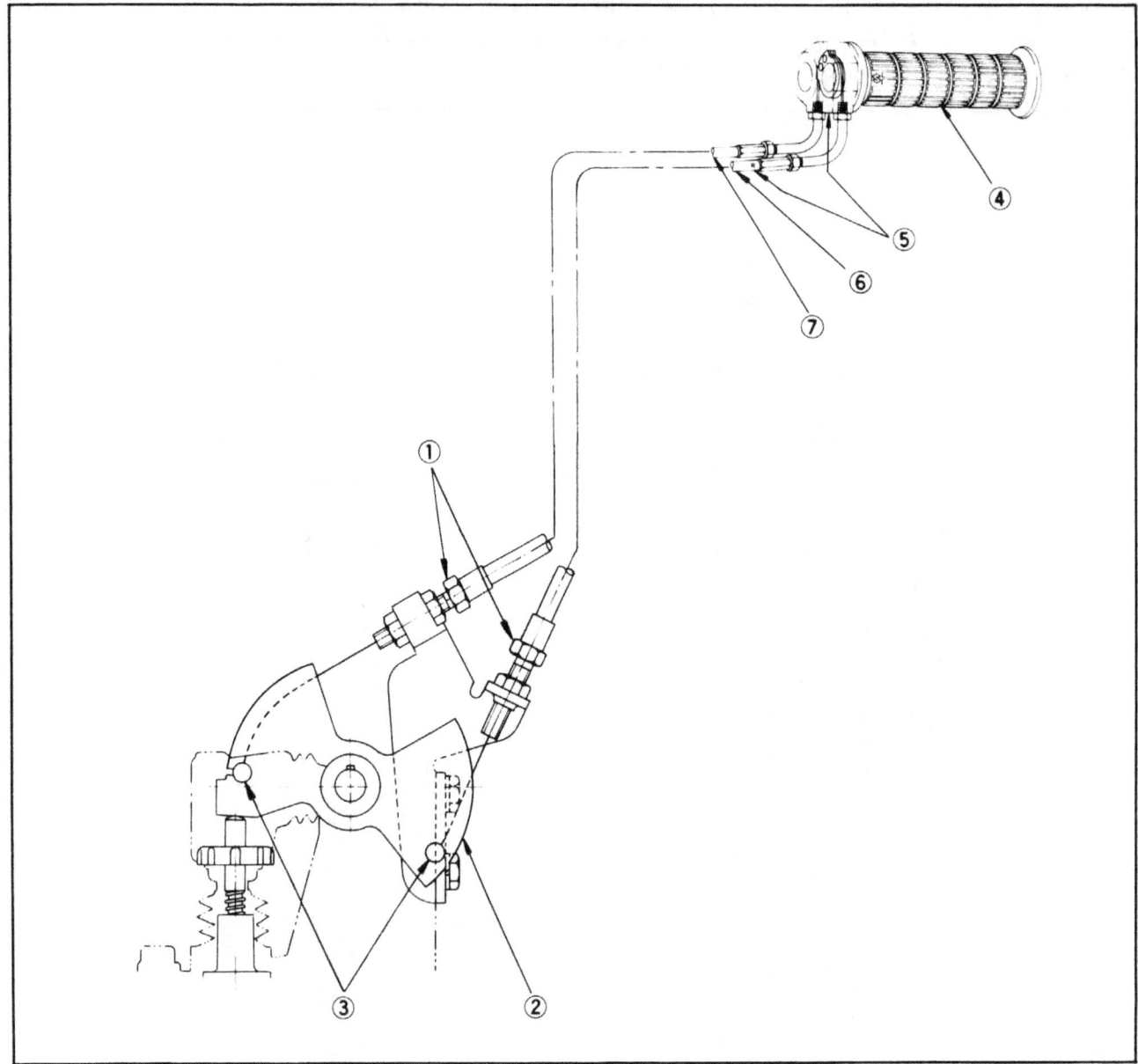

Fig. 3-2

1. Throttle cable adjuster
2. Pulley
3. Cable end
4. Throttle grip
5. Identification letter "R" (return side)
6. Throttle cable (return side)
7. Throttle cable (pull side)

The forced throttle-return system provides an added means of returning the throttle valve to the closed position. Fig. 1 shows an exaggerated view of the system to understand the operation that takes place when the system is operated.

When the throttle grip is turned inward, the pulley is pulled up by a cable; i.e., the throttle is opened.

Now, when the grip is twisted outward, a spring produces some further closing of the throttle valve and spring-loads it in the closed position.

The system forces the throttle valve toward the closed position even when the valve has stuck or the spring has been broken.

b) Slow system

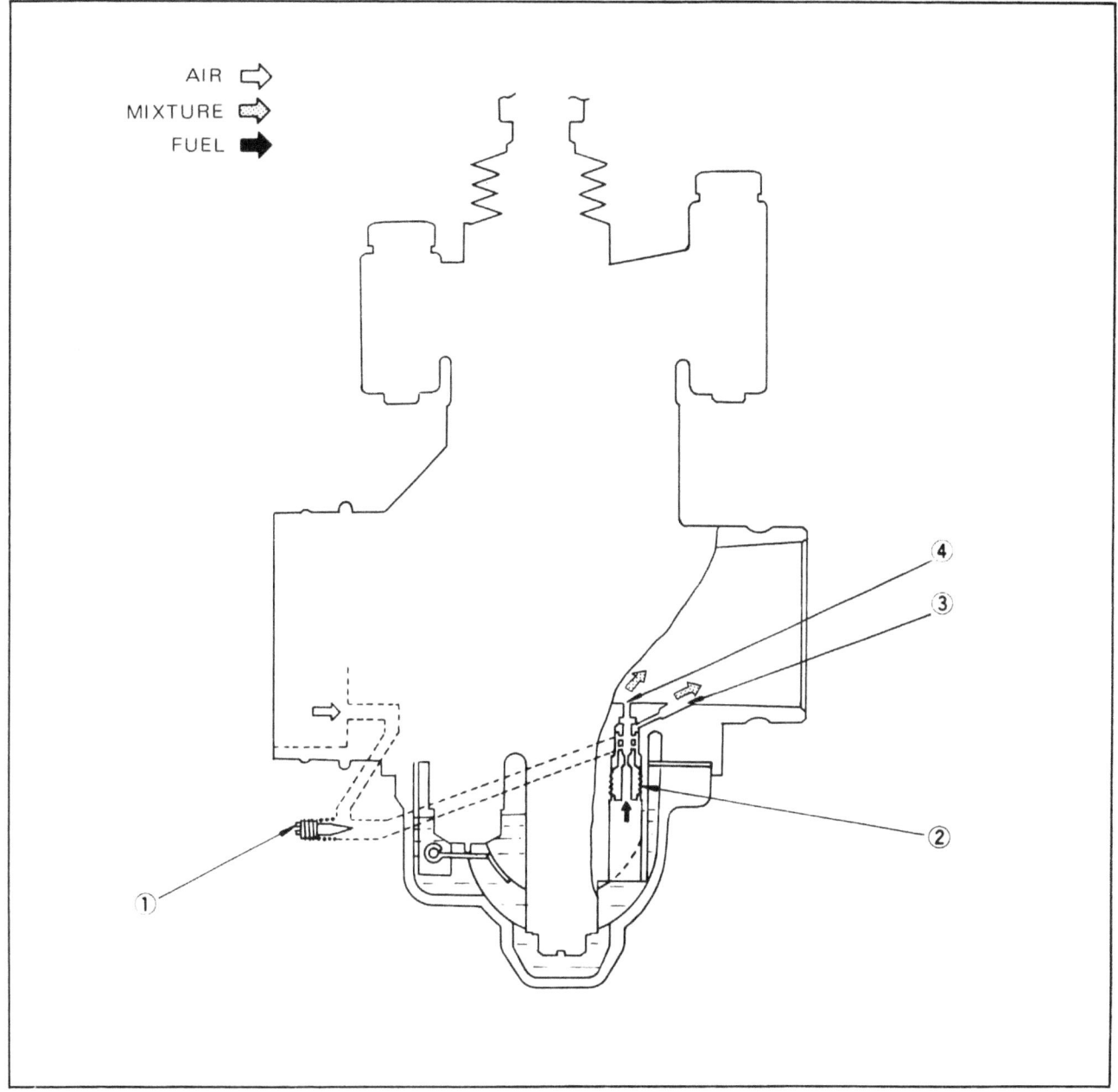

Fig. 3-3

1. Pilot air screw
2. Pilot jet
3. Bypass
4. Pilot outlet

When the throttle valve is closed or only slightly opened, the speed of air flowing through the air horn is low. As a result, there will be very little vacuum at the venturi to draw fuel from the needle jet. The slow system supplies fuel during operation with the throttle closed or almost closed.
The fuel from the float chamber is first metered by the pilot jet, where it mixes with air passing by the pilot air screw. The resultant mixture will then discharge out into the carburetor air horn through the pilot outlet and bypass port where it is to be mixed with the main incoming air stream passing through the throttle valve.

c) Main system

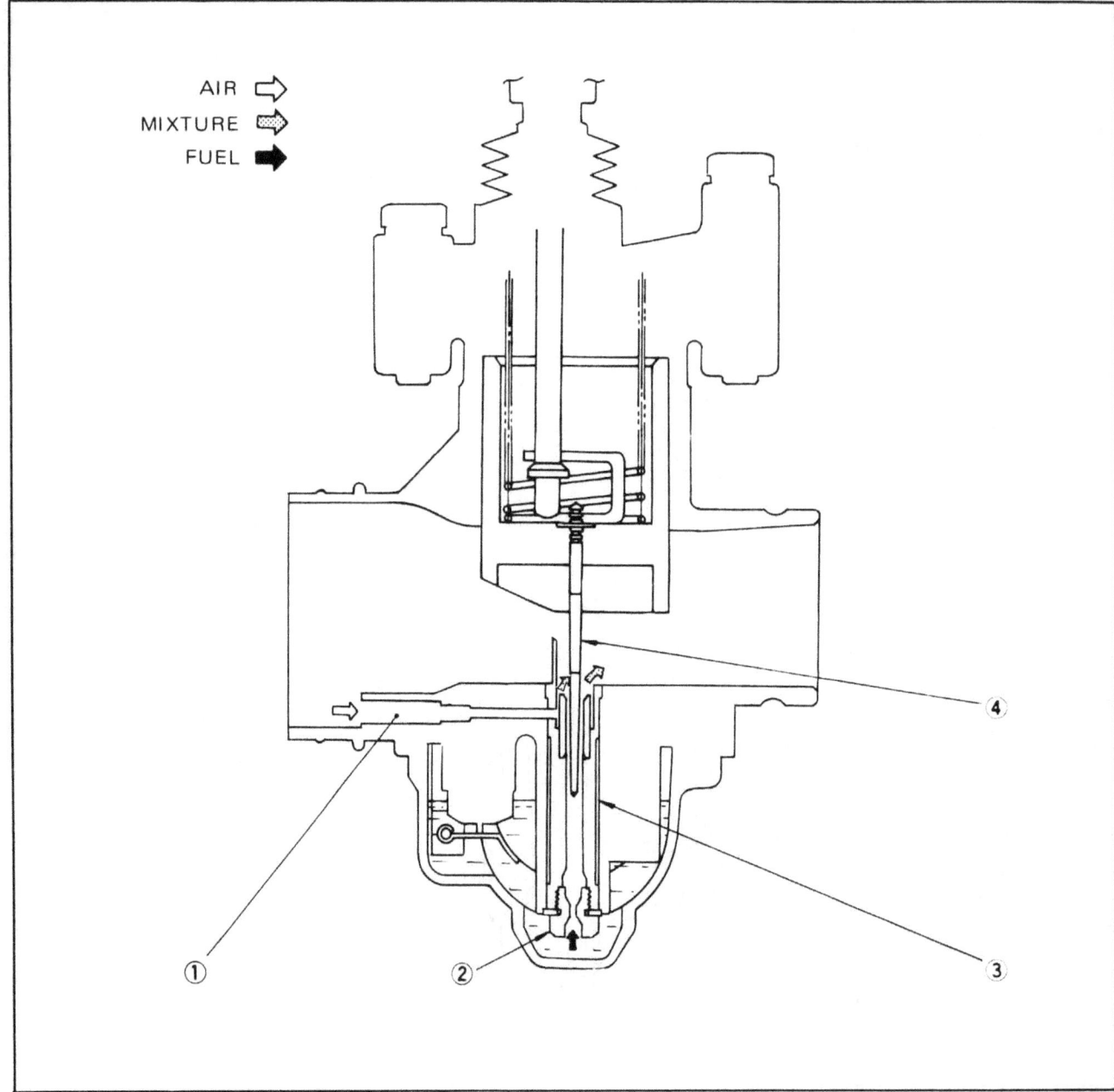

Fig. 3-4

1. Main air passage
2. Main jet
3. Needle jet
4. Jet needle

When the throttle is opened, the fuel in the float chamber is subject to strong engine suction since the vacuum at the venturi is increased.

The fuel in the float chamber is then metered by the main jet as it passes through it. The fuel is again metered by the clearance between the needle jet and jet needle, being mixed with air flowing from the main air passage. The mixture will then be discharged into the carburetor venturi. At the venturi, the mixture meets another air flowing from the main bore, being drawn into the engine.

The fuel is given correct mixture proportions as it passes through the needle jet since the effective size of the needle jet depends on the throttle position.

d) Starter system

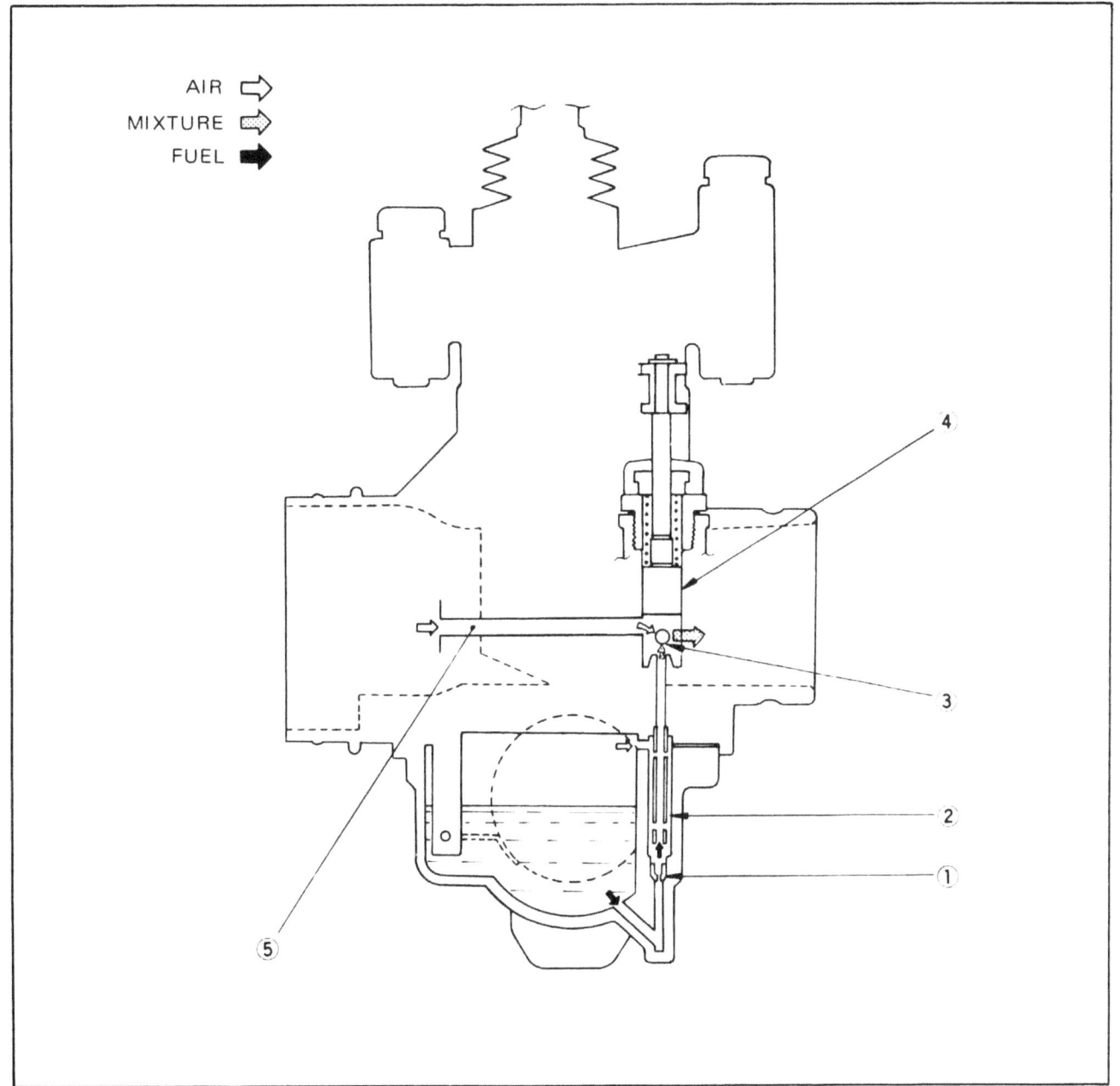

Fig. 3-5

1. Starter jet
2. Starter pipe
3. Starter outlet
4. Starter plunger
5. Starter air passage

When the choke lever at the left side of the carburetor is pulled up, the starter plungers are pushed up by the starter rod. The action allows the fuel to bleed into the starter circuit.

The starter jet is supplied with fuel directly from the float chamber. The fuel is first metered by the starter jet as it passes through it. The metered fuel then goes up into the starter pipe where it enters air from the float chamber.

This rich mixture meets air flowing from the starter air passage when it reaches the starter plunger chamber and is discharged through the starter outlet into the engine directly.

The right side carburetor receives the mixture from the starter system of the main carburetor through a pipe.

5

e) Float system

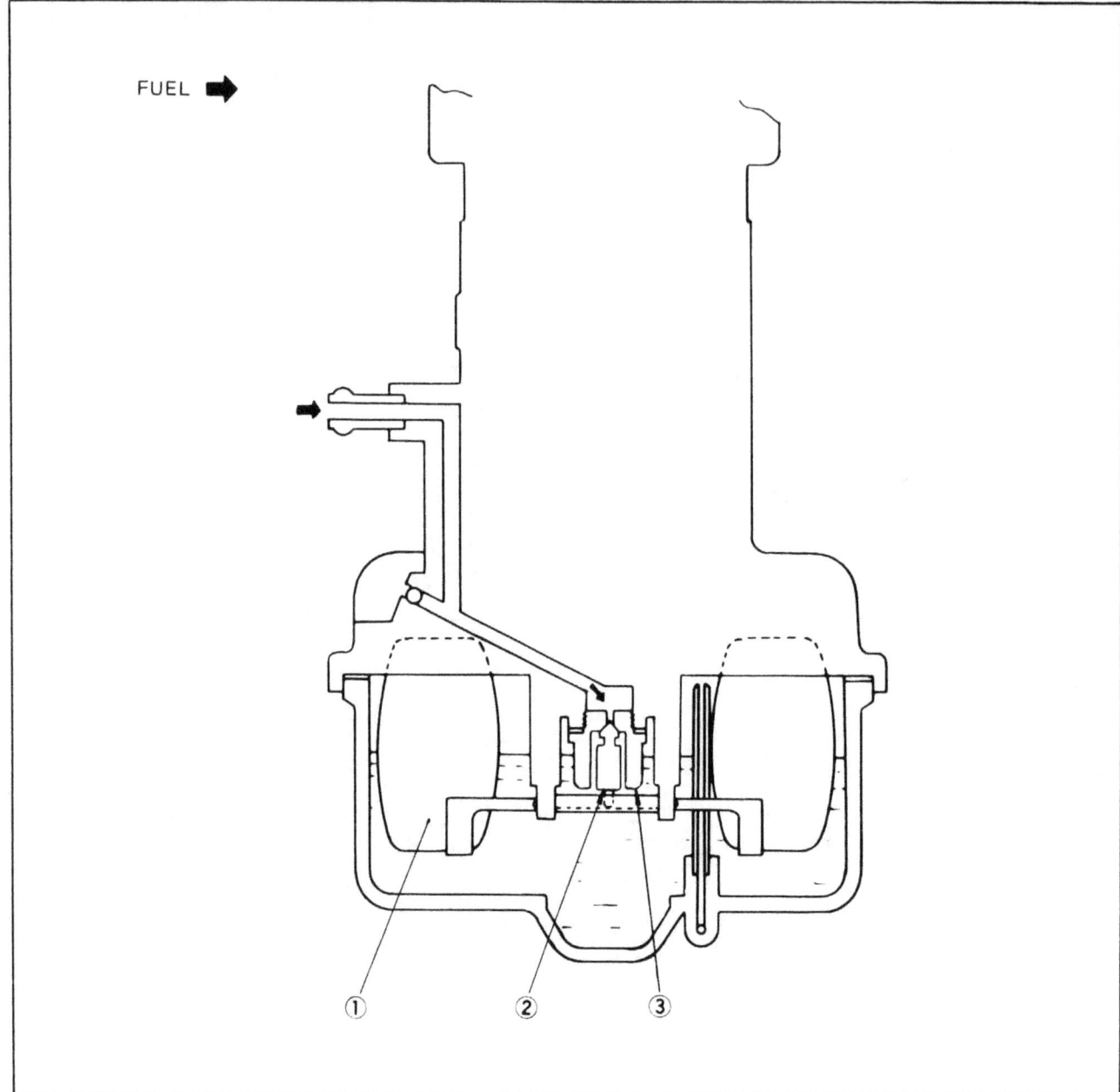

Fig. 3-6

1. Float
2. Needle valve
3. Valve seat

The float system consists of float, needle valve and valve seat, assembled to maintain a constant level of fuel in the float chamber. When fuel enters the float chamber, this causes the float to move up. The valve is so designed that, if the float moves up, it is pushed up into the valve seat. This shuts off the fuel inlet so that no fuel can enter. If the float level lowers, the float moves down; i.e., fuel can now enter since this releases the needle valve.
The same sequence of events takes place to maintain a constant level of fuel in the float chamber.

2. Specifications

		GT380	GT550
Type		VM24SC	VM28SC
Bore Size		24 mm	28 mm
Main Jet	R & L	#80	#97.5
	C	#80	#95
Jet Needle		4DH7-2nd	5DH21-4th
Needle Jet		O-2	P-0
Cutaway		3.0	2.5
Bypass		1.4 mm	1.4 mm
Pilot Outlet		0.8 mm	0.8 mm
Air Screw Opening		1 ¼	1 ½
Valve Seat		2.0 mm	2.0 mm
Starter Jet		#80	#90
Bypass		3.75 mm	5.15 mm
Float Level		25.75 mm	25.75 mm
Identification Mark		33110 R,M,L	34110 R,M,L

3. Troubleshooting Guide

Symptom	Probable Cause	Remedy
Rough idling or slow speed	1. Clogged pilot jet or loose pilot jet	Clean and retighten
	2. Leaky float chamber gasket	Retighten. If necessary, replace gasket
	3. Carburetor out of adjustment	Adjust
	4. Improper float level	Adjust. Check needle valve and float and, if necessary, replace
	5. Pilot air screw out of adjustment	Adjust
	6. Clogged bypass and pilot outlet	Clean
Improper part- and full-throttle operation	1. Clogged main jet	Clean or retighten
	2. Carburetor out of adjustment	Adjust
	3. Improper float level	Adjust. Check needle valve and float and, if necessary, replace
Hard starting (with choke lever in operation)	1. Improper throttle valve opening	Adjust
	2. Clogged starter jet	Clean
	3. Starter plunger out of order	Retighten starter rod screw

4. Special Tools, Adhesive and Grease

a) Throttle valve adjust tool
This tool is designed to adjust carburetor without removing it from the motorcycle. It is a combination of a 10 mm box wrench and plain head screwdriver.

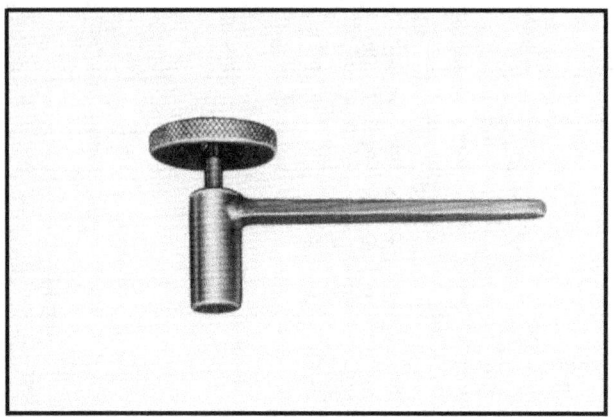

Fig. 3-6

Part Name	Throttle Valve Adjust Screw
Part No.	09913-13110

b) Thread lock cement

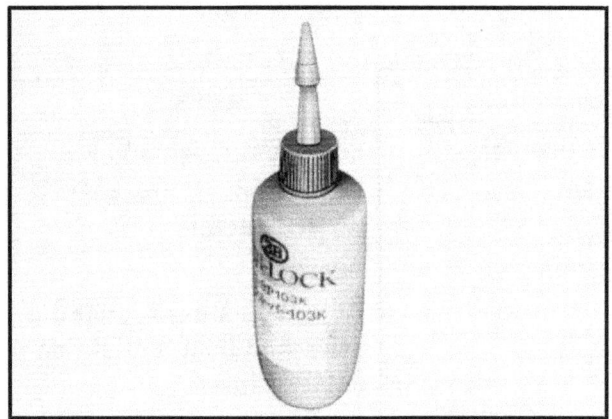

Fig. 3-7

Part Name	Thread Lock Cement "103K"
Part No.	99000-32030

The thread lock cement is used to lock the starter rod screw.

c) Grease

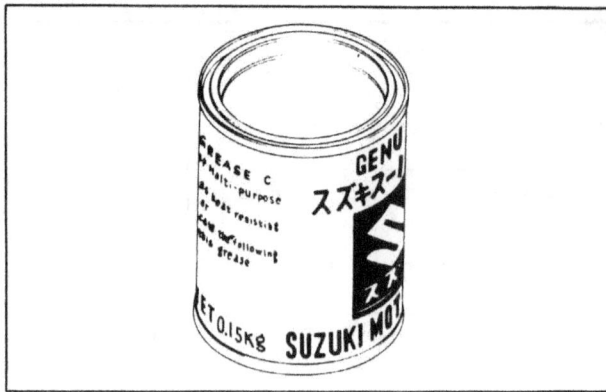

Fig. 3-8

Part Name	Suzuki Super Grease "C"
Part No.	99000-25030

Suzuki Super Grease "C" is used to lubricate the throttle valve rod and throttle valve arm.

CHAPTER 2. REPAIR AND ADJUSTMENT

1. **Disassembly**

a) Remove the fuel and vacuum hoses; take out the fuel tank. Remove the air cleaner.

| 1. Vacuum hose | 2. Fuel hose | Fig. 4-1 |

b) Loosen the throttle cable adjuster and disconnect the cable end from the pulley.

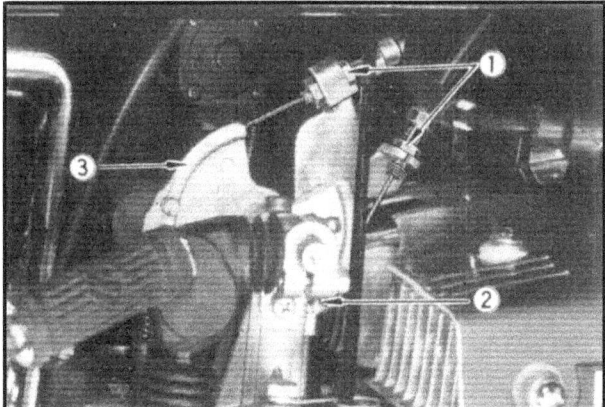

| 1. Throttle cable adjuster | 3. Pulley | Fig. 4-2 |
| 2. Cable end | | |

c) Loosen the clamp at the carburetor inlet and take out the carburetor.

d) Unscrew screw securing the choke lever in place to the carburetor.
Be careful when removing the lever since the steel ball is spring-loaded. Loosen the starter rod screws and pull off the starter rod.

| 1. Choke lever | 3. Starter rod | Fig. 4-3 |
| 2. Choke lever screw | 4. Starter rod screw | |

e) Remove the mixing chamber top complete with the throttle valve.

f) Remove the boot; loosen and upper and lower throttle valve adjust nuts. Separate the throttle valve from the chamber.

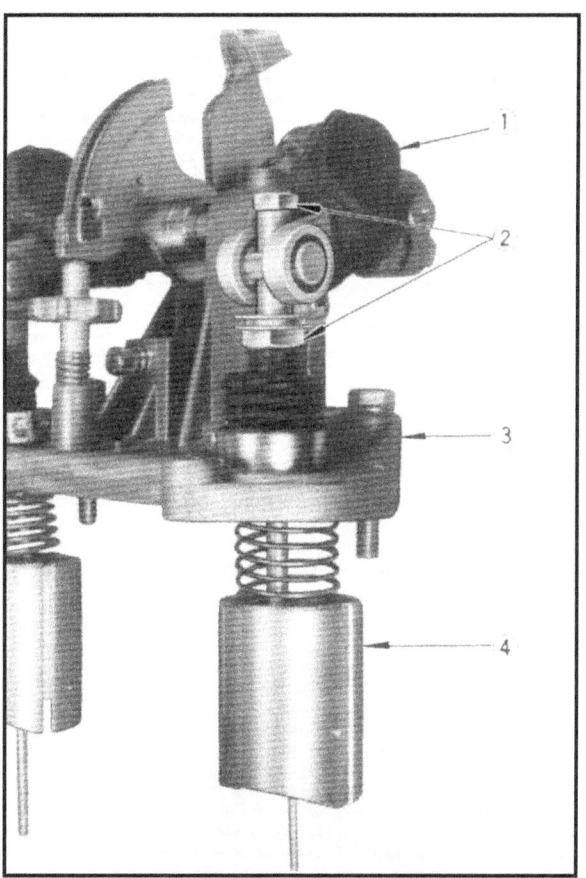

Fig. 4-4

| 1. Boot | 3. Mixing chamber top |
| 2. Throttle valve adjust nut | 4. Throttle valve |

g) Loosen the jet needle set plate screw inside the throttle valve.

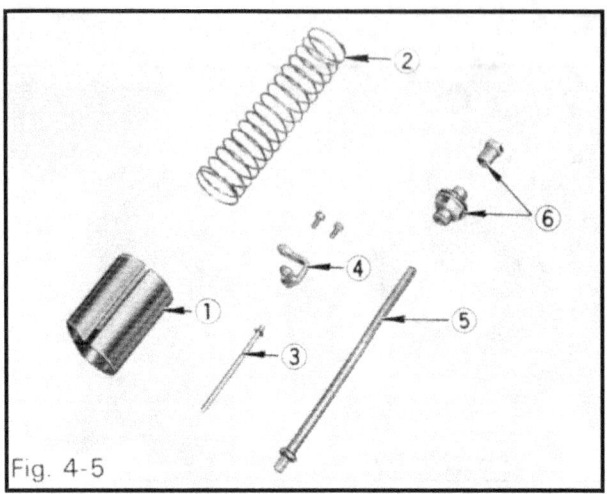

Fig. 4-5

1. Throttle valve
2. Throttle valve spring
3. Jet needle
4. Jet needle set plate
5. Throttle valve rod
6. Throttle valve adjust nut

h) Unscrew bolts securing the throttle valve arm and pulley in place; back off the throttle valve shaft stopper screw.

1. Throttle valve arm
2. Throttle valve shaft
3. Throttle valve shaft stopper
4. Pulley   Fig. 4-6

i) Pry off the woodruff key from the keyway in the throttle valve shaft while moving the pulley and throttle valve arm right and left. Remove shaft from the mixing chamber top.

1. Woodruff key   2. Throttle valve shaft   Fig. 4-7

j) Remove the float chamber; take out the main and pilot jets.

1. Main jet   2. Pilot jet   Fig. 4-8

k) Remove the main jet washer. Carefully drive out the needle jet toward the mixing chamber by tapping it on the bottom.

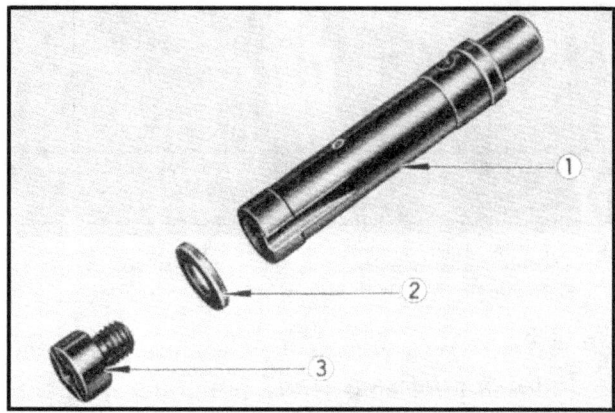

1. Needle jet   3. Main jet   Fig. 4-9
2. Main jet washer

2. Inspections

a) Throttle valve

Examine the throttle valve, and make sure that it is in good condition, particularly on its sliding surface.
Replace the carburetor as an assembled unit if the valve is scored or stepped excessively.

b) Needle valve and valve seat

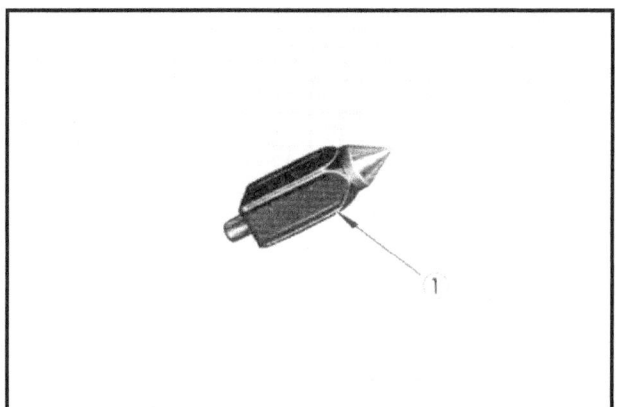

1. Needle valve   Fig. 4-10

Check the tapered point of the needle valve to see if it is not worn. If otherwise, replace the needle valve and valve seat as a set.

c) Float level

A. Float height   Fig. 4-11

Remove the float chamber and gasket. With the carburetor tilted at 10-30° from vertical, measure the distance from the gas- ket surface and top of the float. Adjustment can be made by bending the float arm as necessary.

Standard float height	25.75 ± 1 mm (1.01 ± 0.04 in)

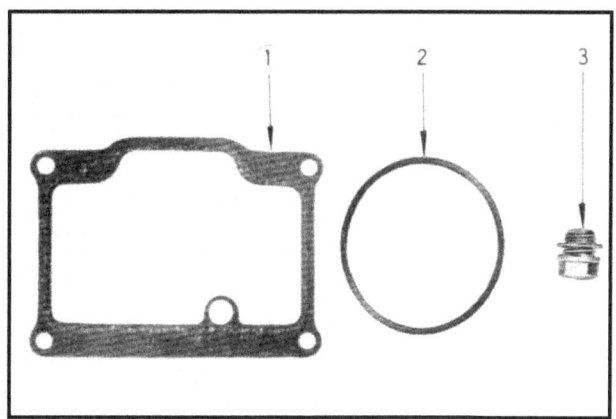

1. Float chamber gasket   3. Valve seat gasket
2. Mixing chamber top O-ring   Fig. 4-12

Check the float chamber gasket, mixing chamber O-ring and valve seat to be certain that these are not broken or weakened. If otherwise, discard the old ones and install new ones.

3. Assembly and Adjustment

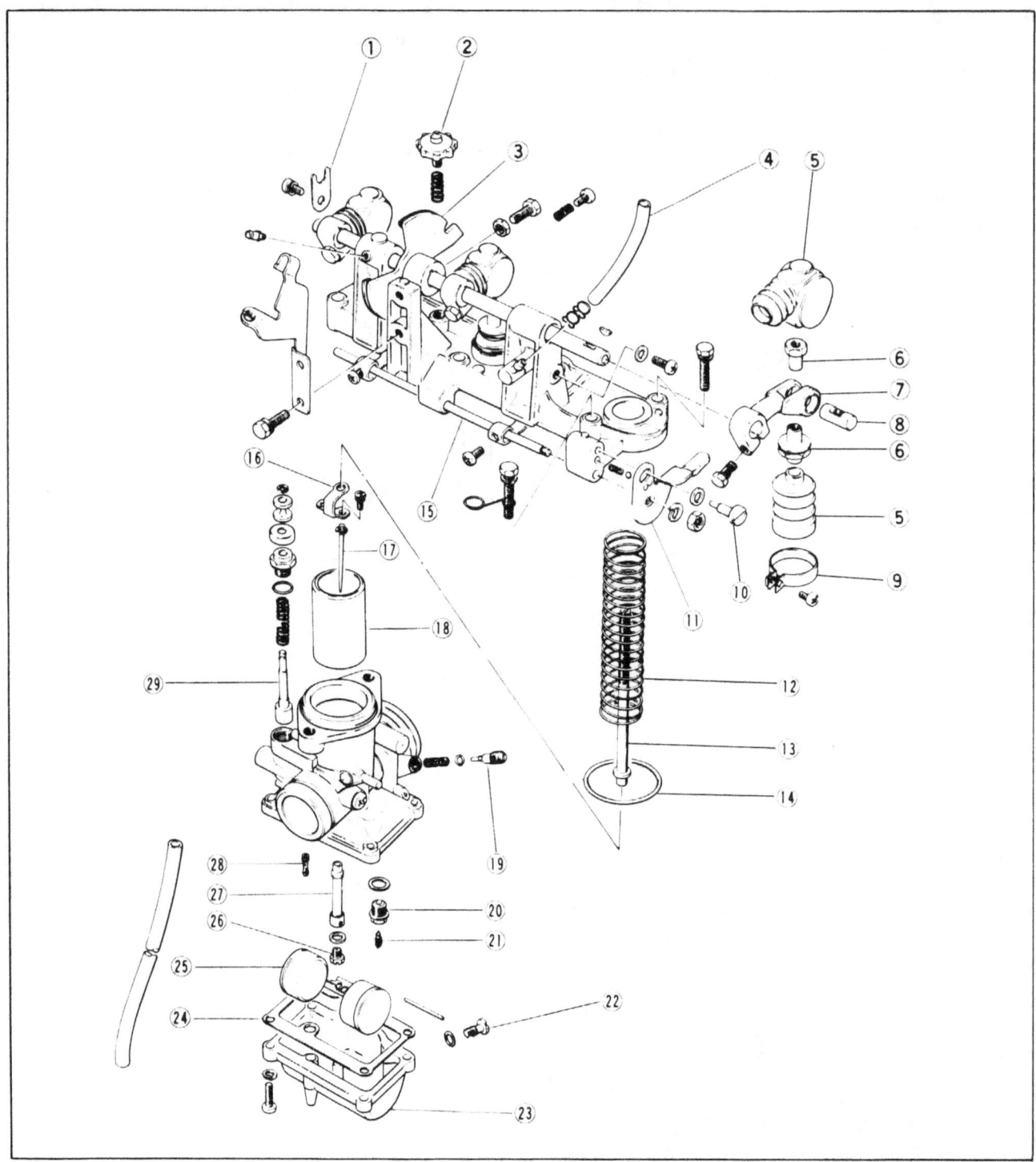

Fig. 4-13

1. Throttle valve shaft stopper
2. Throttle valve stop screw
3. Pulley
4. Vacuum hose
5. Boot
6. Throttle valve adjust nut
7. Throttle valve arm
8. Arm shaft
9. Clamp
10. Choke lever screw
11. Choke lever
12. Throttle valve spring
13. Throttle valve rod
14. Mixing chamber top O-ring
15. Starter rod
16. Jet needle set plate
17. Jet needle
18. Throttle valve
19. Pilot air screw
20. Valve seat
21. Needle valve
22. Drain plug
23. Float chamber
24. Float chamber gasket
25. Float
26. Main jet
27. Needle jet
28. Pilot jet
29. Starter plunger

Wash all parts in clean solvent and dry with compressed air.

a) Reaching from the mixing chamber side, install the needle jet in place.
   Make sure that the needle jet groove aligns with the needle jet holder dowel pin.

1. Dowel pin 2. Needle jet holder Fig. 4-14

b) Install the main and pilot jets in their respective positions.
c) Install the needle valve and float; place the float chamber in position.
d) Install the jet needle in the throttle valve; assemble the needle valve set plate and throttle valve rod with the throttle valve.
e) Position the pulley between the right mixing chamber top column and throttle cable bracket. Run the throttle valve shaft through the right column, pulley, throttle valve arm and left column.

Note:
Install the mixing chamber bolts before installing the throttle valve arm. If this caution is neglected, the bolt cannot be installed.

1. Throttle valve shaft   4. Mixing chamber top column
2. Throttle cable bracket 5. Mixing chamber top bolt
3. Pulley   Fig. 4-15

f) Press three woodruff keys in to place in the keyways in the throttle valve shaft. Install the pulley, being careful that the groove in the pulley is lined with the keys. Align lug of the throttle valve shaft stopper and hole in the mixing chamber top column; secure the throttle valve shaft.

1. Wooderuff key   3. Throttle valve shaft stopper
2. Lug   Fig. 4-16

g) Pump "Suzuki Super Grease C" through the grease fitting at the top column until excess grease shows out on the throttle vale shaft.

1. Grease fitting   Fig. 4-17

h) Approximate the pulley so that the thicker area is in line with the throttle valve stop screws. Secure the pulley with the pulley bolt, being careful not to disturb the above setup.

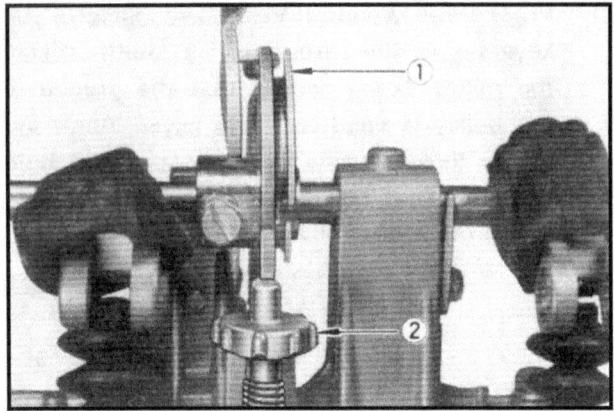

1. Pulley 2. Throttle valve stop screw Fig. 4-18

i) Apply a coating of "Suzuki Super Grease C" to the bearing surfaces of the throttle valve arm. Enter the throttle valve arm shaft through the holes in the arm.

1. Throttle valve arm shaft Fig. 4-19
2. Throttle valve arm

j) Enter the throttle valve into place in the carburetor body. Be sure to line up the groove in the valve with the dowel on the carburetor. Be extremely careful that the throttle valve be installed in the night side carburetor when it carries a marking (dent) on the left side of the groove as shown.

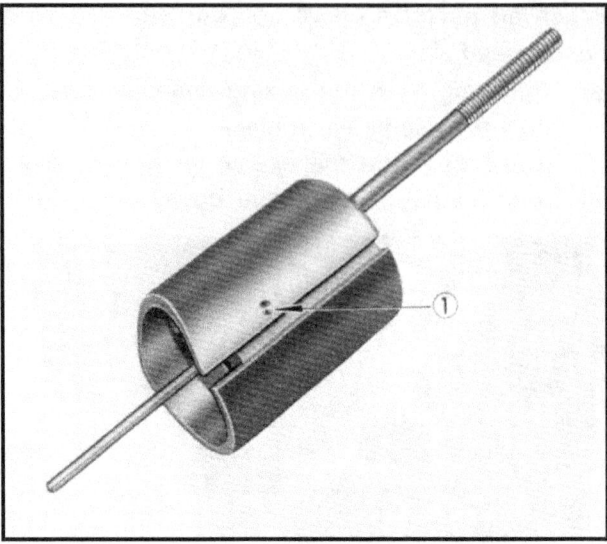

1. Dent mark Fig. 4-20

k) Put the mixing chamber top on the carburetor body and screw in the throttle valve adjust nut until the end of the throttle valve rod comes out from the nut slightly.

1. Throttle valve arm Fig. 4-21
2. Throttle valve adjust nut 3. Throttle valve rod

1) Tighten the throttle valve arm on the shaft with the arm bolt as per the instruction given in the accompanying sketch below.

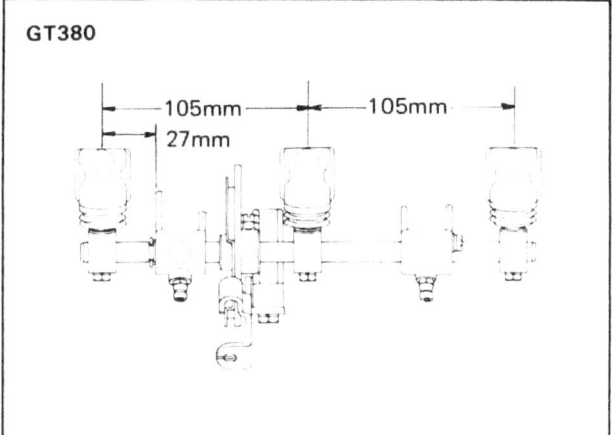

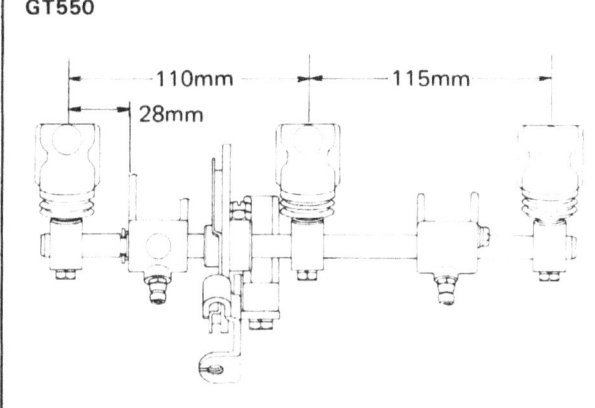

Fig. 4-22

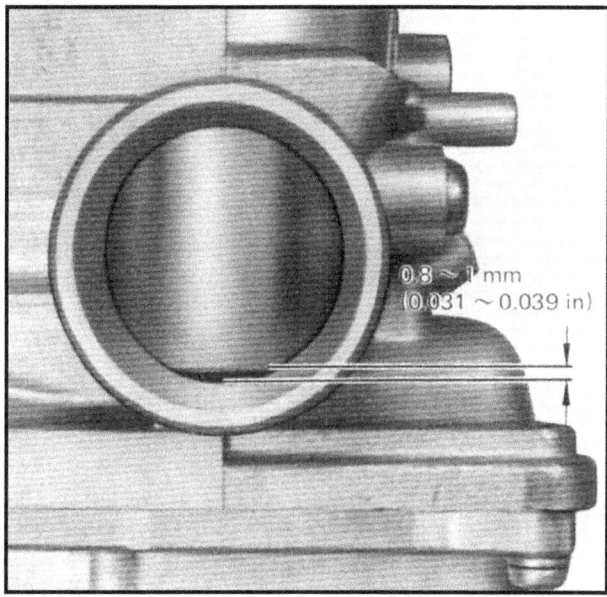

Fig. 4-23

After the above step has been completed, move the pulley several times to make sure that the arm is not interfering with the throttle valve adjust nut. If otherwise, relocate the arm on the shaft.

m) Turn in the throttle valve stop screw all the way until it bottoms; turn it out 1-1/2 turns. Without disturbing the above setup, turn the throttle adjust nut either in or out as necessary until the clearance between the lower end of the throttle valve and main bore is 0.8 ~ 1 mm (0.03 ~ 0.04 in) as viewed from the carburetor outlet (on each carburetor).

n) Turn in or out the throttle valve full-open stop screw so that the lower end of the throttle valve is 0.5 ~ 1 mm (0.02 ~ 0.04 in) above the main bore as viewed from the carburetor inlet. Be sure to keep the throttle fully open during operation.

Fig. 4-24

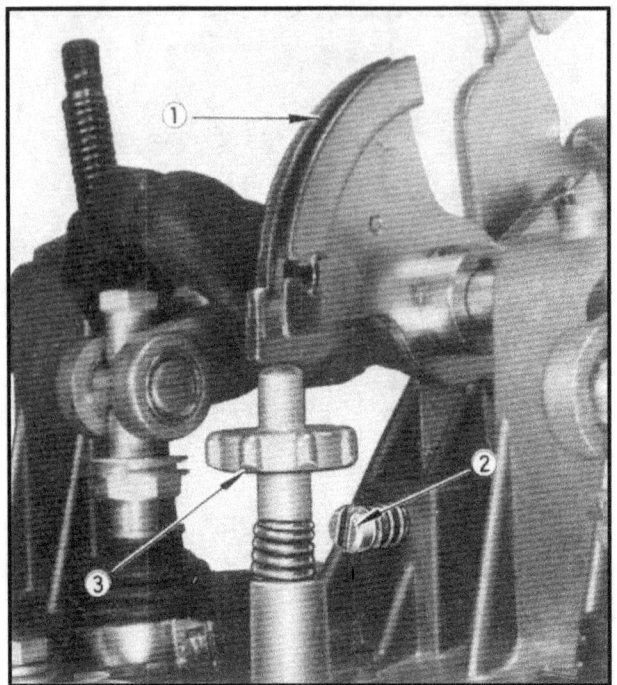
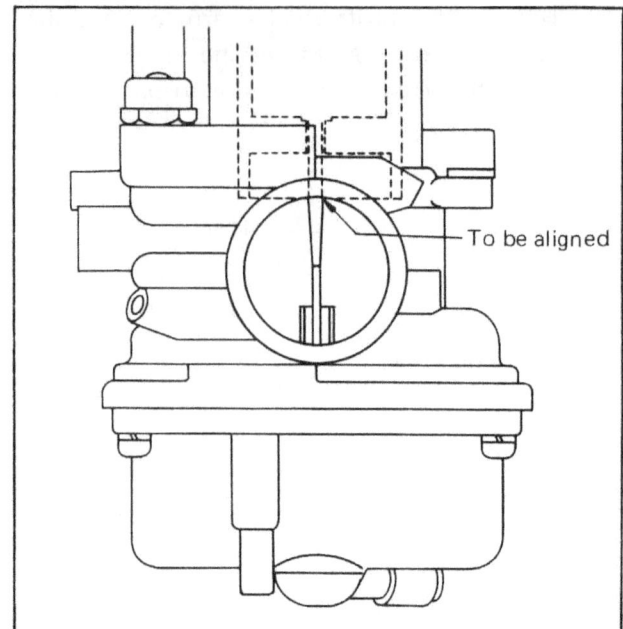

Fig. 4-26

1. Pulley
2. Throttle valve full-open stop screw
3. Throttle valve stop screw

Fig. 4-25

o) Hold any throttle valve so that it is in line with the edge of the main bore as viewed from the inlet. Using this valve as a reference, line up the remaining valves with throttle valve adjust nut. Tighten the throttle adjust nuts securely.

p) Assemble in the reverse order of the disassembly. Start and warm up the engine for about five minutes. Turn the throttle stop screw either in or out as necessary so that the engine will run approx. 1,100 rpm.

q) Adjust the throttle cables (pull side and return side) so that the deflections are 3 ~ 5 mm (0.12 ~ 0.20 in) when thumb pressure 100 ~ 200 g (0.22 ~ 0.44 lb) is applied at a point midway between the cable end and cable adjuster.

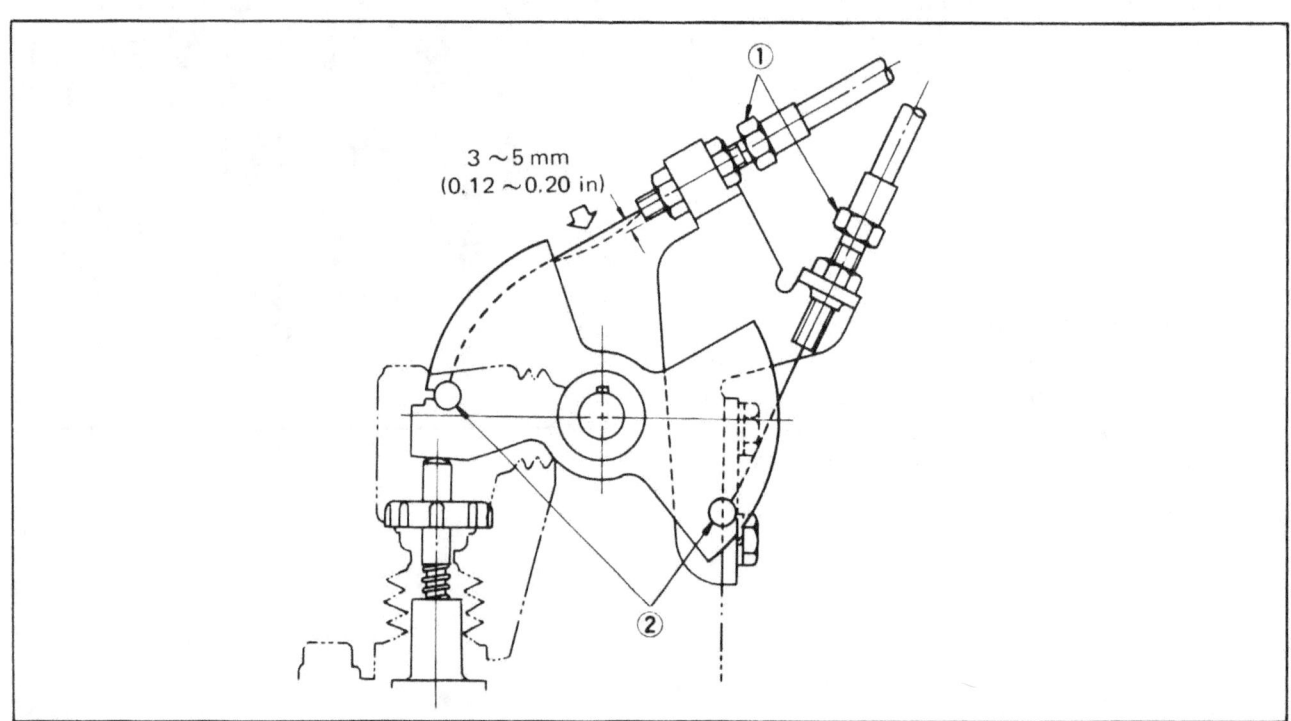

1. Throttle cable adjuster
2. Cable end

Fig. 4-27

r) Remove the plug screw from the right carburetor. Make sure that the marking on the oil pump control lever aligns with that on the oil pump when the dent mark is at the top edge of the vacant hole made by removing the plug screw. Adjustment can be made by turning the oil pump cable adjuster in or out as required.

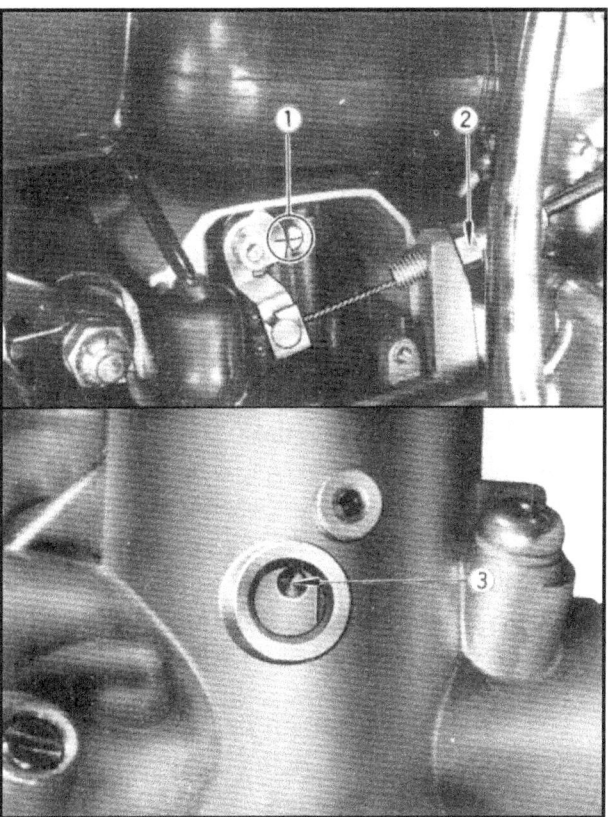

1. Aligning mark
2. Oil pump cable adjuster
3. Dent mark

Fig. 4-28

4. Carburetor Adjustment

Observe either of the following procedures when it becomes necessary to make a throttle-opening (carburetor balance) adjustment during periodic maintenance service etc.

Off-motorcycle adjustment:
   Follow the steps "o" thru "h" under ASSEMBLY in Chapter 3.

On-motorcycle adjustment:
   Proper procedure for adjustment of carburetor on motorcycle is as follows. However, carburetor should not be adjusted unless the following items are properly adjusted.
   - Contact breaker point gap
   - Spark plug gap
   - Ignition timing
   - Pilot air screw opening
   - Throttle cable play

1. Start and warm up the engine for about five minutes.
2. Turn in the throttle valve stop screw so that the engine will run at approx. 1,500 rpm.
3. Ground the breaker point or remove the spark plug cap so that the right cylinder will not fire. Turn the center throttle valve adjust nut so that the engine will run at 1,000 rpm. Use tool "Throttle Valve Adjust Tool No. 09913-13110" to turn the adjust nut and screw.

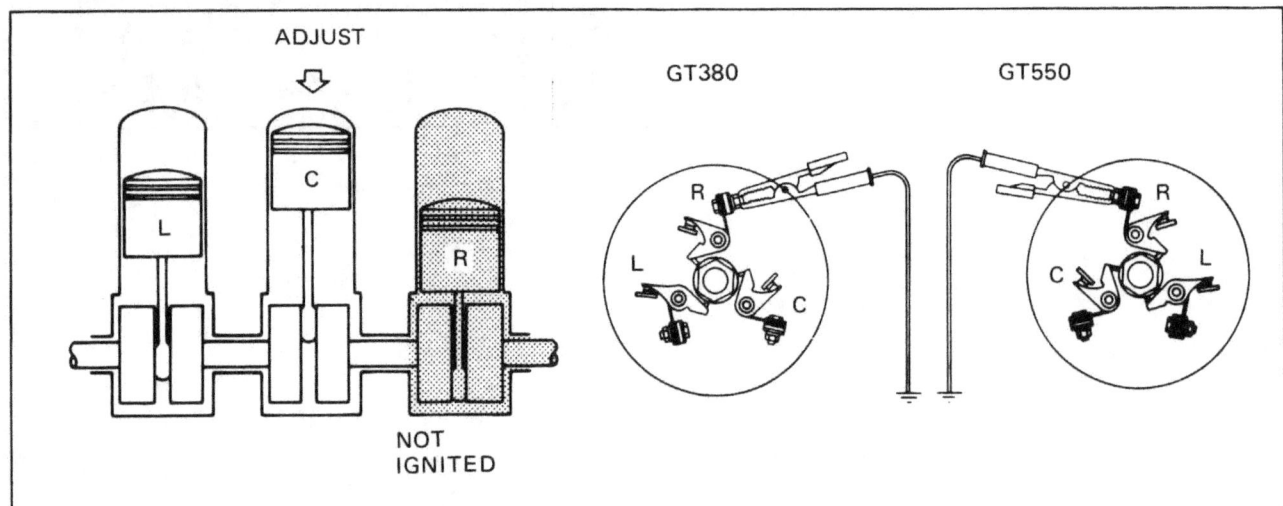

4. In like manner as above, disable the center cylinder. Adjust the engine speed to 1,000 rpm by means of the right carburetor throttle valve adjust nut.

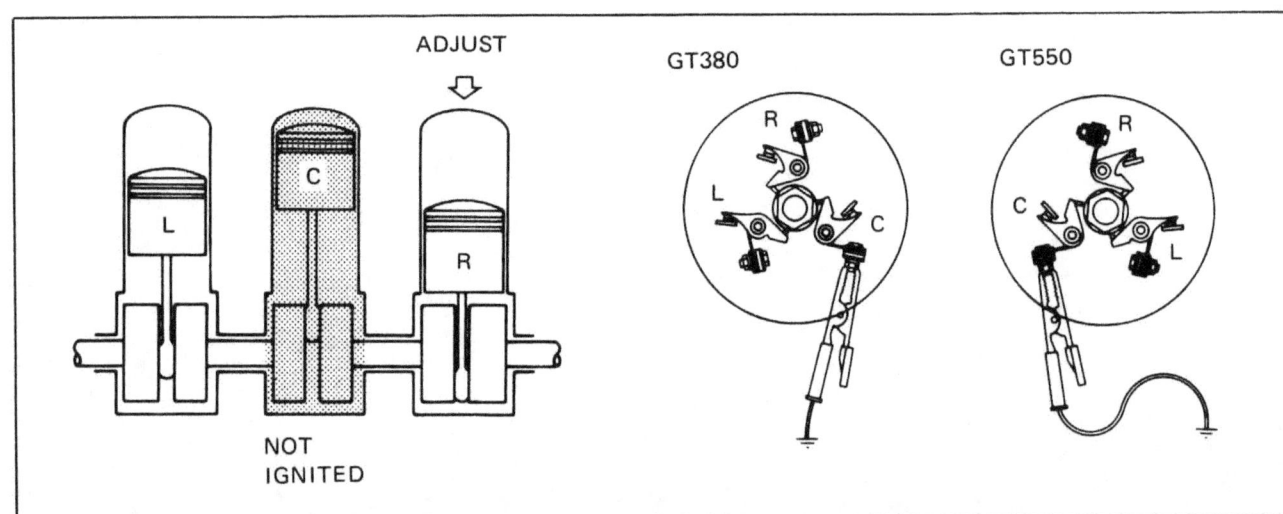

5. Disable the left cylinder. Read the engine speed.

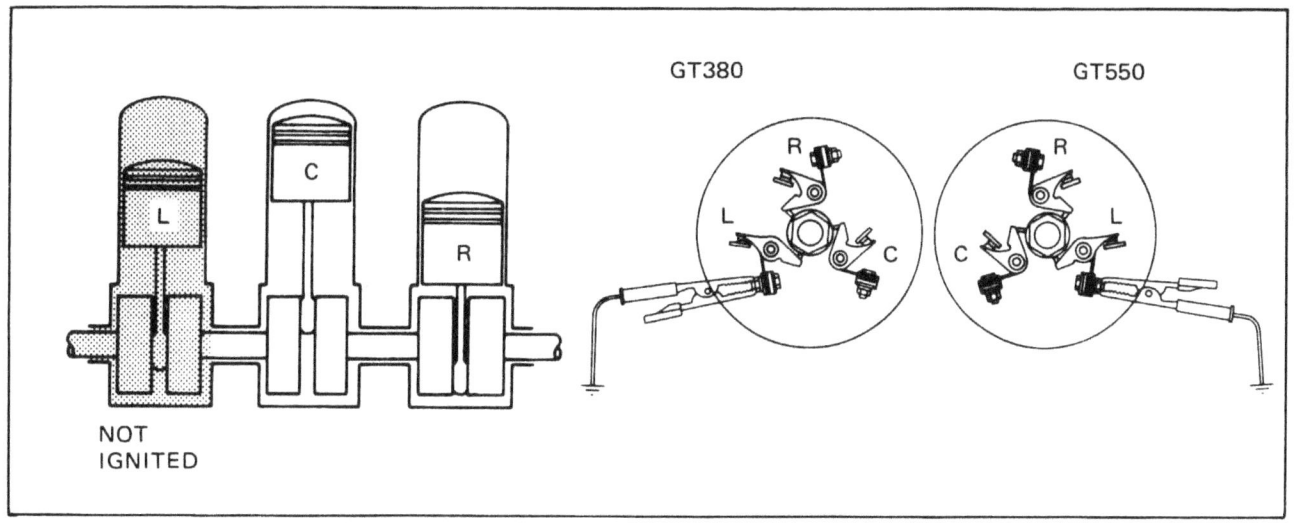

6. Disable the right cylinder. Rotate the left carburetor throttle valve adjust nut so that the engine will run at the same speed as that taken in Step (5) above.

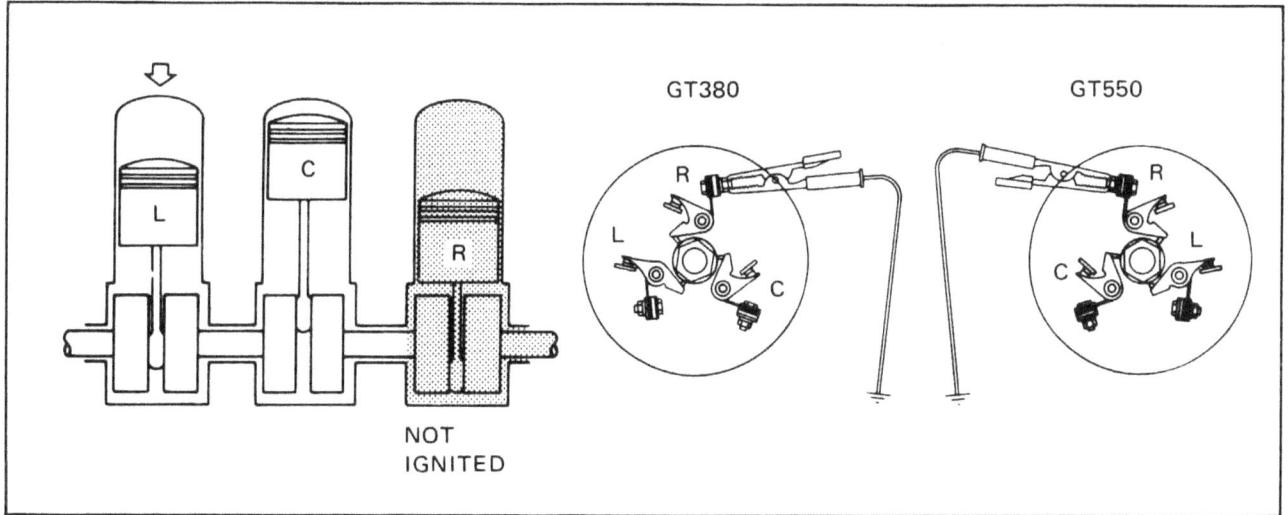

7. Finally, fire all cylinders. Turn out the throttle stop screw so that the engine will run at 1,100 rpm.

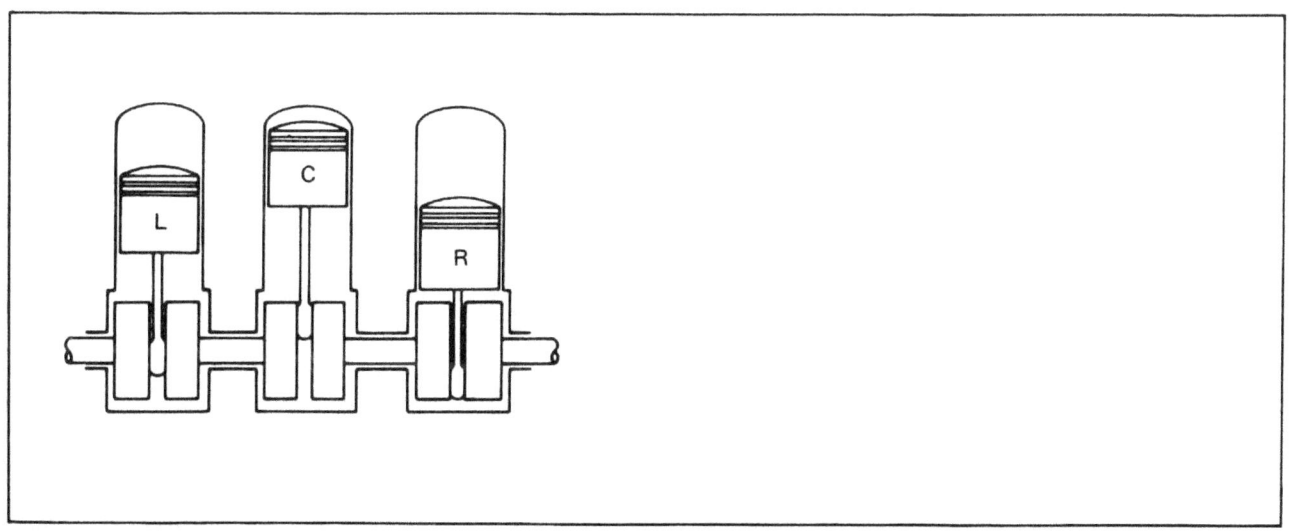

SUZUKI MOTOR CO., LTD.

VELOCEPRESS.com - MOTORCYCLE MANUALS BY MAKE

AJS 1932-1948 SINGLES & TWINS 250cc THRU 1000cc (BOOK OF)
AJS 1945-1956 SINGLES RIGID & SPTRING FACTORY WSM & PARTS
AJS 1945-1960 SINGLES MODELS 16 & 18 350cc & 500cc (BOOK OF)
AJS 1948-1956 TWINS MODELS 20 & 30 FACTORY WSM & PARTS
AJS 1955-1965 SINGLES MODELS 16 & 18 350cc & 500cc (BOOK OF)
AJS 1957-1966 SINGLES & TWINS (ALL) FACTORY WSM
AJS 1959-1969 G80CS G85CS & P11 OFF ROAD FACTORY WSM
AJS 1968-1974 STORMER FACTORY WSM & PARTS LIST
ARIEL UP TO 1932 (BOOK OF)
ARIEL 1932-1939 PREWAR MODELS (BOOK OF)
ARIEL 1933-1951 (WORKSHOP MANUAL)
ARIEL 1939-1960 4 STROKE SINGLES (BOOK OF)
ARIEL 1958-1964 LEADER & ARROW FACTORY WSM & PARTS LIST
ARIEL 1958-1964 LEADER & ARROW (BOOK OF)
BMW R26 R27 (1956-1967) FACTORY WORKSHOP MANUAL
BMW R50 R50S R60 R69S (1955-1969) FACTORY WORKSHOP MANUAL
BMW R50/5 R60/5 R75/5 (1969-1973) FACTORY WORKSHOP MANUAL
BRIDGESTONE 90 SERIES FACTORY WSM & PARTS CATALOGUE
BRIDGESTONE 175 SERIES FACTORY WSM & PARTS CATALOGUE
BRIDGESTONE 350 SERIES FACTORY WSM & PARTS CATALOGUES
BSA SERVICE SHEETS MASTER CATALOGUE ALL MODELS 1945-1967
BSA BANTAM D1 TO D7 1948-1966 FACTORY SERVICE SHEETS MANUAL
BSA BANTAM ALL MODELS FROM 1948 ONWARDS (BOOK OF)
BSA BANTAM D14 FACTORY SERVICE MANUAL
BSA DANDY FACTORY WORKSHOP MANUAL (COMPILATION)
BSA SINGLES & V-TWINS UP TO 1926 inc. 1927 SUPPLEMENT (BOOK OF)
BSA SINGLES & V-TWINS UP TO 1930 (BOOK OF)
BSA SINGLES & V-TWINS UP TO 1935 (BOOK OF)
BSA SINGLES & V-TWINS 1936-1939 (BOOK OF)
BSA C10, C11 & C12 1945-1958 FACTORY SERVICE SHEETS MANUAL
BSA OHV & SV SINGLES 250-600cc 1945-1959 (BOOK OF)
BSA C15 & B40 1958-1967 FACTORY SERVICE SHEETS MANUAL
BSA OHV & SV SINGLES 250cc (ONLY) 1954-1970 (BOOK OF)
BSA B31, B32, B33 & B34 1945-60 FACTORY SERVICE SHEETS MANUAL
BSA OHV SINGLES 350 & 500cc 1955-1967 (BOOK OF)
BSA M20, M21 & M33 1945-1963 FACTORY SERVICE SHEETS MANUAL
BSA TWINS A7 & A10 1948-1962 FACTORY SERVICE SHEETS MANUAL
BSA TWINS A7 & A10 1948-1962 (BOOK OF)
BSA TWINS A50 & A65 1962-1965 FACTORY WORKSHOP MANUAL
BSA TWINS A50 & A65 1962-1969 (SECOND BOOK OF)
BULTACO 125cc to 37cc SINGLES 1968-1979 WORKSHOP MANUAL
CZ 125cc to 380cc SINGLES 1967-1974 WORKSHOP MANUAL
DOUGLAS 1929-1939 PREWAR ALL MODELS (BOOK OF)
DOUGLAS 1948-1957 POSTWAR ALL MODELS FACTORY SHOP MANUAL
DUCATI 160cc, 250cc & 350cc OHC MODELS FACTORY SHOP MANUAL
HODAKA 90cc,100cc & 125cc SINGLES 1964-1978 WORKSHOP MANUAL
HONDA 50cc ALL MODELS UP TO 1970 INC MONKEY & TRAIL (BOOK OF)
HONDA 90cc ALL MODELS UP TO 1966 (BOOK OF)
HONDA TWINS & SINGLES 50cc THRU 305cc 1960-1966 (BOOK OF)
HONDA TWINS ALL MODELS 125cc THRU 450cc UP TO 1968 (BOOK OF)
HONDA C100 50cc SUPER CUB O.H.C. 1959-1962 FACTORY WSM
HONDA C110 50cc SPORT CUB O.H.C. 1960-1962 FACTORY WSM
HONDA 50-65-70-90cc O.H.C. SINGLES 1959-1983 WSM
HONDA 100-125cc SINGLES CB/CD/CL/SL/TL 1970-1984 FACTORY WSM
HONDA 125-150cc TWINS C/CS/CB/CA 1959-1966 FACTORY WSM
HONDA 125-160-175-200cc TWINS 1965-1978 WORKSHOP MANUAL
HONDA 250-305cc TWINS C/CS/CB 1961-1968 FACTORY WSM
HOHDA 250-350cc TWINS CB/CL/SL 1968-1973 FACTORY WSM
HONDA 250-360cc TWINS CB/CL/CJ 1974-1977 FACTORY WSM
HONDA 350F & 400F 4-CYLINDER 1972-1977 FACTORY WSM
HONDA 450cc TWINS CB/CL 1965-1974 K0 TO K7 WORKSHOP MANUAL
HONDA 500cc & 550cc 4-CYL 1971-1978 FACTORY WORKSHOP MANUAL
HONDA 750cc SHOC 4-CYL 1969-1978 K0~K8 WORKSHOP MANUAL
HUSQVARNA 125cc to 450cc SINGLES 1965-1975 WORKSHOP MANUAL
INDIAN PONYBIKE, BOY RACER & PAPOOSE ILL PARTS LIST & SALES LIT
J.A.P. ENGINES 1927-1952 & MOTORCYCLES 1934-1952 (BOOK OF)
KAWASAKI TRIPLES 1968-1980 ALL MODELS 250cc to 750cc WSM
MAICO 250cc to 501cc 1968-1978 WORKSHOP MANUAL

MATCHLESS 1931-1939 ALL MODELS 250cc THRU 990cc (BOOK OF)
MATCHLESS 1945-1956 RIGID & SPRING FACTORY WSM & PARTS
MATCHLESS 1945-1956 SINGLES G3 & G80 350cc & 500cc (BOOK OF)
MATCHLESS 1948-1956 TWINS G9 & G11 FACTORY WSM & PARTS
MATCHLESS 1955-1966 SINGLES G3 & G80 350cc & 500cc (BOOK OF)
MATCHLESS 1957-1966 SINGLES & TWINS (ALL) FACTORY WSM
MONTESA 1962-1978 125cc to 360cc ALL MODELS WORKSHOP MANUAL
NEW IMPERIAL ALL SV & OHV FROM 1935 ONWARDS (BOOK OF)
NORTON 1932-1939 PREWAR MODELS (BOOK OF)
NORTON 1932-1947 (BOOK OF)
NORTON 1938-1956 (BOOK OF)
NORTON 1945-1963 MODELS 16H, Big4, ES2, 19 & 50 WSM'S & PARTS
NORTON 1955-1963 MODELS 19, 50 & ES2 (BOOK OF)
NORTON 1948-1970 DOMINATOR TWINS FACTORY WSM'S & PARTS
NORTON 1955-1965 DOMINATOR TWINS (BOOK OF)
NORTON 1960-1970 TWIN CYLINDER FACTORY WORKSHOP MANUAL
NORTON 1970-1975 COMMANDO 850 & 750cc FACTORY WSM
NORTON 1975-1978 MK 3 COMMANDO 850 cc FACTORY WSM
OSSA 1971-1978 125cc, 175cc, 250cc, 310cc WSM
PANTHER 1932-1958 LIGHTWEIGHT MODELS 250 & 350cc (BOOK OF)
PANTHER 1938-1966 HEAVYWEIGHT MODELS 600 & 650cc (BOOK OF)
PENTON-KTM-SACHS 1968-1975 100cc & 125cc WORKSHOP MANUAL
PENTON-KTM 1972-1975 175cc, 250cc & 400cc WSM & PARTS MANUALS
PENTON-KTM 1972-1979 125cc to 400cc ENGINE WSM & PARTS MANUAL
RALEIGH MOTORCYCLES 1919-1933 (BOOK OF)
ROYAL ENFIELD 1934-1946 SINGLES & V TWINS (BOOK OF)
ROYAL ENFIELD 1937-1953 SINGLES & V TWINS (BOOK OF)
ROYAL ENFIELD 1946-1962 SINGLES (BOOK OF)
ROYAL ENFIELD 1948-1962 350cc & 500cc PRE-UNIT BULLET WSM
ROYAL ENFIELD 1948-1963 500cc TWINS FACTORY WORKSHOP MANUAL
ROYAL ENFIELD 1952-1963 700cc TWINS FACTORY WORKSHOP MANUAL
ROYAL ENFIELD 1956-1966 250cc CRUSADER & 350cc NEW BULLET WSM
ROYAL ENFIELD 1958-1966 250cc & 350cc SINGLES (SECOND BOOK OF)
ROYAL ENFIELD 1962-1970 INTERCEPTOR WSM'S & PARTS (Compilation)
RUDGE 1933-1939 (BOOK OF)
SACHS 1968-1975 100cc & 125cc ENGINES WSM & M/CYCLE PARTS LIST
SUNBEAM 1928-1939 (BOOK OF)
SUNBEAM 1946-1957 S7 & S8 (BOOK OF)
SUZUKI 50cc & 80cc UP TO 1966 (BOOK OF)
SUZUKI T10 1963-1967 FACTORY WORKSHOP MANUAL
SUZUKI T20 & T200 1965-1969 FACTORY WORKSHOP MANUAL
SUZUKI TWINS 1962 ONWARDS 125-500cc WORKSHOP MANUAL
SUZUKI GT550 1972-1977 A COMPILATION OF 3 FACTORY WSM's
SUZUKI GT750 1971-1977 A COMPILATION OF 4 FACTORY WSM's
TRIUMPH 1935-1949 SINGLES & TWINS (BOOK OF)
TRIUMPH 1937-1961 SINGLES SV & OHV 250cc-600cc + TERRIER & CUB
TRIUMPH 1945-1955 PRE-UNIT 350cc, 500cc & 650cc TWINS WSM No.11
TRIUMPH 1945-1959 TWINS (BOOK OF)
TRIUMPH 1956-1969 TWINS (BOOK OF)
TRIUMPH 1956-1962 PRE-UNIT 500cc & 650cc TWINS WSM No.17
TRIUMPH 1957-1963 UNIT CONSTRUCTION 350-500cc WSM No.4
TRIUMPH 1963-1970 UNIT CONSTRUCTION 350-500cc FACTORY WSM
TRIUMPH 1963-1970 UNIT CONSTRUCTION 650cc FACTORY WSM
TRIUMPH 1968-1974 TRIDENT T150 & T150V FACTORY WSM
TRIUMPH 1971-1973 650cc OIL-IN-FRAME FACTORY WSM
TRIUMPH 1973-1978 750cc BONNEVILLE & TIGER FACTORY WSM
TRIUMPH 1979-1983 750cc T140, TR7 & TR65 FACTORY WSM
VELOCETTE 1925-1970 ALL SINGLES & TWINS (BOOK OF)
VELOCETTE 1933-1952 MOV-MAC-MSS RIGID FRAME FACTORY WSM
VELOCETTE 1953-1960 MAC SPRING FRAME WSM & ILL PARTS LIST
VELOCETTE 1954-1971 MSS-VENOM-THRUXTON-VIPER FACTORY WSM
VILLIERS ENGINES UP TO 1959 INC. 3 WHEELERS (BOOK OF)
VILLIERS ENGINE UP TO 1969 (BOOK OF)
VINCENT 1935-1955 (WORKSHOP MANUAL)
YAMAHA 1961-1967 YA5 & YA6 (WORKSHOP MANUAL & ILL PARTS LIST)
YAMAHA 1963-1976 50cc to 100cc ROTARY VALVE SINGLES WSM
YAMAHA 1968-1971 DT1 & MX SERIES Inc. GYT WORKSHOP MANUAL
YAMAHA 1971-1972 JT1& JT2 (WORKSHOP MANUAL & ILL PARTS LIST)

VELOCEPRESS.com – SCOOTER MANUALS

BSA SUNBEAM SCOOTER WORKSHOP MANUAL 1959-1965
BSA SUNBEAM SCOOTER 1959-1965 (BOOK OF)
LAMBRETTA 1947-1957 ALL 125 & 150cc MODELS (BOOK OF)
LAMBRETTA 1957-1970 LI & TV MODELS (SECOND BOOK OF)
NSU PRIMA 1956-1964 ALL MODELS (BOOK OF)
TRIUMPH TIGRESS SCOOTER WORKSHOP MANUAL 1959-1965
TRIUMPH TIGRESS SCOOTER (BOOK OF)
VESPA 1951-1961 (BOOK OF)
VESPA 1955-1963 125 & 150cc & GS MODELS (SECOND BOOK OF)
VESPA 1955-1968 GS & SS (BOOK OF)
VESPA 1963-1972 90, 125 & 150cc (THIRD BOOK OF)

VELOCEPRESS.com - MOPEDS & MOTORIZED BICYCLES MANUALS

CYCLEMOTOR (BOOK OF)
NSU QUICKLY 1953-1963 ALL MODELS (BOOK OF)
PUCH MAXI N & S MAINTENANCE & REPAIR (3 MANUAL COMPILATION)
RALEIGH MOPEDS 1960-1969 (BOOK OF)

VELOCEPRESS.com - THREE WHEELER MANUALS

BOND MINICAR THREE WHEELER 1948-1967 (BOOK OF)
BMW ISETTA FACTORY WORKSHOP MANUAL
BSA THREE WHEELER (BOOK OF)
RELIANT REGAL THREE WHEELER 1952-1973 (BOOK OF)
VINTAGE MORGAN THREE WHEELER (BOOK OF)

VELOCEPRESS.com – MOTORCYCLE TECHNICAL BOOKS

1930'S BRITISH MOTORCYCLE CARBS & ELEC COMPONENTS (BOOK OF)
1930'S BRITISH MOTORCYCLE ENGINES (OVERHAUL & MAINTENANCE)
1930'S BRITISH MOTORCYCLE GEARBOXES & CLUTCHES (BOOK OF)
CATALOG OF BRITISH MOTORCYCLES (1951 MODELS)
LUCAS ELECTRONICS BRITISH M/CYCLES REPAIR & PARTS (1950-1977)
MOTORCYCLE ENGINEERING (P.E. Irving)
MOTORCYCLE ROAD TESTS 1949-1953 (Motor Cycle Magazine UK)
SPEED AND HOW TO OBTAIN IT (Motor Cycle Magazine UK)
TUNING FOR SPEED (P.E. Irving)
WIPAC (COMBO) MANUAL NUMBER 3 + M/CYCLE & SCOOTER MANUAL

www.VelocePress.com

VELOCEPRESS.com - AUTOMOBILE MANUALS BY MAKE

ALFA ROMEO GIULIA WORKSHOP MANUAL 1300 TO 2000cc 1962-1975
ALFA ROMEO GIULIA TECH MANUAL CARBURETED CARS FROM 1962
ALFA ROMEO GIULIA TECH MANUAL FUEL INJECTED CARS FROM 1969
ALFA ROMEO GIULIETTA & GIULIA 750 & 101 SERIES 1955-1965 WSM
AUSTIN-HEALEY SPRITE & MG MIDGET WORKSHOP MANUAL 1958-1971
BMW 600 LIMOUSINE FACTORY WORKSHOP MANUAL
BMW 600 LIMOUSINE OWNERS HAND BOOK & SERVICE MANUAL
BMW 2000 & 2002 1966-1976 WORKSHOP MANUAL
BMW 2500, 2800, 3.0 & BARVARIA WORKSHOP MANUAL
CORVAIR 1960-1969 WORKSHOP MANUAL
CORVETTE V8 1955-1962 WORKSHOP MANUAL
FERRARI HANDBOOK ROAD & RACE CARS (SERVICE/SPECS) 1948-1958
FERRARI 250GT SERVICE & MAINTENANCE by JIM RIFF 1956-1965
FERRARI 250GT & 250GTE FACTORY PARTS AND REPAIR MANUALS
FIAT 500 FACTORY WORKSHOP MANUAL 1957-1973
FIAT 600, 600D & MULTIPLA FACTORY WORKSHOP MANUAL 1955-1969
FORD MUSTANG 1965-1973 TRANSMISSION WORKSHOP MANUAL
JAGUAR E-TYPE 3.8 & 4.2 SERIES 1 & 2 WORKSHOP MANUAL
JAGUAR MK 7, 8, 9 & XK120, 140, 150 WORKSHOP MANUAL 1948-1961
MERCEDES-BENZ 230 SERIES 1963-1968
MERCEDES-BENZ 280 SERIES 1968-1972
METROPOLITAN FACTORY WORKSHOP MANUAL
MGA & MGB OWNERS HANDBOOK & WORKSHOP MANUAL
MG MIDGET TC, TD, TF & TF1500 WORKSHOP MANUAL
PORSCHE 356 1948-1965 WORKSHOP MANUAL
PORSCHE 911 2.0, 2.2, 2.4 LITRE 1964-1973 WORKSHOP MANUAL
PORSCHE 911 2.7, 3.0, 3.2 LITRE 1973-1989 WORKSHOP MANUAL
PORSCHE 912 WORKSHOP MANUAL
PORSCHE 914/4 & 914/6 1.7, 1.8, 2.0 LITRE 1970-1976 WSM
TRIUMPH TR2, TR3, TR4 1953-1965 WORKSHOP MANUAL
VOLKSWAGEN TRANSPORTER, TRUCKS & WAGONS 1950-1979 WSM
VOLVO 1944-1968 ALL MODELS WORKSHOP MANUAL

VELOCEPRESS.com - AUTOMOBILE TECHNICAL BOOKS

HOW TO BUILD A FIBERGLASS CAR
HOW TO BUILD A RACING CAR
HOW TO RESTORE THE MODEL 'A' FORD
MASERATI OWNER'S HANDBOOK
PERFORMANCE TUNING THE SUNBEAM TIGER
SOUPING THE VOLKSWAGEN
SOLEX CARBURETORS (EMPHASIS ON UK & EU AUTOMOBILES)
SU CARBURETORS (EMPHASIS ON UK AUTOMOBILES)
WEBER CARBURETORS (EMPHASIS ON ALFA & FIAT)

VELOCEPRESS.com – AUTOMOBILE BOOKS & GUIDES

COMPLETE CATALOG OF JAPANESE MOTOR VEHICLES
FERRARI 308 SERIES BUYER'S AND OWNER'S GUIDE
FERRARI BROCHURES AND SALES LITERATURE 1968-1989
FERRARI SERIAL NUMBERS PART I - ODD NUMBERS TO 21399
FERRARI SERIAL NUMBERS PART II - EVEN NUMBERS TO 1050
HENRY'S FABULOUS MODEL "A" FORD
MASERATI BROCHURES AND SALES LITERATURE

VELOCEPRESS.com - AUTO RACING BOOKS

BOOK OF THE 1950 CARRERA PANAMERICANA - MEXICAN ROAD RACE
DIALED IN - THE JAN OPPERMAN STORY
VEDA ORR'S NEW REVISED HOT ROD PICTORIAL
LIFE OF TED HORN – AMERICAN RACING CHAMPION

www.VelocePress.com

www.ingramcontent.com/pod-product-compliance
Lightning Source LLC
Chambersburg PA
CBHW080744300426
44114CB00019B/2645